TABLE OF CONTENT

"I will lift up mine eyes unto the hills, from whence cometh my *HELP*. My *HELP* cometh from the LORD, which made heaven and earth." Ps.121:1,2 (emphasis mine)

"Woe to them that go down to Egypt for *HELP*; and stay on horses, and trust in chariots, because they are many; and in horsemen, because they are very strong; but they look not unto the Holy One of Israel, neither seek the LORD!" Isai.31:1 (emphasis mine)

"O Israel, thou hast destroyed thyself; but in me is thine help." Hos.13:9

All Scriptures are taken from the King James Version or as otherwise stated.

SECTION FOUR
HYMNS/ORIN IYIN

SECTION FIVE
YORUBA TRANSLATION
OJO KINI DE OGOJI (IJEWO ATI KOKO ADURA)

12. IPELE IRANLOWO: IRANLOWO IBI

13. IPELE IRANLOWO: IRANLOWO NI KIAKIA / IRANLOWO WAKATI KOKANLA

14. IPELE IRANLOWO: IRANLOWO TI KO SISE

15. RIRAN OLORUN LOWO

16. IRANLOWO TI A KO FOJURI: IRANLOWO LATOKE

17. IRANLOWO OKUNKUN

18. KIKIGBE FUN IRANLOWO

19. IDIWO SI IRANWO: ESE

20. IDIWO FUN IRANLOWO: AWON IWA ODI

21. IDIWO FUN IRANLOWO: AIMOKAN ATI IKUNA LATI BEERE

22. GBIGBOGUN TI EMI TI N TAKO IRANLOWO

23. AMUSEYA IRANLOWO: AAWE ATI ADURA

24. AMUSEYA IRANLOWO: ORE, IRUBO ATI IFURUGBIN

25. AMUSEYA IRANLOWO: SISE IRANLOWO

26. AMUSEYA IRANLOWO: IMORE

27. AMUSEYA IRANLOWO: IGBAGBO

SECTION SIX

APPENDIX

1. PRAYERS FOR SPIRITUAL RENEWAL
2. **PRAYERS AGAINST BESETTING SINS**
3. PRAYERS FOR AWAITING MOTHERS
4. PRAYER FOR THE CHRONICALLY ILL
5. PRAYER FOR BUSINESS EXPANSION
6. PRAYER FOR THE UNSAVED
7. **PRAYER AGAINST BUSINESS OPPOSITION**
8. PRAYER FOR THE GRADUATES SEEKING JOB
9. PRAYER FOR MARRIAGEABLE SINGLES
10. **PRAYER AGAINST THE SPIRIT OF UNTIMELY DEATH**
11. **PRAYER AGAINST EATING IN THE DREAM**
12. **PRAYER FOR MINISTRY GROWTH AND & FRESH FIRE**
13. **PRAYER FOR GOD'S VESSELS**
14. **PRAYER AGAINST THE SPIRIT OF DEBT**
15. **PRAYER AGAINST THE SPIRIT OF BACKSLIDING**
16. **PRAYER FOR OUR CHILDREN**
17. **PRAYER FOR RECOMMENDATION**
18. **PRAYER FOR THE CHURCH OF GOD**
19. **PRAYER WHEN IN FOREIGN LAND**
20. **PRAYER WHEN APPLYING FOR VISA**
21. **PRAYER FOR SPIRITUAL FREEDOM**

AFIKUN

1. ADURA FUN SISO DI TITUN NINU EMI
2. ADURA LODI SI AWON ESE TO SORO KO SILE
3. ADURA FUN AWON TIN WOJU OLUWA FUN OMO
4. ADURA FUN AWON TI NSE AISAN OJO PIPE
5. ADURA FUN IMUGBORO OKOOWO
6. ADURA FUN AWON TI WON KO TI MO OLORUN
7. ADURA LODI SI IDOJUKO OKOOWO
8. ADURA FUN AWON AKAWE YEGE TI NWA ISE
9. ADURA FUN AWON APON TO TI TO SE IGBEYAWO
10. ADURA LODI SI EMI IKU OJIJI
11. ADURA LODI SI OUNJE OJU ORUN
12. ADURA FUN ITESIWAJU ISE-IRANSE ATI INA TITUN
13. ADURA FUN AWON OUN ELO OLORUN
14. ADURA LODI SI EMI GBESE
15. ADURA LODI EMI IPEYINDA
16. ADURA FUN AWON OMO WA
17. ADURA FUN IFINISIPO
18. ADURA FUN ILE OLORUN
19. ADURA FUN AWON TI O WA NI ILE AJEJI
20. ADURA FUN IWE IRIN AJO SI OKE OKUN
21. ADURA FUN ITUSILE TI EMI

SECTION SEVEN

PRAISE REPORTS

PREFACE

'I will lift up mine eyes to the hills'. Said the Psalmist. 'Where will my help come from'? He asked. 'My help comes from the Lord'. He answered! Psalm 121 is a profound Scripture that describes what happens when men trust in God.

Beloved, I welcome you to another Mercy Rain Fasting and Prayer. It is a season of revival, a season of revisiting our relationship with God. It is a season of beseeching the Lord. A season of receiving from the Lord. Oh Lord, our help in ages past, we thank You for the possibility of this year's Mercy Rain. We thank You for past years' testimonies. We are grateful for the coming together of the saints in a unified purpose; seeking to know and do Your will. We thank You for the grace to do Your will. We thank You for forgiving all of our failings. Thank You Lord for showing us a better way. Thank You for Your sure mercies. We will forever be grateful.

Dearly beloved, it is our custom every year to seek the face of the Lord in fasting and prayer for 40 Days and nights. Every year has its own area of concentration as the Spirit of God directs. Last year, the Holy Spirit led us to our INHERITANCE and this year, He wants to help us understand the importance of HELP and how only the HELP FROM ABOVE can truly be of value to the saints.

You can testify to the fact that help is an essential commodity when it comes to man and his existence. No one was created to live without the input of another. You remember that immediately God noticed a certain lapse concerning Adam in the Garden, He quickly created the needed help for him. Two are better than one, the Bible says. While some people try to live their lives as if they have no need of help, the Bible condemns such practices. It says, *'woe unto him who is alone...'* *(Ecc.4:10).*

We could see in the Book of Genesis that God Almighty sought the assistance of 'others' when creating man. He said, *'let **Us** make man in **Our** image...' (Gen.1:26).* The emphasis is on US and OUR. By utilizing these 'us' and 'our' is an indication that God could not have been talking to himself. So, if God did not act alone, why are you acting alone, failing to seek help when you badly need it?

Man has been programmed by God to need assistance in his life. Majority of us know this and we spend a greater part of our lives seeking this assistance in order to fulfill our purpose in life. The problem now is not just seeking assistance (help) but seeking it from the right source.

As earlier said, man has need of help. Where will he get help? That question has driven many to unfortunate ends because they were unable to locate the right channel of help. Many have gone to the opposite end of the spectrum in order to get aids and their lives have terrible endings. For your case not to be like that, God has inspired us to create this platform for spiritual wisdom, knowledge and understanding (people perish for lack of these) of where to get the best help and that is the reason why this book is in your hand.

One major problem this Prayer Manual has come to solve is to open people's eyes to the understanding of the fact that they have been seeking help from the wrong channels and the time has come for them to come to the right source. This Prayer Manual is not written to judge anyone. Even Jesus said He has not come to judge nor condemn (Mt.3:17). It is not written to condemn your going to the wrong places for help, I understand that you did not know better.

People condemn our fore-mothers for subscribing to the witchcraft society which is now having adverse effect on their offspring. The point however needs be understood that what people do is largely a product of how much they know as at the time the action is being taken. At that point in time, the LIGHT has not shone through; so gross darkness prevailed and the people walking in darkness cannot help falling into ditches.

Now, the LIGHT has come and it is the desire of God for no one to fall into ditches again. This manual is a help guide to circumnavigate such ditches by shining light upon your path. It is written with the hope that it will help you realise where you have gotten it wrong concerning seeking help outside of God and how you can re-establish your relationship with God and how that decision can positively affect your destiny fulfilment.

This Prayer Manual is written to affirm the dominance of God in the School of Help and how any help sourced outside of Him will end in futility. It is written to establish the fact that every one has need of help. It is written to explain the importance and categories of help. It is written to help you discern diverse forms of false help and how to do away with them. This timely Prayer Manual is written to open up your own understanding concerning rising up to help others – help received is help given.

My hope is that this Prayer Manual will help you fulfill your destiny with the appropriate help. There are hundreds of fire-brand prayer points to clear the spiritual blockers of help. There are also Confessions aimed at enforcing your faith. It is loaded with beautiful hymns to elevate your soul. A major plus is the appendix written to widen your scope. You will also find many testimonies added to encourage you.

Friend, do not think otherwise. You need this manual. Do not stop there though. Just like Jesus advised Peter, when you have achieved your aim, pass it on to others. Assist them in fulfilling their own purpose too. May you encounter always, the needed help to fulfill your purpose in life in Jesus' name.

Amen!

God bless you.

SCRIPTURES ON HELP

Gen. 2:18 And the LORD God said, It is not good that the man should be alone; I will make him an help meet for him.

Gen. 49:25 Even by the God of thy father, who shall help thee; and by the Almighty, who shall bless thee with blessings of heaven above, blessings of the deep that lieth under, blessings of the breasts, and of the womb:

Exod. 18:4 And the name of the other was Eliezer; for the God of my father, said he, was mine help, and delivered me from the sword of Pharaoh.

Deut. 22:4 Thou shalt not see thy brother's ass or his ox fall down by the way, and hide thyself from them: thou shalt surely help him to lift them up again.

Deut. 33:7 And this is the blessing of Judah: and he said, Hear, LORD, the voice of Judah, and bring him unto his people: let his hands be sufficient for him; and be thou an help to him from his enemies.

Deut. 33:26There is none like unto the God of Jeshurun, who rideth upon the heaven in thy help, and in His excellency on the sky.

Deut. 33:29 Happy art thou, O Israel: who is like unto thee, O people saved by the LORD, the shield of thy help, and who is the sword of thy excellency! And thine enemies shall be found liars unto thee; and thou shalt tread upon their high places.

Josh. 10:6 And the men of Gibeon sent unto Joshua to the camp to Gilgal, saying, Slack not thy hand from thy servants; come up to us quickly, and save us, and help us: for all the kings of the Amorites that dwell in the mountains are gathered together against us.

Judg. 5:23 Curse ye Meroz, said the angel of the LORD, curse ye bitterly the inhabitants thereof; because they came not to the help of the LORD, to the help of the LORD against the mighty.

1Sam. 7:12 Then Samuel took a stone, and set it between Mizpeh and Shen, and called the name of it Ebenezer, saying, Hitherto hath the LORD helped us.

1Sam. 11:9 And they said unto the messengers that came, thus shall ye say unto the men of Jabeshgilead, tomorrow, by that time the sun be hot, ye shall have help. And the messengers came and shewed it to the men of Jabesh; and they were glad.

2Sam. 10:11 And he said, If the Syrians be too strong for me, then thou shalt help me: but if the children of Ammon be too strong for thee, then I will come and help thee.

2Kings 6:26 And as the king of Israel was passing by upon the wall, there cried a woman unto him, saying, help, my lord, O king.

2King 6:27 And he said, If the LORD do not help thee, whence shall I help thee? Out of the barn floor, or out of the winepress?

1Chr. 12:22 For at that time day by day there came to David to help him, until it was a great host, like the host of God.

1Chr. 19:12 And he said, If the Syrians be too strong for me, then thou shalt help me: but if the children of Ammon be too strong for thee, then I will help thee.

2Chr. 14:11 And Asa cried unto the LORD his God, and said, LORD, it is nothing with thee to help, whether with many, or with them that have no power: help us, O LORD our God; for we rest on thee, and in thy name we go against this multitude. O LORD, thou art our God; let not man prevail against thee.

2Chr. 19:2 And Jehu the son of Hanani the seer went out to meet him, and said to king Jehoshaphat, Shouldest thou help the ungodly, and love them that hate the LORD? Therefore is wrath upon thee from before the LORD.

2Chr. 20:4 And Judah gathered themselves together, to ask help of the LORD: even out of all the cities of Judah they came to seek the LORD.

2Chr. 20:9 If, when evil cometh upon us, as the sword, judgment, or pestilence, or famine, we stand before this house, and in thy presence, (for thy name is in this house,) and cry unto thee in our affliction, then thou wilt hear and help.

2Chr. 28:23 For he sacrificed unto the gods of Damascus, which smote him: and he said, Because the gods of the kings of Syria help them, therefore will I sacrifice to them, that they may help me. But they were the ruin of him, and of all Israel.

2Chr. 32:8 With him is an arm of flesh; but with us is the LORD our God to help us, and to fight our battles. And the people rested themselves upon the words of Hezekiah king of Judah.

Ezra 1:4 And whosoever remaineth in any place where he sojourneth, let the men of his place help him with silver, and with gold, and with goods, and with beasts, beside the freewill offering for the house of God that is in Jerusalem.

Ezra 8:22 For I was ashamed to require of the king a band of soldiers and horsemen to help us against the enemy in the way: because we had spoken unto the king, saying, the hand of our God is upon all them for good that seek Him; but His power and His wrath is against all them that forsake Him.

Job 8:20 Behold, God will not cast away a perfect man, neither will He help the evil doers:

Job 29:12 Because I delivered the poor that cried, and the fatherless, and him that had none to help him.

Ps.10:14 Thou hast seen it; for thou beholdest mischief and spite, to requite it with thy hand: the poor committeth himself unto thee; thou art the helper of the fatherless.

Ps. 12:1 Help, LORD; for the godly man ceaseth; for the faithful fail from among the children of men.

Ps. 22:11 Be not far from me; for trouble is near; for there is none to help.

Ps. 22:19 But be not thou far from me, O LORD: O my strength, haste thee to help me.

Ps. 27:9 Hide not thy face far from me; put not thy servant away in anger: thou hast been my help; leave me not, neither forsake me, O God of my salvation.

Ps. 33:20 Our soul waiteth for the LORD: he is our help and our shield.

Ps. 35:2 Take hold of shield and buckler, and stand up for mine help.

Ps. 37:40 And the LORD shall help them, and deliver them: he shall deliver them from the wicked, and save them, because they trust in him.

Ps. 38:22 Make haste to help me, O Lord my salvation.

Ps. 40:13 Be pleased, O LORD, to deliver me: O LORD, make haste to help me.

Ps. 40:17 But I am poor and needy; yet the Lord thinketh upon me: thou art my help and my deliverer; make no tarrying, O my God.

Ps. 42:5 Why art thou cast down, O my soul? and why art thou disquieted in me? hope thou in God: for I shall yet praise him for the help of his countenance.

Ps. 44:26 Arise for our help, and redeem us for thy mercies' sake.

Ps. 46:1 God is our refuge and strength, a very present help in trouble.

Ps. 59:4 They run and prepare themselves without my fault: awake to help me, and behold. [can be deleted]

Ps. 60:11 Give us help from trouble: for vain is the help of man.

Ps. 63:7 Because thou hast been my help, therefore in the shadow of thy wings will I rejoice.

Ps.68:6 God setteth the solitary in families: he bringeth out those which are bound with chains: but the rebellious dwell in a dry land.

Ps. 70:1 Make haste, O God, to deliver me; make haste to help me, O LORD.

Ps. 70:5 But I am poor and needy: make haste unto me, O God: thou art my help and my deliverer; O LORD, make no tarrying.

Ps. 71:12 O God, be not far from me: O my God, make haste for my help.

Ps. 79:9 Help us, O God of our salvation, for the glory of thy name: and deliver us, and purge away our sins, for thy name's sake.

Ps. 94:17 Unless the LORD had been my help, my soul had almost dwelt in silence.

Ps. 107:12 Therefore he brought down their heart with labour; they fell down, and there was none to help.

Ps. 108:12 Give us help from trouble: for vain is the help of man.

Ps. 109:26 Help me, O LORD my God: O save me according to thy mercy:

Ps. 115:9 O Israel, trust thou in the LORD: He is their help and their shield.

Ps. 115:11 Ye that fear the LORD, trust in the LORD: He is their help and their shield.

Ps. 119:86 All thy commandments are faithful: they persecute me wrongfully; help thou me.

Ps. 119:175 Let my soul live, and it shall praise thee; and let thy judgments help me.

Ps. 124:8 Our help is in the name of the LORD, who made heaven and earth.

Ps. 146:3 Put not your trust in princes, nor in the son of man, in whom there is no help.

Ps. 146:5 Happy is he that hath the God of Jacob for his help, whose hope is in the LORD his God:

Prov.3:5,6 Trust in the LORD with all thine heart; and lean not unto thine own understanding. In all thy ways acknowledge him, and he shall direct thy paths.

Ecc. 4:9,10 Two are better than one, because they have a good reward for their labour. For if they fall, the one will lift up his fellow: but woe to him that is alone when he falleth; for he hath not another to help him up.

Isa. 31:1 Woe to them that go down to Egypt for help; and stay on horses, and trust in chariots, because they are many; and in horsemen, because they are very strong; but they look not unto the Holy One of Israel, neither seek the LORD!

Isa. 41:10 Fear thou not; for I am with thee: be not dismayed; for I am thy God: I will strengthen thee; yea, I will help thee; yea, I will uphold thee with the right hand of my righteousness.

Isa. 41:13-14 For I the LORD thy God will hold thy right hand, saying unto thee, Fear not; I will help thee. Fear not, thou worm Jacob, and ye men of Israel; I will help thee, saith the LORD, and thy redeemer, the Holy One of Israel.

Isa. 44:2 Thus saith the LORD that made thee, and formed thee from the womb, which will help thee; Fear not, O Jacob, my servant; and thou, Jesurun, whom I have chosen.

Isa.50:7 For the Lord GOD will help me; therefore shall I not be confounded: therefore have I set my face like a flint, and I know that I shall not be ashamed.

Isa. 50:9 Behold, the Lord GOD will help me; who is he that shall condemn me? lo, they all shall wax old as a garment; the moth shall eat them up.

Lam. 4:17 As for us, our eyes as yet failed for our vain help: in our watching we have watched for a nation that could not save us.

Dan. 10:13 But the prince of the kingdom of Persia withstood me one and twenty days: but, lo, Michael, one of the chief princes, came to help me; and I remained there with the kings of Persia.

Hosea 13:9 O Israel, thou hast destroyed thyself; but in me is thine help.

Mt.7:7 Ask, and it shall be given you; seek, and ye shall find; knock, and it shall be opened unto you.

Mt. 15:25 Then came she and worshipped him, saying, Lord, help me.

Mk. 9:22 And ofttimes it hath cast him into the fire, and into the waters, to destroy him: but if thou canst do anything, have compassion on us, and help us.

Mk. 9:24 And straightway the father of the child cried out, and said with tears, Lord, I believe; help thou mine unbelief.

Luke 5:7 And they beckoned unto their partners, which were in the other ship, that they should come and help them. And they came, and filled both the ships, so that they began to sink.

John 14:26 But the Comforter, which is the Holy Ghost, whom the Father will send in my name, he shall teach you all things, and bring all things to your remembrance, whatsoever I have said unto you.

Acts 16:9 And a vision appeared to Paul in the night; There stood a man of Macedonia, and prayed him, saying, come over into Macedonia, and help us.

Acts 26:22 Having therefore obtained help of God, I continue unto this day, witnessing both to small and great, saying none other things than those which the prophets and Moses did say should come:

Rom.8:26 Likewise the Spirit also helpeth our infirmities: for we know not what we should pray for as we ought: but the Spirit itself maketh intercession for us with groanings which cannot be uttered.

Rom.16:3 Greet Priscilla and Aquila my helpers in Christ Jesus:

Rom.16:9 Salute Urbane, our helper in Christ, and Stachys my beloved.

2Cor.1:11 Ye also helping together by prayer for us, that for the gift bestowed upon us by the means of many persons thanks may be given by many on our behalf.

2Cor.1:24 Not for that we have dominion over your faith, but are helpers of your joy: for by faith ye stand.

Php. 4:3 And I intreat thee also, true yokefellow, help those women which laboured with me in the gospel, with Clement also, and with other my fellow labourers, whose names are in the book of life.

Heb. 4:16 Let us therefore come boldly unto the throne of grace, that we may obtain mercy, and find grace to help in time of need.

Heb.13:6 So that we may boldly say, The Lord is my helper, and I will not fear what man shall do unto me.

(KJV)

ARTICLES

1.

WHY DO YOU NEED HELP?

'But the manifestation of the Spirit is given to each one for the profit *of all* (1 Cor 12:7; NKJV)

It has been well and unarguably established the fact that without the Help of God, we cannot be what God wants us to be. We are what we are today by reason of the help of God that has come our way. Apostle Paul put this very succinctly when he says: But by the grace of God *I am what I am*, and His grace toward me was not in vain; (1 Cor 15:10; NKJV)

Show me a man whose journey in life is fast or quick, and I will tell you a man who has enjoyed the help (or Grace) of God. In life we are *Help / Grace Rated*. The completion of the above Scriptures from Apostle Paul confirms this as we read further below:

"But by the grace of God I am what I am*, and His grace toward me was not in vain; but* I *labored more abundantly than they all, yet not* I*, but the grace of God which was with me."* (1 Cor 15:10; NKJV).

Various Scriptures confirm that there is common understanding by God and men that as humans, we are not self-sufficient without the help of God (2 Cor 3:5 KJV - *not that we are sufficient of ourselves to think anything as of ourselves; but our sufficiency is of God*); we need God's help. (Ps.124:8 reads: *Our help is in the name of the Lord, who made heaven and earth).* Also Ps.121:2 confirms that *'My help comes from the Lord.*

The question, which is the focus of this message is "What do we do with God's Help? Or put in another form, "Why do we need God's help? Other Posers that we intend to answer in this message are: "Is God's help meant for our ultimate and final consumption?" "When helping us, does God have any expectation of us?" "How are we going to demonstrate to God that helping us is well justified and fulfilling to Him?"

GOD'S HELP AS INVESTMENT

'But the manifestation of the Spirit is given to each one for the profit *of all* (1 Cor 12:7; NKJV)

For God so loved the world that He gave His only begotten Son, that whoever believes in Him should not perish but have everlasting life (John 3:16; NKJV)

The scriptures above establishes that whatever God gives is intended for a purpose, a benefit, and an eternal reward. God's gifts are not 'make-feel-good' gifts but rather, a form of investment in which God is expecting good returns or profits.

Let us consider another scripture that shows the investing nature of God with respect to His gifts.

For as the rain comes down, and snow from heaven, and do not return there, but water the earth, and make it bring forth and bud, that it may give seed to the sower and bread to the eater, so shall my word be that goes forth from my mouth; it shall not return to me void, but it shall accomplish what I please, and it shall prosper in the things for which I sent it. (1Cor.55:10-11; NKJV**)**

From the above, we clearly see the following:

> God gives Rain & Snow (i.e. **The Help of God, the Investment**)
> The Earth, as recipient of the help of God bring forth & bud (i.e. **The Investment platform**)
> Seed is given to the Sower and Bread to the Eater (i.e. **Return on Investment; Outcome)**

God's WORD is also an investment in man as shown in Ps.107:20
- ➢ Sent to accomplish what pleases God **(Investment and Investment expectation)**
- ➢ It shall prosper in the particular case / instance / situation, God sent it to (**Outcome**)

God's investment in Jesus Christ was in the form of the spirit of God in Him and the anointing was to bless mankind. In the scripture following (Isai.61:1–3), we can see clearly all the components of God's Investments in the Lord Jesus Christ: The Investment **(The Spirit of the Lord)** and the numerous investment returns / outcomes as listed.

Isai.61: 1 – 3 reads The Spirit of the Lord GOD *is* upon me; *because the LORD hath anointed me to preach good tidings unto the meek; he hath sent me to bind up the brokenhearted, to proclaim liberty to the captives, and the opening of the prison to them that are bound; to proclaim the acceptable year of the LORD,* and the day of vengeance of our God; to comfort all that mourn; to appoint unto them that mourn in Zion, to give unto them beauty for ashes, the oil of joy for mourning, the garment of praise for the spirit of heaviness; that they might be called trees of righteousness, the planting of the LORD, that he might be glorified."

BEING AN AGENT OF HELP & THE OUTCOME

One of the greatest lessons we learnt from the LORD is that we have been made as an agent of HELP and the earlier we recognize and discover this, the better for us in realizing and fulfilling the essence of our being.

Rev 4:11b (NKJV) .. For You created all things, And by Your will they exist and were created.

One way of really showing help to people is to demonstrate and extend God's help towards them even without asking or seemingly undeserving of it. This is when it is more rewarding and fulfilling with regard to God's expectation and purpose. (**Read Matt 5:43 – 47;** ... *Love them that hate you;* ... *bless them that persecute and despitefully use you...*)

Acts 20:35b "... And remember the words of the Lord Jesus, that He said, 'It is more blessed to give than to receive."

We must always seek / look for opportunity to be a giver. God is looking for *distributor/ source of help, not terminator / sink of help.*

OUTCOME / REWARD OF BEING AN AGENT OF HELP

➤ The first benefit of being helpful or an agent of help or mercy is that you will receive more help / mercy from God in return.

Matt 5:7 – **"Blessed *are* the merciful: for they shall obtain mercy."**

➤ The LORD himself becomes your Rewarder.

Proverb 19:17 (NKJV) - **He who has pity on the poor lends to the Lᴏʀᴅ, And He will pay back what he has given**

Ephesians 6:8 **Knowing that whatever good anyone does, he will receive the same from the Lord,** whether *he is* a slave or free.

Case Studies:

1. Cornelius ➔ Acts 10: 1 – 6
2. Shunamite Woman ➔ 2 Kings 4:8-17
3. Dorcas ➔ Acts 9:36 – 42
4. The first Christians after Pentecost - ➔ Acts 4:32-37 (They had all things in common)

Conclusion

The surest way to attract God's help is to first reach out to others; helping them from the little God has blessed us with. Then God will respond by helping us. We must show to God that we are really deserving of His investment of HELP in us by demonstrating that we are DISTRIBUTORS of His GRACE / HELP / MERCY and not an END-CONSUMER / TERMINATOR.

2.

SEEKING BUT NOT GETTING HELP: THE PLACE OF PERSISTENCE

Luk.18:1-8; Luk.11:5-8; 1Ki.18:41-45; Dan.10:12-13

"I will lift up mine eyes unto the hills, from whence cometh my help. My help cometh from the Lord, which made heaven and earth." Ps.2-1:121

The above statement from the Psalmist underscores the point that man always seeks help from higher power. From the days of Adam till the last man that will ever walk on the face of the earth, help will always be a recurring decimal in man's life. Help is the currency which defines man's greatness and prosperity. Consequently, each man's present reality now is a function of the cumulative helps received in life's sojourn. Someone once said, "there are no great men, but men greatly helped". Therefore, seeking help is universal to man.

Furthermore, two key things stand out in this topic of discourse, seeking help and persistence.
We shall therefore be looking at, why men seek help, where men seek help, why people don't get help while seeking and getting help through persistency.

Why Do Men Seek Help?

Humanity is interdependent therefore everyone at one point or the other will require help. Interestingly, our Lord Jesus Christ while on earth received help provided by women who ministered to him in material things. Also, Peter once provided his boat as a platform to preach for the Lord Jesus Christ which was a help required for that purpose. Luk.8:1-3; Luk.5:1-3.
Undoubtedly, there are various reasons why men seek help, amongst which are:

No man is self-sufficient. We all require somebody to lean on, irrespective of our level of skill, anointing and wealth. For example, cook, driver, caregiver (with due respect to the named professions) provide such assistance to the high and mighty. Naaman in the Scriptures was helped by a maid or slave girl. 2Ki.5:1-3. Joseph also got to the palace through the chief butler, Esther became the queen not necessarily because of her charm and beauty but with help from Mordecai who provided godly counsel and training for her. Lastly, Daniel required a word before King

Belshazzar to utilize his gift to interpret the writings. Dan.5:10-11; Gen.49:1

Help reduces period for accomplishing a task, destiny, or project. The daughters of Jethro are a good example whilst running their father's errand. They returned earlier than expected and responded, "an Egyptian helped us". Therefore, help will reduce the time to get to the top. Do you want to fulfill destiny in time? Help is the answer. Exod.2:19

Help multiplies effort. The Bible states "one shall chase a thousand and two ten thousand".

The multiplying effect of help is geometric thus attracting men to seek it. Deut.32:30

Help takes away shame and confusion. Isa.50:7 Imagine if God did not come through for the three Hebrew men in the fiery furnace, or if he let down Daniel in the lion's den or if help didn't come for Mordecai when it did; shame and confusion will have been theirs. That's why bible describe God as "a very present help in trouble" Ps.46:1; Esth.6:4-10, Dan.3:23-25; 6:20-22

Help delivers from destruction. The woman and her son were to be swallowed by the flood from Satan, but the earth helped the woman. David was to be killed by the giant, but help came and delivered him. Rev.12:16; 2 Sam.21:15-17

Help reduces stress of accomplishment. A good analogy is using the stairs as against an elevator. Getting to each level of the building could be with effort or seamless. That's help. Exd. 17:12-14. There are men God has ordained to take the burden of stress off you on the journey of destiny. He has laid help on one that is mighty Ps 89:19

Help brings success in ministry. Paul ascribed his success in ministry to, "having therefore obtained help of the Lord". Acts 26:22, Acts 23:12-22, Lk 8:1-3

May we never lack help in Jesus' name. May the oil of helpers never run dry in our lives. I sincerely pray God will both beautify and surround our lives with help.

WHERE DO MEN SEEK HELP?

The above tremendous benefits of help make men from the day of Adam to devise means to help themselves. Adam sewed fig leaves to help himself; though this was a non-lasting help.

Basically, man has been looking for help in four ways and it shows why many don't get help when required:

Self-Help. The slogan, "Heaven helps those who help themselves" has been the motto of men. But the Bible categorically stated that, "by strength shall no man prevail" Self-help is futility as it has great limitation. 1 Sam.2:19

Seeking Help from Fellow Man. Truthfully man can only help to the limit of their ability and power. Even Pastors and Prophets are men, and their God is who we should be looking for help from. Man's help has some challenges among which are:

Man, who wants to help has his power in his nostril. He can die before he is able to help you. Isai. 2:22

Man's help is vain. Ps.60:11

Relying on Man for help hinders seeing God's help. It is impossible to look up and down at the same time. Jer.17:5-6;

Man's help is full of trouble and sorrows.

Satan. Men looking for help have often turned to Satan, devils, demon and evil spirit. Examples abide of men that ran to devil for help.

King Ahaziah ran to Beelzebub, god of Ekron for help. 2Ki.1:2-4

Saul went to the necromancer woman seeking help. Isai.31:1, 1Sam.28:3-25

Many so-called men of God have run to devil to seek for power. Act.13:8; 8:19-25

God is the ultimate, best and dependable helper. He is a faithful helper. He is the supreme helper that can use any of the preceding helpers to do his bidding.

He is a very present help in trouble Ps 46:1

God's help is early. Ps.46:5

Believers' help should come from God Ps.121:1

If God didn't help you nobody can. 2Ki.6:26-27

God is the helper of the fatherless Ps.10:14

Undoubtedly, your reading this prayer rain book, I believe, is an indication that you know the right place to seek help, from God the Father of light with whom there is no variableness nor shadow of turning. I congratulate you because I know the God of Mercy you have come to is a specialist in helping men. I'm a testimony and so are many others. Just hold on to Him alone because He is a jealous God. You can't combine Him with mammon.

WHY MEN DON'T GET HELP WHILE SEEKING?

It has been established that, men will always seek for help, so why do some get and others don't. There are various reasons but let's consider a few.

1. **Seeking Help in Wrong Places**: Many don't get help because they are looking for help in wrong places;

from man, self and Satan. If God didn't help you, no man, no matter how close, will help you. Many have spent all their substances for false prophet and physicians like King Asa did in the Bible. They look at the wrong places, to Physicians and not God, therefore real help eluded them. (2Chr. 16:12; Mk.5:26)

2. **Stopping too early**: Many don't get help from above because they stopped too early. Elisha opened the window eastward and asked the King to shoot the arrow of the Lord's deliverance from Syria. He shot thrice and stopped. He stopped too early. He could have gotten total help but stopped too early. Learn from him, keep on keeping on till your help come. (2Ki.13:16-19)

3. **Unbelief**: Nothing can be gotten from the Father including help without faith for he that cometh to God must believe that he is and is a rewarder of them that diligently seek him. Heb 11:6 You need help, come with faith. A double minded person cannot receive help from God. (Jas.1:8-10)

4. **Fear**: It has paralyzed many from getting help. We always come to the throne of grace with boldness to obtain help in time of need. Boldness required not fear. (Heb.4:16; 1Joh.4:18-20)

5. **Not sowing help**. It is an eternal law, the law of sowing and reaping. You need help therefore sow help. Whatever a man sows that he will reap. Seedtime and harvest time won't cease. Help is

also a seed you can sow to reap help too. (Gal.6:7; Gen.8:22)

6. Persistence: The Key to Getting Help from Above

Having established the fact that true help comes from God. Help that adds no sorrow comes from God. The question that should then be begging for answer is how to get this help from God.

Fortunately, the Psalmist has provided an answer, "looking up to the hill" or as the writer of the book of Hebrews says, "coming to the throne of grace". These are phrases used to describe the art of Prayer. Prayer is the only approved means by which we can obtain help from God. So, persistence, ability to hold on till the desired result is received in prayer is the key to getting help from God.

The days we live in are days of fast food, fast money, quick this and quick that. Persistence and perseverance seem alien to this generation. But the Lord Jesus while on earth taught us via His life and teachings the importance of persistence to get help.

Let us take a closer look at his prayer in the garden of Gethsemane. His only prayer request throughout that night was, "father let this cup pass over me not as I will but thy will be done" He persistently continued all night in a single prayer request. Tarrying in prayer, persistence in prayer, continuing in prayer till help comes is the key. Hallelujah! Help came the Lord's way as an angel was sent to strengthen Him. If you'll get help from God, this year's 40 days, please persist in prayer till he sends help. Mt.26:39-44

The parable of the widow and the unjust judge, the friend that went to meet his friend at midnight and his prayer life all throughout the night are to teach us – persistency.

The unjust judge won't be perturbed at the initial request of the widow, but her continual coming wearied him and had to succumb to her request. The two main gist in the parable are, "her continual coming" and "which cry day and night". You want help, then continuously come to him day and night in prayer. Help is always found in prayer through persistency. (Luk.18:1-8)

The friend that came to his friend for help at midnight got an initial no from his friend to his request for help. His friend went further to give fairly an inconvenient excuse but when he persisted, the man who had initially said no arose and gave more than his friend required so he can have his peace. Importunity, another side of persistence got help for him not his friendship. Luk.11:5-8 Being a child of God might not be enough to get the help required but adding persistency will do the magic and bring result.

Elijah was a man given to power and prayer. He prayed down fire from heaven to consume the sacrifice. He consumed soldiers of fifties not once with fire but when he announced the coming of shower of rain, he sent his servant and there was nothing. He persisted in prayer sending his servant seven times till heaven gave rain. Help came his way through persistency in prayer. (1Ki. 18:41-45)

Shall we talk of the famous Daniel 21 days of fasting and the Prince of Persia withholding his answers. Only one thing brought help to Daniel, he persisted in the place of prayer. (Dan.10:12-13)

You wonder why God wanted us to persist in prayer before he helps us? To punish us? No. Not because he wanted us to force his unwillingness, but he delighted in our fellowship to empower us above the forces of darkness to enjoy the blessings.

Let me conclude by prophesying to someone reading this manual that as you persist in prayer seeking his help, the following will happen in your life:

Men will help you with silver, with gold and goods. (bolden) According to Ezra 1:4 *"And whosoever remaineth in any place where he sojourneth, let the men of his place help him with silver, and with gold, and with goods, and with beasts, beside the freewill offering for the house of God that is in Jerusalem."*

God will send you help from his sanctuary. According to Ps.20:1-2 *"The Lord hear thee in the day of trouble; the name of the God of Jacob defends thee; Send thee help from the sanctuary, and strengthen thee out of Zion;"*

By this time tomorrow you will receive help that will gladden your heart. According to 1Sam.11:9 *"And they said unto the messengers that came, Thus shall ye say unto the men of Jabesh–Gilead, Tomorrow, by that time the sun be hot, ye shall have help. And the messengers came and shewed it to the men of Jabesh; and they were glad."*

Please seek help persistently not from man, Satan or self but from God and you shall have help.

3.

GOD - THE SOURCE OF ALL HELP

For I the LORD thy God will hold thy right hand, saying unto thee, Fear not; I will help thee. (Isai.40:41)

Help means to make it easier or possible for someone to do something by offering one's services or resources.

Man was created to need help. He does not have all he needs within Him. Man was created specially to look unto God his maker for assistance in all things. Since the purpose of God for making man was primarily for fellowship with Himself, God in His love and mercy has positioned Himself within the reach of man to supply all his needs. Unfortunately, man fell from this position of privilege until his restoration by our Lord Jesus Christ.

God offered man the first help he needed in Gen.2:18:

"And the Lord God said it is good that man should be alone. I will make an help meet for him"

No suitable companion was found for Adam until God provided a help meet for him which was Eve, the first woman.

Everything God created practically needs God for survival. He is the eternal God who runs the universe. He is the source of all power, strength, grace, ability and wisdom. No matter where we get something from, the ultimate source is always God.

In Job 38: 4, in trying to make Job understand that God runs the universe and man cannot claim to understand all or help himself, God asked a question: "*Where was thou when I laid the foundations of the earth? declare if thou hast understanding*".

Therefore, the Scriptures enjoins that man should utterly depend on God for help. He must look unto God to whom nothing is impossible to supply him with the ability and resources to make anything meaningful out of life.

Ps.121:1-2 declare that:" *I will lift up my eyes unto the hills, from where hence cometh my help. My help cometh from the lord which made heaven and earth*".

Help is sent from the sanctuary or habitation or presence of the Lord God. (Ps.20:2). The lord is the commander of the universe, the director of the hearts of men. He is the only one who knows exactly what we need and where to get it. No wonder He said vain is the help of man (Ps 108:12), only God can give us help from trouble because of His everlasting love, limitless resources and omnipotent powers. None of these can we get from any man. (Ps 146:3-6) says we should not put our trust in princes nor in the son of man for these is no help in them. They will eventually die and their influence will come to an end forever. Man is infinite, limited and temporary in nature.

WHY IS GOD'S HELP TO BE DESIRED?

(1)   Gods' help is timely:

Ps 46:5 says God will help us right early. He is never late. He always comes through at the right time. What usually appears as delay or lateness to us may just be for us to learn the lessons we need to learn or acquire the virtue we lack. He is never too late even if He comes in at a time, we think irreparable damage has been done. (total recast was done here to remove observed clumsiness in the thought flow) In John11, the sisters of Lazarus thought Jesus had come too late because Lazarus was dead but Jesus, the resurrection and the life demonstrated that he was right on time when he raised Lazarus from the dead.

(2)   God's help is very close

Psalm 46:1 says God is a very present help in trouble. When we need His help and intervention, God is just a cry away. Man may delay his help and leave us stranded, frustrated and ashamed. Man will not be there when we need him but God is ever present. He said He will never leave us nor forsake us, He said He will be with us when we pass through waters or fire and He was present with the three Hebrew boys in the fire of affliction (Heb13:5, Isa43:2, Dan3:25).

(3)   God is never short of resources to help

All things belong to God, therefore whatever is necessary to make our life easier and our destinies fulfilled can be supplied by God. God commanded the locusts, the sea, hail, darkness, lightening, thunder and even the spirit of death to assist the Israelites to be delivered from the hand of pharaoh in the book of Exodus. Only the living God could have rescued a nation from the hand of another wicked nation so spectacularly as God did for Israel.

(4)   God is eager and willing to help us

Isa41:13-14 says:" For I the lord, thy God will hold thy right hand saying unto thee, fear not, I will help thee...".
God is not reluctant to help His own. He has graciously stretched out His hand of mercy and help unto us. Man may have what we need but may not be willing to help us except God compels him.

(5)   God arises for our help

God is so concerned when we are stranded and call upon him for help. Jesus said the good shepherd will leave 99 sheep and personally go and look for the one that has strayed away and needs help. (Luk.15:4). Deut.36:26 says, *"There is none like unto the God of Jeshurun, who ride upon the heaven in thy help and in his excellency on the sky"*. Only God can show such care, love and concern for us.

(6)   God can compel anyone to help us.

No one has power over every single human being or creature except God their maker. When God decides to help us, it does not matter if the vessel he wants to use is willing or not. The person to be used may not even like us or know us. God will get hold of his heart and instruct him to help us any way. In 1king17:4 -God told Elijah that He had commanded the ravens to feed him. The ravens did so twice a day without fail until God told him to move on as the brook he drank from had dried up.

God did not leave Elijah stranded. In 1king 17:9, God again directed Elijah to Zarephath to go and meet a widow who he had commanded to sustain him. Only God can miraculously organize such help in the time of famine.

Ps 89:19 say God lays our help upon the mighty.

(7)   God's help brings sure deliverance from trouble

Only the help of God can give us total, lasting victory in the battles of life. When we call upon him, he gives us battle strategies that may seem foolish to men, but he uses the foolish things of this world to confound or confuse and defeat the wise. (1Cor.1:18-21).

In Joshua 6, the wall of Jericho came down after the children of Israel had strictly followed God's instructions.2Chron20 also recorded victory for king Jehoshaphat and Judah over the enemies of Judah through God's help.

THOSE THAT GOD WILL NOT HELP

(1)   God will not help evil doers.

We cannot continue in sin and expect grace to abound. It is true that Ps121 enjoins us to lift up our eyes unto the hills and look unto God for help. But Ps.24:3 says *"Who shall ascend unto the hills of the Lord? Ps 24:4 says it is "He that has a clean hand and a pure heart, who has not lifted his soul unto vanity...."*

God will not assist evil doers to perpetrate evil or forge ahead in an unrighteous cause.

(2)   God will not help the proud.

In 2ki.12:6,17 - King Ahaziah fell down from the top floor of his palace. He did not humble himself to ask God for healing and deliverance but he sent messengers to go to Ekron to ask Baal-zebub whether he would recover from the sickness. God sent word to him through Elijah that he would surely die because of this folly and he did.

We must always humbly ask God for help in every situation and never seek word or help from other gods. God resists the proud but gives grace to the humble. (Jas.4:6).

THOSE THAT GOD WILL HELP

(1)   Those who call upon His name with all their heart

Jer33:3 says we should call upon God and he will answer us. Blind Bartimaeus called unto Jesus earnestly and got his miracle. (Mk.10:46-52). We are to call upon God as if there is no alternative and indeed he is our only option. Such a mindset provokes God's help.

(2)   Those who put their hope in him

Ps146:5 says *"Happy is he that hath the God of Jacob for his help, whose hope is in the lord his God".*

The expectation of such a person will not be cut off. If God's help is our only hope then surely, we will not be frustrated for the eyes of all who wait upon him will get their meat in due season. (Ps.145:15)

(3)   The righteous

'The righteous are those who have put their trust in Jesus Christ and have received him as their Lord and Saviour. The Bible says "Christ is our righteousness." (1Cor.1:30).

The Lord loves the righteous and shines His countenance upon them. (Ps 11:7). Ps.34:15-19 teaches us that the eyes of the Lord are upon the righteous and his ears are open unto their cry. The lord delivers the righteous out of all their troubles and afflictions.

Therefore, child of God, rest assured that God is willing and able to help you in every way you desire. He is looking out for you, He is waiting for you to call upon Him so that He can show you great and mighty things. You are not alone; the Lord is with you by His spirit. Ps.34:22 says, *'...**none of those who trust in the Lord shall be desolate.'***

4.

ATTACKING ANTI HELP SPIRITS

"But I will stay in Ephesus until Pentecost because a wide door for effective service has opened to me (in Ephesus a very promising opportunity), and there are many adversaries" 1Cor.16: 8-9 (AMP)

Looking vividly into the Scriptures, we could see that a wide-open-door of help, or a very promising opportunity can be opened for a man and there could be many adversaries or opportunities to it. This shows that there is the reality of help and there is the certainty of its opponents and until they are attacked; stood against forcefully and opposed with hostility, they shall remain unperturbed and poised as blockage to the opportunity or help. This explains, our topic ATTACKING ANTI-HELP SPIRITS.

You can fight violently the enemies to your help and triumph over them. It is then you can free yourself and the opportunities to be helped from their clutches and bondages. But before we go into this I will like us to understand our topic of discussion, this will start with the meaning to its term.

What does the world "ATTACKING" mean? Attacking according to the English Dictionary, means "Launching or engaging in a military or violent physical attack". It is a word gotten from "ATTACK" which means "to set upon in a forceful, violent, hostile, or aggressive way, with or without a weapon. It is to begin hostility or fighting with; or start an offensive against".

The word "HELP "means "to make it easier or possible (for someone to do something by offering one's services or resources".

While the word "ANTI" *means* 'opposition', spirits indicate, "unseen forces or supernatural beings, often but not exclusively without physical form". Thus, anti-help spirits are unseen forces or supernatural beings with or without physical body opposing or fighting against what makes things easier or possible for someone to do something. They are powers that withstand the services or resources offered by somebody to get things done.

In line with these definitions of terms, we could understand that "attacking anti-help spirit is the act and the processes of engaging or launching a forceful, violent, hostile, and offensive fight against the supernatural forces withstanding or opposing your possibilities of doing something easily and without struggle. It is fighting both seen and unseen enemies of your opportunity for help. It is for you to be both physically and spiritually militant to adversaries to your open doors for help. It is you being hostile, aggressive and offensive to unseen or seen enemies to help. It is making sure that doors of help are not closed against you, but help gets to you against all odds. It is for you to be continually in submission to God and in serious resistance to the devil and his angels (Jas 4:7).

You may be wondering who this anti-help spirits are "their nature and characteristics, how can one recognize them, deal with them?

ANTI-HELP SPIRITS, THEIR NATURE, THEIR RECOGNITION AND WAYS TO FIGHT THEM:

There is the reality and certainty of existence of forces against help. The Word of God speaks clearly about them, they have been in existence right from the Biblical world. And they are also real today and they will be forever more. Our text confirms this through Apostle Paul. However, the goodness is that they were defeated foes over whom the death, burial and the resurrection of Jesus Christ has given you victory over if you believe in Jesus Christ and ready to fight them.

Devil is the head of the anti-help spirits. He is described as man's adversary, a roaring lion with his angels, lurking about, devouring any man's help if given opportunity (Jas.4:7; 1Pet.5:8).

The anti-help spirits are the spiritual thieves our Lord Jesus mentioned in His Word. They set out to steal, kill, and destroy. They are spiritual soldiers, killers and destroyers of help. They will not see yours to steal, kill or destroy in Jesus name (Jon.10:10).

The anti-help spirits are spirits of temptations. Living one to be enticed to sin or offend your rightful helper. They would want you to do what will make you fall short of God's grace (Rom. 6:23, 1Cor.10:13).

They are evil strongholds with satanic and evil imagination. They are principalities and powers in high places that do exalt themselves above the knowledge of God. They are unfriendly friends who needs your quick attack. (2Cor.10: 4-5).

They are evil traps against your opportunities and help, your household enemies, your evil foundation, the evil covenants and generational curses of your family. They are the deceptive spirit foiling your destiny helpers; (Gen.3:1-7; 23-24; 2Thess.3:3). They are the evil beast of your family (1Cor.15:3).

They are spiritual wrestlers against your fortunes; the unseen enemies who the Bible described as the principalities, powers, rulers of darkness and spiritual host of spiritual wickedness in high places (Eph.6:10-12).

All in all, the anti-help spirits are your worst enemies, not only to your help but to your rising in life; the adversaries or forces that are evil, set over your life to oppose you and to destroy you. (Phil.3:18).

You need to rise up forcefully against them, fight them aggressively and engage them violently in battle. You need to destroy them before they destroy you. Then engage them with your spiritual weapons, cast them down, bring them all into complete captivity to the obedience of your victory in Christ. You need to resist them vehemently, otherwise they will not let you be.

ATTACKING THEM, HOW?

1. **Humble yourself before God**. Have a link with God. Submitting to the Lordship of the Lord Jesus Christ. Accept His leadership over you. Let Jesus take over from you. Take Him as your Lord and personal Saviour, invite Him into your life (Jas.4:7). He came to give you life unto fullness John 10:10. He is the only gateway to your winning in life. His birth, life on earth, arrest, condemnation, death, burial, and resurrection fortify you against all these anti-help spirits. Just come to Him today, He will help you; (Acts 4:12, Heb.2:14, Phil.2:9-10, Rev.12:11).

2. **Live by faith in the living Word of God**. The sword of the spirit is the word of God. Faith is the shield by which you can quench the fiery darts of the enemy (Eph.6:16-17). Faith to win against the anti-help spirits is located in the Word of God. Rom.10:17, Jesus Christ, the Lord and Saviour defeated them by the Word (Mt.4:1-11). If you

must stand strongly against the evil forces to your help, you must know how to use these weapons. Learn to fellowship with the word of God and the faith to win will rub on you.

3. **Prayer and fasting**. This is another effective weapon you can engage in, when dealing with anti-help spirits in your life. Launch out in violent and aggressive prayers combined occasionally with fasting as the need may arise. The only language your enemy (the devil) understands is violence. Be forceful against him in prayer. Lord Jesus enjoined this weapon and He conquered. Our favourite characters in the Bible used this weapon and were victorious (Est 4:16). Wake up in prayer and fasting and see your life characterized with unusual help.

4. **The weapon of praise and thanksgiving**. Learn to praise God and give Him thanks in any battle of life and victory shall be yours. King Jehoshaphat used this weapon and he gained victory over his allied enemies (2Cor.20). The Lord Jesus' attitude is to give thanks to God in any situation of life. Thanksgiving to God gave Him victory over Lazarus' death (Joh.11:43-44). King David lived a victorious life because he knew how to praise God and thank Him. God's command is that you should give thanks and not to worry, then you will have the hand of victory (Phil 4:6-7). Thanksgiving and praise to God should be your habit and you will see the defeat of your enemies to your progress in life.

5. **The lifestyle of giving**. God loves a cheerful giver. God is a giver, He gave the only one He has to receive many. Giving will give your life victory, turning your life around and giving you material progress. It will help you to defeat demons to your

financial help. The Word of God encourages giving in all circumstances, for God knows it to be a spiritual weapon that can subdue any anti-help spirits in your life (Joh.3:16; Prov.3:9). Learn to be generous and you will see what the results will be.

6. **The grace of higher anointing.** By this I mean seeking help from the genuine anointed man of God for victory over any anti-help spirits attacking your life. What destroys their yoke and lifts their burden from man's life is the anointing of God upon His servants (Isa 10:27). There are demons attacking your help who will not bow to you until you engage them in higher power than them (Mt.12:29; Luk.11:21,22). By this you can go for counseling or deliverance or the grace of God's Prophet. The ministry of these men of God can be of help to you especially if your life is characterized with fruitless efforts continually. By these also you can win battles over the anti-help spirits in your life.

7. **Lifestyle of holiness.** If you must actually build resistance against any evil powers and forces consistently and victoriously and if any of the spiritual weapons mentioned here or not will be effective, you must live a life of holiness. Living by God's principles and standards. Note this "PURITY IS POWER"; (Ps.29:2, 47:8, 93:5, Heb.12:14).

Conclusively, life is full of opportunities and help but great and many are the adversaries and until you engage them in battle, life will not give you what you deserve but what you earn. Fight the enemies of your life. Destroy them before they destroy you. Kill them before they kill you. Rob them before they rob you. Do this by putting to effective use the spiritual weapons God makes available unto you.

Through your relationship and faith in Jesus, victory is yours. Remember always that if you don't attack the anti-help spirits, they will attack you. And this may be too dangerous and life threatening to you. The anti-help spirits are real, attack them and they will surrender to you.

5.

SEASON OF HELP

REFERENCE / INTRODUCTORY SCRIPTURES

The following scriptures set the tone for this write up on 'Season of Help'. It suffices to say from the foregoing that throughout this piece, the Words: HELP, FAVOUR & MERCY are used interchangeably as they are also referenced in most contexts in the Bible.

- Psalms 102:13 NKJV: You will arise and have **mercy** on Zion; **_For the time to favor her, Yes, the set time, has come._**

- Ecclesiastes 3:11 KJV: **_He hath made everything beautiful in His time_**: also, he hath set the world in their heart, so that no man can find out the work that God maketh from the beginning to the end.

- 1 Peter 5:10 NKJV: But may the God of all grace, who called us to His eternal glory by Christ Jesus, ***after you have suffered a while***, perfect, establish, strengthen, and settle you.

- 1 Chronicles 12:32 KJV: And of the children of Issachar***, which were men that had understanding of the times,*** to know what Israel ought to do; the heads of them were two hundred; and all their brethren were at their commandment.

God's Disposition about Season & Biblical Concept of Season

Though God lives in eternity, which is not time bound or time measured, yet for the purpose of relating to humanity, He works in time and season which are what are well understood by us, and we can relate to. To this extent, God thus have time and season that He does set for certain intervention and activity that concerns man, especially His own people.

God lives in a Timeless Space and His notion of Time and Season is quite different from and not in synchronization with ours. It is comparable to the difference between God's Thought and ours or His Plans / Ways and ours as established in Isaiah 55.

"For My thoughts are not your thoughts, Nor are your ways My ways," says the Lord. "For as the heavens are higher than the earth, so are My ways higher than your ways and My thoughts than your thoughts". (Isa 55:8-9; NKJV)

However, an in-depth study of the Word of God reveals that God does appoint a special SEASON, or TIME or DISPENSATION that He reaches out to His Own People, based on His own prerogative, or when His people, based on understanding precipitated the time or season for God's performance.

For example, the following Times / Seasons / Days are mentioned in the Bible and are worthy of studying for a good understanding of our subject:

> **Times of Refreshing**: Acts 3:19 KJV: Repent ye therefore, and be converted, that your sins may be blotted out, when _the times of refreshing_ shall come from the presence of the Lord;

> **Time of Ignorance**: Acts 17:30 KJV: _And the times of this ignorance_ God winked at; but now commandeth all men everywhere to repent:

> **Accepted Time / Day of Salvation**: 2 Corinthians 6:2 KJV: (For he saith, I have heard thee in a _time accepted_, and in _the day of salvation_ have I succoured thee: behold, _now is the accepted time; behold, now is the day of salvation_.)

> **Seedtime & Harvest:** Genesis 8:22 KJV: While the earth remaineth, _seedtime and harvest_, and cold and heat, and summer and winter, and day and night shall not cease.

> **Time to every purpose under heaven**: Ecclesiastes 3:1 KJV: To everything there is a

season, and *a time to every purpose under the heaven*:

> **Set time to favour Zion (God's People):** Psalms 102:13 NKJV: You will arise and have mercy on Zion; *For the time to favor her*, Yes, *the set time*, has come.

And the biggest and most assuring truth is the capacity of God to step in, and change the situation, and the time and season in our favour.

Daniel 2:21 – ***And He (God) changeth the times and the seasons: he removeth kings, and setteth up kings: he giveth wisdom unto the wise, and knowledge to them that know understanding:***

Did you read that? Yes! He (God) changes the times and the seasons! This is amazingly fulfilling and exciting. It means that even if the setting of the 'Season or Timing' is not favorable to you, **God the Changer of Times and Season can step into the stage and change everything in your favour**. What can be more assuring?

THE SEASON OF HELP / SET TIME TO FAVOUR US: WHEN IS IT?

While it is absolutely true that God reserves the prerogative to choose whom He will show His Mercy to, or put in another way, Whom He will Help and the time He will as made known by Apostle Paul in Roman 9:15 -16;

For he saith to Moses, I will have mercy on whom I will have mercy, and I will have compassion on whom I will have compassion. So then it is not of him that willeth, nor of him that runneth, but of God that sheweth mercy. (Rom.9:15 & 16; KJV)

we still can go to God on some platforms to present ourselves as candidates for His Help / Mercy, and to precipitate the timing / the season for the divine intervention as will be shown in the following Biblical references:

1. **When we are chosen of God and become His own**; He automatically assumes the responsibility to HELP us no matter the level of opposition or odds against us. (Isaiah 41:8 - 14)

2. **When we have no other alternative to God**; he steps in to HELP US.

Psalms 20:7-8 KJV: **"Some trust in chariots, and some in horses: but we will remember the name of the Lord our God. They are brought down and fallen: but we are risen and stand upright."**

Ps.125:1-2 KJV: **"They that trust in the Lord shall be as mount Zion, which cannot be removed, but abideth forever. As the mountains are round about Jerusalem, so the Lord is round about his people from henceforth even forever."**

3. **When our FAITH in GOD is in place;** GOD's performance of His Promise to help us and do wonders in our lives will be spontaneously activated.

Luk.1:45 KJV: **"And blessed is she that believed: for there shall be a performance of those things which were told her from the Lord."**

Joh.11:40 KJV: **"Jesus saith unto her, Said I not unto thee, that, if thou wouldest believe, thou shouldest see the glory of God?"**

Mk.9:23 KJV: **"Jesus said unto him, if thou canst believe, all things are possible to him that believeth."**

4. **When our obedience is total and complete in GOD**; God's intervention on our behalf is guaranteed.

2Cor.10:6 KJV: **"And having in a readiness to revenge all disobedience, when your obedience is fulfilled."**

Isai.1:19 KJV: **If ye be willing and obedient, ye shall eat the good of the land:"**

Case Studies:

1. Jesus' Miracle at the Marriage at Cana in Galilee ➔ John 2: 1 - 11
2. Net Breaking, boat-sinking Miracle that Peter received from Jesus Christ ➔ Luke 5:1 - 6
3. The Helpless Impotent Man for thirty-eight years that Jesus Healed with absolute disregard to the traditional 'once-in-a-year' healing time at the troubling of the water by certain Angel. Jesus broke the 'Help Protocol' and healed the man out of the 'Help Season ➔ John 5:5-9

4. The 7 Notable times that Jesus performed healing miracles on a Sabbath Day contrary to the believe and expectations of the Jews as they believed that **Healing, carrying your bed, and walking more than a Sabbath's day journey was forbidden.** According to the Jews, *A Sabbath's day journey equaled to 3,000 feet from your dwelling place.* –

I. Jesus Heals Simon Peter's Mother-in-Law ➔ (*Read:* Mark 1:29-31)

II. Jesus heals a man with a withered hand ➔ (*Read:* Mark 3:1-6)

III. Jesus heals a man born blind ➔ (*Read:* John 9:1-16)

IV. Jesus heals a crippled woman ➔ (*Read:* Luke 13:10-17)

V. Jesus heals a man with Dropsy ➔ (*Read*: Luke 14:1-6)

VI. Jesus drives out an evil spirit ➔ (*Read:* Mark 1:21-28)

VII. Jesus heals a lame man by the pool of Bethesda ➔ (*Read:* John 5:1-18)

Conclusion

Surely, God has gotten times and seasons in His Hands, (Time / Season of Help inclusive). We can however invoke or precipitate the Season of Help to our advantage by becoming God's Own, having absolute Trust and Faith in Him, no alternative to Him and Walking in total Obedience to His words. Even if it seems the times and seasons are not in our favour,

God will change them to our favour and we will enjoy His HELP regardless of Culture, Protocol, Rule, Authority or any contrary verdict.

6.
ACCESSING DIVINE HELP

PSALM 121:1-2
I will lift up my eyes to the hills, from whence comes my help? My help comes from the LORD, who made heaven and earth.

ISAIAH 41:13
For I, the LORD your God, will hold your right hand, saying to you, Fear not, I will help you.

HEBREWS 4:16
Let us therefore come boldly to the throne of grace, that we may obtain mercy and find grace to help in time of need.

Help is a necessity of life. No man becomes great without being helped. It is an action given to provide assistance or aid to someone in need.

Divine help is normally referred to as "Help from above." It is when God Himself organizes help for His people - and He does it in a way that no man will take the glory. When a man is helped he finds it easy to achieve his purpose and fulfill destiny.
Solomon would never have been king over Israel without the invaluable help of Prophet Nathan and King David. (1Ki.1:11-35)

Peter would have gone back home empty handed on the day his efforts delivered nothing on his fishing expedition without the help of our Lord Jesus Christ. (Luk.5:1-8)

Divine help is to the destiny of man what soil is to seeds. It usually arises from expected and unexpected sources or known and unknown sources.

The man who helped David and his men to recover their losses in the hands of the Amalekites was unknown to them (1Sam.30:10-16) while Jonathan, who helped him against his father, King Saul, was known to him (1Sam.20:1-4).

The man who had spent thirty-eight years at the Pool of Bethesda received his deliverance when Jesus unexpectedly approached him (Joh.5:1-9).

The four friends who brought their paralyzed friend to Jesus expected him to be healed on that day (Mk.2:1-12).

There are four things to know about divine help. They are:

1. It comes from God alone. Ps.121:1-2; Gen.49:25; Deut..33:29; 2Ki. 6:27; Acts 26:22.

2. He uses men as His channel of help. 1Sam.16:1-13; Exod.3:7-9; Acts 9:10-18; Acts 8:5-8.

3. Helpers sent by God don't usually appear as helpers. 2Ki.5:3; Mk.1:6; 2Ki.7:3-4; 1Sam. 17:33;43.

4. Some sent helpers are unwilling to help. Jon.1:1-3; Exod.4:10-14.

Examples of divine help in the scriptures:

1. Num.22,24

When Balak, the king of the Moabites contracted Balaam to curse Israel.

2. Exod.14:1-31
Crossing the Red Sea and deliverance from the army of Egypt.

3. 2Chr.20:1-30
The battle between the Israelites and the people of Ammon, Moab and Mount Seir.

4. Luk.23:39-43
The criminal crucified with Jesus on Calvary.

5. Joh.9:1-7
The man born blind.

6. Acts 12:1-11
The deliverance of Peter from the hand of Herod.

The help of God is always available but there are keys to accessing them. They are -

1. You must be known to Him. If He doesn't know you, He can't help you. Mt.15:22-28; Amos 3:3.

2. You must ask for it. There are things He might not do if we do not ask.
Luk.15:31; Mt.7:8-11.

3. Position yourself for help. There are things a man does that tell God such a man is ready for help.
Luk.5:2-3; Phil.4:15-19.

4. Sow the seed of help. If you desperately need help from above, help people below.
Prov.19:17; Ps.41:1; Mt.5:7.

5. Faith in the Word of God. Absolute reliance on the promises of God releases His help.
Gen.21:1-2; Heb.13:5-6.

7.

THE ROLE OF ANGELS IN HELP MINISTRY

"Bless the LORD, ye his angels, that excel in strength, that do his commandments, hearkening unto the voice of his word."
Psalms 103:20

Although there will be challenges, troubles and affliction in human history, there will be opposition, persecution and disaster. Jesus said, 'In the world, there will be trouble.' We Christians are involved in this world but Jesus has prayed for us to be kept. How do we go about overcoming these challenges?

There are human limitations and restrictions. How then do we achieve our God-given goals and assignments here on earth? God promised that He will deliver us from troubles that Satan, the trouble maker can throw at us. One way He delivers us is through the ministry of angels. Our angels are here on earth right now, having been sent to minister to our needs as an *heir of salvation* (Heb.1:14)

WHO ARE THE ANGELS?

1. They are supernatural beings
2. They have extra ordinary powers

3. They are spirits
4. They reside in heaven, the dwelling place of God.
5. They are fearful beings with wings which they use to fly
6. They do not marry; they cannot procreate
7. They are not limited by time, distance or obstacles.
8. They can assume or change into shapes, humans or objects as the need or occasion arises
9. They are ageless and swift in movement
10. They were created and not deities
11. They are light; dazzling lights
12. They take directives
13. They are numerous in number and many times more than human beings
14. They are in hierarchies and in different forms
15. They don't die neither are they subject to natural or human laws
16. They are not robots; they have expression
17. They are in categories or levels:
    i.   Cherubims and Seraphims
    ii.   Elders, Dignitaries, Thrones
    iii. Arch-angels
    iv.   Angels

THEIR ROLES AND EXAMPLES OF WHAT THEY DID IN THE BIBLE:
1. WARRING ANGELS: they fight
2. WORSHIP ANGELS: they sing and worship God
3. MESSAGE: they deliver good news
4. DEFENCE: they defended Daniel in the lion's den
5. PROTECTION: they will carry you so that you don't dash your feet against stone

6. LEAD: they will go ahead of you; do not provoke them.
7. They appear in dreams for guidance and direction, e.g. an angel appears to Joseph to carry the baby Jesus to Egypt.
8. They killed Herod – maggot ate him up
9. They killed 185,000 armies of Syria
10. They emboldened Elijah
11. They called on Hagar to see the well in the desert
12. They rolled the grave away from the tomb of Christ for resurrection or during resurrection
13. They instructed Cornelius to send Peter
14. They advised Joseph not to leave Mary his wife
15. The angel of death killed the entire firstborn in Egypt
16. They ministered to Jesus after forty days of fasting and praying
17. They appeared to Jacob to give Him divine ideas when Laban wanted to cheat him.
18. They strengthened Jesus during the prayer of Gethsemane
19. They were sent to hand over revelation of the God of Daniel
20. They appeared to Elizabeth and Mary for divine order.
21. They will be reapers of the last days.
22. They will blow the last trumpet.
23. They will come with Jesus during the Second Coming.
24. They are real and they exist.
25. They released Peter from prison.

26. They broke his chains and shackles
27. They assisted early Believers in evangelism by opening prison doors for them
28. Angels understand the Word of God
29. Angels understand the name of Jesus
30. Angels recognize and honour the Believers' authority
31. Angels await the Believers' instructions
32. Angels know how to get a job done.

8.
POSITIONED FOR HELP

'Arise, go to Zarephath, which belongs to Sidon, and dwell there. See, I have commanded a widow there to provide for you.' 1Ki.17:9

The book of 1Kings 17:1-22 is a record of events that establishes the fact that positioning is a condition for accessing the right help. If you are wrongly located, you may miss your desired help because those who may have been sent to help and raise you will not get to you, and they will not wait forever. After praying and waiting upon the Lord one must be rightly located so that one's efforts in prayer will not go to waste. The right location in this context does not mean a physical or geographical place but things that one can do that can position him for the help one needs.

When drought came upon Israel because of the word of Prophet Elijah, the Lord instructed him to proceed to Brook Cherith where he would drink the water there and also be fed with ravens (1Kings 17:2-6). He did and was spared the sorrow that came upon the whole land. When the water from the brook dried up, God commanded him to proceed to Zarephath where a certain widow would take care of him (1Kings 17:7-9). He did and was provided for. The widow was also spared because she accommodated the Prophet of God. She not only had enough to eat throughout the famine (1Kings 17:15-16), her only son was brought back to life by the prophet when the son died (1Kings 17:17-22).

Let us consider three things that can position a man for help - even from unlikely sources from 1Kings 17:1-22.

1. INTIMACY WITH GOD

Elijah was so close to God that he was able to hear the instructions for his help clearly. He heard when it was time to go to Brook Cherith and he heard when it was time to go to Zarephath and who to go and meet there. God knows where you help is and how to bring it to you. Your closeness to the Lord will enhance your visibility for help spiritually and physically. Mary's relationship with Jesus saved the newly wed couple in Cana of Galilee from shame on their day of joy (John 2:1-10). The disciples of Jesus were given the meaning of His parables because they were close to Him (Matthew 13:36-42). Other followers did not have that benefit. Isaac was close enough to hear that he must not go to Egypt during the famine in his days (Genesis 26:1-3; 12-14).

Intimacy with God is cultivated and improved by regular personal prayer and worship sessions, Bible study and praying in the Spirit. That is when you hear what others are not hearing and see what others can't see.

2. OBEDIENCE TO INSTRUCTIONS

God honours obedience. When He gives an instruction concerning a place, He goes there ahead awaiting our response.

If Elijah did not go to the brook or Zarephath, he would have suffered the way others suffered. If Peter did not throw his net into the river as commanded by the Lord in Luke 5:1-8, he would have missed the great success he got in one throw. Jesus once asked a man whose hand was withered to stretch out that hand, he did and was made whole (Mark 3:1-4). Imagine if he did not comply.

When we obey God, we commit Him to perform what He has promised. Abraham became great because he followed instructions. Obedience positions you to receive from God and man.

3. SACRIFICE

To sacrifice is to give away what is of a present benefit or what can be of benefit in the nearest future.

The widow sacrificed her family's last meal to Elijah and got more than a meal in return. Her last meal became her first and when sickness took her son, she got him back. Genuine sacrifice opens up the gates of a man's life to great things. Abraham agreed to sacrifice Isaac and God swore by Himself to bless him (Genesis 22:1-2; 16-17). Solomon offered a unique sacrifice to God and he got from God what nobody before him ever had (1Kings 3:4-5; 11-13). Apostle Paul compared our giving to a sacrifice (Philippians 4:18). Our seeds and first fruits are sacrifices.

What have you given to God recently? The sacrifice of the widow in our text opened her up for the best of God. We get the best of God when we give Him the best of us.
If a man is rightly positioned the good things he does not ask for will come looking for him.

SECTION TWO

DAY ONE TO FORTY (EXHORTATION, CONFESSIONS AND PRAYER POINTS)

DAY ONE
THE MYSTERY OF HELP

EXHORTATION

Until help is available, insult is inevitable! - P A Olowoporoku

"And the LORD God said, It is not good that the man should be alone; I will make him an helpmeet for him." (Gen.2:18)
Two are better than one, Because they have a good reward for their labor.
For if they fall, one will lift up his companion. But woe to him who is alone when he falls, For he has no one to help him up. Again, if two lie down together, they will keep warm; But how can one be warm alone? Though one may be overpowered by another, two can withstand him. And a threefold cord is not quickly broken. (Eccl.4:9-12)

Help is an active force in the actualization of man's destiny. When God created man, He felt there is the need for that man to have a 'helpmeet' a helper if you please that is different from every other creature. The purpose of this helpmeet is to assist in ensuring that the man reaches his full potentials and of course to curb loneliness.
While some will readily assume that the helpmeet intended in the Scripture quoted above relates solely to marriage, it will be wrong to so assume; because there are

other Scriptural references that prepare individuals for purpose achievement, that do not necessarily relate to marriage alone (Eccl.4:9-12; Amos 3:3).

The essence of this discourse is to expose us to the mystery behind help. It is mysterious because without it there is no way you can get to where you are going. Why? Because you don't know where you are going and you need a **Navigational Guide** to lead you. The **Supreme Navigational Guide** is God Almighty Himself and He disperses Himself in other beings to distribute help. Many people are unaware of this fact and are thus languishing on the pathway of life. Such people are living a rudderless life which makes them purposeless in life. The essence of help is to give guidance towards life's destination.

Let's quickly examine the reason why help is mysterious.

- **MAN IS HELPLESS WITHOUT GOD (Hosea 13:9; Isai.41:14)**. Whether you like it or not, the fact remains that everyone of us will be lost without God. As our Spiritual 'Birther', our spiritual umbilical cord is still attached to Him. With this, He directs and orders our lives. When we try to detach ourselves from this cord, we suffer. Operating outside of His jurisdiction is perilous to our existence. Don't run away from God. Rather, run towards Him.

- **EVERYONE NEEDS HELP (Luk.6:13)**. Jesus, our Supreme Leader needed help for the continuation of His earthly ministry so He chose some men. When He was spiritually weak, the angels came to help Him (Mk.1:13; Luk.22:43). When He was tired while bearing His Cross, someone was sent to help Him (Mt.27:32). All these go to show that if Jesus could need help we all need help.

- **HELP BIRTHS HELP (Gal.6:7).** One of the mysteries of help is that when you render help, it will come back to you not necessarily in the format in which you rendered it. The Scriptures is filled with instances where people who render help were not stranded.
- **HELP ATTRACTS MORE HELP (1Chr.12:22).** David was a beneficiary of such help. He was able to locate one help, the floodgate opened and more help came pouring in. If you are able to locate the right help, it will cause a chain reaction of more help.
- **HELP GOTTEN OUTSIDE OF GOD IS WITH DEADLY PENALTY (Isai.31:1).** When men leave the 'Fountain of Life' to dig cisterns for themselves, they court death. There is a curse waiting for whoever ventures out of God for help. I beg you, do not try it. If you have, humbly seek His face in repentance.
- **ABSENCE OF HELP THWARTS PROGRESS (Mt.20:6).** Those labourers in Jesus' parable were stagnant until help came. When there is no help, one's life will either be oscillating or regressing. Only help guarantees progress.
- **ONLY GOD CAN DETERMINE THE KIND OF HELP YOU NEED (Isai.41:14).** We fall into trouble because we think we know what we need but God knows best (Isai.55:8,9). He likens us to a worm which is very helpless. You need God to help you determine the perfect help you really need.
- **IF GOD DOES NOT ORDAIN HELP, IT WILL BE INEFFECTUAL (2Ki.6:26,27).** Beloved, please beware of any form of help that does not originate from God. If God does not send you help, do not

take it because it will not work. It is only God's ordained help that will profit your life.

- **THE HEIGHT OF ACHIEVEMENT IS DEPENDENT ON THE LEVEL OF HELP RECEIVED (Luk.11:31).** Jesus only compared His greatness to one earthly man – Solomon. Solomon's wealth and wisdom was far-reaching. He was able to accomplish these because of the unusual help he received from God.
- **GOD'S HELP IS THE BEST OF ALL (Ps.60:11).** To anyone relying on mere mortal for help without first looking unto God (Ps.121:1), my counsel for you is, desist. When you look unto God like the Israelites in the Book of Exodus, He will send you a Moses. If you first look for Moses without God, he will put you in trouble.

CONFESSIONS

❖ I am entitled to help because the Great Helper is my Heavenly Father. Help is my redemption package, help is readily available for me in the Lord. Help is coming my way today. There is help with my name written on it, and I cannot miss my appointed help.

❖ The Spirit of God is my helper, I am therefore strengthened, oil of help is on my head, I receive uncommon help, I receive direct help, I receive indirect help, I receive unusual help, I receive divine help, and I receive pure help.

- Help is not scare in my life, I call for help, I pray for help, I believe in help, help brings unusual apportion my way, help brings my deliverance.
- The heaven of help is opened to me, I cannot be in bondage, I cannot be frustrated, help brings joy into my heart, and help brings perfect correction into my life.
- The Lord is my helper. Therefore, I receive reliable help, I receive fulfilling help, I receive continuous help, and I receive international help.
- Helping hands are stretched towards me. Therefore, I cannot fall, I cannot lack, I cannot be stranded, I cannot remain on a spot, I am not abandoned.
- He that helps me is near me, I am not alone, help is available for me, help is within reach for me, no more delay, no more waiting in vain, no more empty expectations, and no more dry places.
- God is at work on my behalf, all things works for good in my life, my helpers cannot be tired, my helpers cannot be lost, my helpers cannot die because it is God that sends helpers to me. Therefore, I have hope of a better life.
- Help opens impossible doors for me, help break impossible barriers for me, help is the leg that claims my dominion, help is the power to break all limitation.

❖ Help is the mouth that speaks for me, help makes impossible become possible. Hallelujah, I am helped!

PRAYER POINTS
(ISAI.40,41)

1. Lord, I thank You for Your Divine plan and purpose for this year's Mercy Rain.
2. I thank You because what You have in store for us is beyond human comprehension.
3. I celebrate God for His faithfulness and the past help we have received. Sing a song to the King of kings.
4. Lord, cleanse me from all unrighteousness and forgive all my sins.
5. Shout, God of mercy 21 times. Then, say, give me an encounter that will move me into my next level.
6. I refuse to be alone, make a help meet for me (Gen.2:18).
7. Where there is no help, find help for me (Gen.2:20).
8. Let the earth help me and my children (Rev.12:16).
9. God, from every garrison of judgment arise for my help and redeem me in Jesus' name (Ps.44:26).

10. A Very Present help locate me now (Ps.46:1).
11. My Father, my Father, awake the sleeping helpers for my sake   (Mk. 4:37-39).
12. Turn, oh Lord, every evil intention against my life to my uttermost, in Jesus' name (Gen.50:20).
13. Lord, help me to overcome anything I am doing now that might eventually make You find substitute for me in Your kingdom (ISam.15:28).
14. My Father, My Father, fill me with the consciousness of Your second coming at all times (Eph.5:14-16).
15. God of mercy, have mercy on all my unseen family members. See them and heal all of their sicknesses (Luk.19:10).
16. My Father, my Father, forgive me for my past misdeeds and give me another chance to live my life for You (Jon.8:11).
17. My Father, my Father, terminate every unfruitfulness effort in my life (Gen.27:20-30).
18. Connect me oh Lord, with the people who have what I need and the people who need what I have (Gen.41:14-46).

DAY 1 PROPHECY

1. A hero will emerge from something reputable to be a hero.
2. A major issue will be resolved mysteriously.
3. We will receive grace to discern the strategies of the enemy.

DAY TWO
JESUS – HELP PERSONIFIED
EXHORTATION

"Grace does not depend on what we have done for God but rather what God has done for us. Ask people what they must do to get to heaven and most reply, 'Be good.' Jesus' stories contradict that answer. All we must do is cry, 'Help!'"
- Philip Yancey
Who saved us and called us to a holy calling, not because of our works but because of His own purpose and grace, which he gave us in Christ Jesus before the ages began. (2Tim.1:9)

Help is beyond an act or offer. Help can also be a Person - Jesus is help personified. He does this through a special gift called GRACE. Of a truth, we can't properly understand Help until it begins and ends with Jesus. At a time when the human race was in jeopardy, great darkness and confusion, bound to be doomed forever. Jesus was the only worthy Lamb of God who volunteered and took up our suffering, gave us hope and helped us out of our misery.

Rev.5.12 - Saying in a loud voice, Deserving is the Lamb, who was sacrificed, to receive all the power and riches and wisdom and might and honor and majesty (glory, splendor) and blessing!

One of the ways Jesus helped us out was through GRACE. Every good and perfect gifts comes from God, found in Jesus and delivered to us through GRACE. Since the introduction of grace (help) to the life of man, we have been able to do all that is expected of us through this divine grace (help).

Ephesians 4:7 But to each one of us grace has been given as Christ apportioned it.

WHAT IS GRACE?

Grace is God's free and unmerited favor for singular human.

WAYS BY WHICH JESUS HELPS US THROUGH GRACE:

1. **GRACE SAVES US**: Eph.2.8 - *For it is by free grace (God 's unmerited favor) that you are saved (delivered from judgment and made partakers of Christ 's salvation) through [your] faith. And this [salvation] is not of yourselves [of your own doing, it came not through your own striving], but it is the gift of God. We were doomed, condemned and judged at a time, but through Grace we were delivered, discharged and acquitted. (AMP.)*

2. **GRACE IS SUFFICIENT TO HELP OUR WEAKNESSES:** 2Cor.12:9 - *But he said to me, "My grace is sufficient for you, for my power is made perfect in weakness."* Therefore, I will boast all the more gladly of my weaknesses, so that the power of Christ may rest upon me. We all have our weak points, which affects our relationship, our walk with God, or our ventures in life. The availability of Grace. Makes the weak achieve great feat.

3. **GRACE OBTAINS MERCY FOR US**: Heb.4:16- *Let us then approach the throne of grace with confidence, so that we*

may receive mercy and find grace to help us in our time of need. Upon our salvation, we still err as humans, we make bad decisions, we hurt our relationships, we make mistakes and hurt God most times. Each time we sin against God, we must approach the throne of Grace to obtain Mercy.

4. **GRACE GIVES UNCTION TO FUNCTION**: Eph.3:20... *according to the power that works within us...* Matt.25.15 - *To one he gave five talents [probably about 5,000], to another two, to another one - to each in proportion to his own personal ability. Then he departed and left the country* (AMP).

The level of God's power working in us is called Grace. Our abilities vary from each other. The proportion to which we function and display strength is fueled by God's grace within us.

5. **GRACE INTERCEDES FOR US**: Rom.8.34 - *Who is there to condemn [us]? Will Christ Jesus (the Messiah), Who died, or rather Who was raised from the dead, who is at the right hand of God actually pleading as He intercedes for us?* What would we have done if Christ would have not died for us? Yet after he ascended he never left us, he keeps interceding for us.

CONFESSIONS

- ❖ I am an heir of salvation, I boast in my relationship, I am accepted amongst the beloved, I am adopted in the common wealth of Israel, I am a seed of Abraham, I am a child of God.
- ❖ There is therefore no condemnation for me, because I am in Christ Jesus, I have been

justified, because I was predestined for glory.

❖ Jesus has taken my place, He paid the price of the sin He did not owe, He took the punishment I cannot bear, He paid the ransom in full measure, He finished everything, He conquered on my behalf.

❖ Now I am born again, I am alive unto righteousness, death has no power over me, Jesus is my substitute, I was weak, now I am strong, I was condemned, now I am justified, I was appointed to wrath, now I am the apple of God's eye.

❖ The law of the Spirit of life in Christ Jesus has set me free from the law of sin and death, my weak flesh cannot satisfy the laws of God, Jesus's life in me has given me victory over the flesh.

❖ I can do all things through Christ who strengthens me. Christ lives in me so, I have the hope of glory. Heaven is not closed on me, I know Jesus, who is the Door of Heaven.

❖ Jesus is the Light of the world. Therefore, darkness cannot rule over me. I belong to Jesus, so, I have victory over darkness.

❖ Jesus is the bread of life therefore, I cannot be hungry. Jesus is the water of life, I am a satisfied person. Jesus is the resurrection and the life therefore, I cannot die, Jesus is the way, therefore I cannot be lost. I am glad I belong to Jesus.

❖ Help is readily available for me, because Jesus is my helper. Jesus helped me know God the Father, Jesus helped know the Spirit. Jesus helped me fulfill my ministry, Jesus has helped me identify my divine purpose, Jesus helped me conquer sin and lust.

❖ Jesus is my reliable help, Jesus is my dependable help, Jesus is my available help, Jesus is my never exhausted helper, Jesus is my sure help. Hallelujah!

PRAYER POINTS

PSALM 22

1. Jesus, I thank You for working alongside me as I grow in my relationship with You.
2. Thank You Jesus. You are bigger than any giant in my life (Ps. 20:7)
3. Lord, baptize me with the anointing of ease in Jesus' Name.
4. My Father, my Father, in these perilous times, hide me under the shadow of Your wings.

5. Holy Spirit, open my eyes to the hidden things in the kingdom (ICor.29:10).
6. Father, help me to be worthy of the ultimate reward for profitable stewardship in Jesus' name (Rev.22:12).
7. Jesus, draw me close to You like never before (Gal.4:6).
8. Lord, cancel all appointment with death in my life (Jon.8:1-8).
9. Lord, show me how to achieve help and attract helpers (Mk.10:46-52).
10. Demonic dreams assigned to chase helpers from me cease! In the name of Jesus.
11. Jesus! walk into my life and help me (Mt.14:25).
12. Jesus! have compassion on me and settle me (Mt.15:32).
13. Oh Lord, thou son of David, have mercy on me and help me (Mt.20:20).
14. Whatever is sponsored to make me a victim of untimely death, Jesus the death swallower, swallow it (2Cor.15:54).
15. Oh Lord, arise and ordain terrifying noises against my oppressors in Jesus' name (Mt.28:1-3)
16. Disappeared helpers, re-appear to move my destiny forward in Jesus' name (Jon.11:11).

17. Lord, help me to lay a very solid foundation for every member of my family (2Tim.6:9).
18. Lord, increase my faith and help me to be completely dependent on You in all I do (Heb.11:6).

DAY THREE
HOLY SPIRIT, OUR DIVINE HELPER
EXHORTATION
When we pray for the Spirit's help ... we will simply fall down at the Lord's feet in our weakness. There we will find the victory and power that comes from His love.
- Andrew Murray

"But you shall receive power (ability, efficiency, and might) when the Holy Spirit has come upon you, and you shall be My witnesses in Jerusalem and all Judea and Samaria and to the ends (the very bounds) of the earth." Acts.1:8

Our Lord Jesus Christ knew how miserable we would be if left alone without help. So, when he was leaving, he promised to send us a new Helper - The Holy Spirit. Every Christian can only succeed when the Holy Spirit is present in his or her life.
WHO IS THE HOLY SPIRIT?
1. **A Person.** Rev.22.17 - The Spirit and the Bride say, "Come." And let the one who hears say, "Come." And let the one who is thirsty come; let the one who desires take

the water of life without price. He can talk, he has feelings. Personal pronouns are used for him throughout the Bible.

2. **The Helper.** Jon.16.7 - Nevertheless, I tell you the truth: it is to your advantage that I go away, for if I do not go away, the Helper will not come to you. But if I go, I will send him to you. Romans 8:26. In the same way, the Spirit helps us in our weakness. We do not know what we ought to pray for, but the Spirit himself intercedes for us through wordless groans.

3. **The one that convicts.** Jon.16.8 - And when he comes, he will convict the world concerning sin and righteousness and judgment:

4. **The Guide.** Joh.16.13 - When the Spirit of truth comes, he will guide you into all the truth, for he will not speak on his own authority, but whatever he hears he will speak, and he will declare to you the things that are to come.

5. **The Teacher**. Joh.14.26 - But the Helper, the Holy Spirit, whom the Father will send in my name, he will teach you all things and bring to your remembrance all that I have said to you.

7 WAYS THE HOLY SPIRIT HELPS EVERY BELIEVER

1. **He forms Christ's character in us.** Gal.5.22-23 But the fruit of the [Holy] Spirit [the work which His presence within accomplishes] is love, joy (gladness), peace, patience (an even temper, forbearance), kindness, goodness (benevolence), faithfulness, gentleness (meekness, humility), self-control (self-restraint, continence). Against such things there is no law [that can bring a charge].

2. **He clothes us with Christ's power so that we can do the works that Jesus did, and even greater ones. Isai.61.1** - The Spirit of the Lord God is upon me, because the Lord has anointed and qualified me to preach the Gospel of good tidings to the meek, the poor, and afflicted; He has

sent me to bind up and heal the brokenhearted, to proclaim liberty to the [physical and spiritual] captives and the opening of the prison and of the eyes to those who are bound.

3. **He increases our faith. Jude.1.20** - But you, beloved, build yourselves up [founded] on your most holy faith [make progress, rise like an edifice higher and higher], praying in the Holy Spirit.

4. **He enables us to pray even when you don't know what to pray Rom.8.26** - The [Holy] Spirit comes to our aid and bears us up in our weakness; for we do not know what prayer to offer nor how to offer it worthily as we ought, but the Spirit Himself goes to meet our supplication and pleads on our behalf with unspeakable yearnings and groanings too deep for utterance.

5. **He allows us to receive spiritual gifts from Jesus for the common good. 1Cor.12.4** - Now there are distinctive varieties and distributions of endowments (gifts, extraordinary powers distinguishing certain Christians, due to the power of divine grace operating in their souls by the Holy Spirit) and they vary, but the [Holy] Spirit remains the same (I Cor.12, 13 & 14)

6. **He allows us to operate in specialized spiritual functions. Rom.12.5** - So we, numerous as we are, are one body in Christ (the Messiah) and individually we are parts of one another [mutually dependent on one another]. (Rom.12:4-8; I Cor.12:27-31; Eph.4:11-13).

7. **He fulfills the prophecy of Joel 2:28-32** - And afterward I will pour out My Spirit upon all flesh; and your sons and your daughters shall prophesy, your old men shall dream dreams, your young men shall see visions (Acts 2:16-21).

CONFESSIONS

- ❖ I receive divine help, I receive divine guidance, I receive supernatural assistance, I receive Holy Ghost support.

- ❖ The help of man is not enough: I have access to divine wisdom, he that lack wisdom should ask from God who gives liberality and upbraided not, I enjoy Open Heaven, I enjoy divine support.

- ❖ I am born again, I am baptized in the Holy Ghost, I shall profit in my life, my fellow men shall benefit from me. I shall be a profit to heaven, Holy Spirit is my guidance.

- ❖ What is difficult for men is possible with God, I shall not fail, I have access to divine secrets, I have access to godly wisdom, power is available to me. Word of knowledge is also available to me.

- ❖ I belong to the light, I cannot walk in darkness, Jesus is the light of the world, I reject the spirit of deception, I reject the seducing spirit, I reject the spirit of end-times, and I reject darkness.

- ❖ If I do not know what to do, I know who to meet, the Holy Spirit does not deny. The Holy Spirit will inspire me, and lead me to the truth, I cannot be stranded.

- ❖ There is a way that seems right to a man, but the end thereof is the way of death. The Holy Spirit will lighten my path, I will not fall nor stumble, I will not reduce in size, I will increase.

❖ Shame is the promotion of fools, I have the wisdom of the Ancient of Days, I cannot fall like the foolish, God is my teacher, I cannot fail. God is my helper, I cannot lose my relevance.

❖ There is help for me in God, there is hope for me, there is a way for me, and I cannot be lost.

❖ Death is not my portion, I belong to the living God, I am blessed. Hallelujah!

PRAYER POINTS

Romans 8

1. Father, I thank You for Your power to rescue me in Jesus' name.
2. Father, I am grateful that I am valued by You.
3. Lord, help me to trust in Your provision for every of my potential problem (Ps.18:32).
4. Lord, help me to respond positively to Your ongoing work in my life   (Luk.2:19).
5. Lord, order my steps and help me walk like You (Ps.119:133).
6. Unction of the Holy Spirit, give me insight into all things (2Cor.2:10).

7. Boldness of the Holy Spirit to enter territories and occupy them for God, possess me.
8. The power of the Holy Spirit to destroy the works of the devil, possess me, in Jesus' name.
9. Spirit of wisdom, possess me to be productive (Exo. 28:3).
10. Shout Holy Spirit 21 times, reveal me to my helpers in Jesus' name.
11. Every spirit of error, that hinders prophecies, catch fire in Jesus' Name.
12. Anointing of wisdom that attract helpers, possess me in Jesus' name.
13. Holy Spirit equip me with what will make me acceptable before my helpers.
14. Spirit of promise and fail monitoring my life your time is up, leave me and be wasted, in the name of Jesus.
15. Holy Spirit, fill me with the Spirit of Joy in Jesus' name.
16. My altar of prayer, receive fresh fire.
17. God of mercy, reveal Yourself to me.
18. Poison of sin in my fluid and blood, Blood of Jesus flush it away.

DAY FOUR

THE MINISTERING ANGELS
EXHORTATION

Angels descending, bring from above, Echoes of mercy, whispers of love
Fanny J. Crosby

"Are not the angels all ministering spirits (servants) sent out in the service [of God for the assistance] of those who are to inherit salvation?" Heb.1.14

Angels are supernatural beings and Messengers of God who do God's will. Ps.103.20 - Bless (affectionately, gratefully praise) the Lord, you His angels, you mighty ones who do His commandments, harkening to the voice of His word.

The Bible is filled with instances of how angels came to the aid of man. For instance, God sent an angel to free Apostle Peter after he was jailed by King Herod (Acts 12:7-11). An angel of the Lord appeared to Joseph three times in a dream to make Mary his wife, to take baby Jesus and family on the Flight to Egypt when King Herod sought after his life and then to return to Nazareth (Mt.1:18-2:23).

Also, we can cite instances where angels in human forms have helped people in Bible times. The Bible recorded it that Angels came to minister to Christ after his temptation in the desert (Mt.4:11). Angels also comforted Jesus in His agony in the garden (Luk.22:43). In our contemporary world, there are situations where angels in human forms have helped people their daily existence too. A certain lady was kidnapped and driven deep into the forest. Fortunately, she was a child of God so the oracle rejected her for rituals. The kidnappers had to return her to the highway in the midnight so she couldn't find her way home. Suddenly a man appeared beside her and escorted her through certain shortcuts. Before she knew what was happening, she opened her eyes to her street. Before she would say thank you, the man had disappeared.

WAYS BY WHICH ANGELS HELP US

1. **They guide and guard us. Acts.12.15** ... *'They said, it is his (Peter's) angel!* Every believer has a guardian angel, just like dignitaries have bodyguards so also do we have. Ps.91:11 says *He will give his angels charge over us to accompany us.* While the Church was interceding for Peter to be released from prison. An angel rescued him so he came home knocking. Unfortunately, the other disciples who were praying for him couldn't believe he could be released so quickly, wgich made them argue and thought it was Peter's guardian angel.

2. **They protect us: Ps.91.12** – *'They shall bear you up on their hands, lest you dash your foot against a stone.'* There are several evils in the day, invisible arrows fly in the day and in the night, and so many evils roam the night while we sleep. While we sleep the Bible says enemies do come. They come with various attacks unknown to us but our angels protect us from many of these evils. Hallelujah!

3. **They are agents of good news (spiritual marketers): Luk.2.13,14** – *'Then suddenly there appeared with the angel an army of the troops of heaven (a heavenly knighthood), praising God and saying, - Glory to God in the highest [heaven], and on earth peace among men with whom He is well pleased [men of goodwill, of His favor].'* Many children of God who are into business or ministry are yet to understand how to engage the ministry of angels to help their trade. Angels have always been known to proclaim news. Without them, the shepherds would not have known Jesus was born. As ministers of God, engage the ministry of REAPER ANGELS to go forth into your harvest field and drive multitude to your ministry as you embark on evangelism. Rev.14.17 – *'Then another angel*

came out of the temple [sanctuary] in heaven, and he also carried a sharp scythe (sickle).'

4. **They rescue us from dangers. Act.12.7** – *'And suddenly an angel of the Lord appeared [standing beside him], and a light shone in the place where he was. And the angel gently smote Peter on the side and awakened him, saying, Get up quickly! And the chains fell off his hands.'* Apart from their abilities to protect us from encountering evils, they also have the capabilities to deliver us peradventure we fall into trouble. Peter was imprisoned and was planned to be executed, the Church prayed and an angel rescued Peter from Prison. *'The angel of the Lord, who encamps with them, delivers all who fear God.'* Ps.34:8

5. **They minister to refresh and comfort our soul during distress. Luk.22.43** – *'And there appeared to Him an angel from heaven, strengthening Him in spirit.'* In the hustle and bustle of life, unpleasant circumstances, stress, temptations, hard times etc. Will surface. In such difficult times, Angels can minister to our souls.

6. **They are agents of direction: Exod.23.20** - *"See, I am sending my angel before you to lead you safely to the land I have prepared for you.'* Angels are God's representatives for leading us to our destinations in life. This is why when you have met your prophet, honour and obey him. Many instances where people claim they dreamt of the prophet giving them profitable instructions in their dream; little do they know it wasn't the prophet himself but his angel.

7. **They fight on our behalf: Dan.10.13** – *'But for twenty-one days the spirit prince of the kingdom of Persia blocked my way. Then Michael, one of the archangels, came to help me, and I left him there with the spirit prince of the kingdom of Persia.'* Angels are also warriors. That is why God is called the Lord of host, the Lord of the armies of heaven armies made of angels etc. Mt.26.52-53- *"Put*

away your sword," Jesus told him. *"Those who use the swrod will be killed by the sword. - Don't you realize that I could ask my Father for thousands of angels to protect us, and he would send them instantly?"*

CONFESSIONS

- ❖ I am entitled to angelic help, Angels are my servants, Angels have assignments over me, Angels carry out divine purposes for me.
- ❖ Angels bring messages from God to me, Angels support me in battle, Angels go on errands for me, and Angels surround me always.
- ❖ Angels guide my properties, Angels move around my environment, Angels listen to my instructions, Angels make weapons of warfare available for me, Angels carry me in their hands.
- ❖ I cannot dash my foot against a stone, I cannot be a victim of accident. I cannot be kidnapped. I cannot die untimely death.
- ❖ My angels are not asleep, my angels are not weak, my angels are not corrupt, my angels are good. My angels watch over me.
- ❖ My angels bring good news to me, my angels connect me with great opportunities, and my angels will clear road blocks for me.
- ❖ My angels are not missing, my angels did not abandon me, my angels are not sluggish;

my angels are not powerless, my angels are not cruel.

❖ My angels will guide me to where I will locate help, my angels guide me to where to obtain mercy, my angels guide me to prosperity, my angels influence people to favour me.

❖ I receive angelic help, I receive my ministering angels, I enjoy divine favor, I enjoy divine intervention, I enjoy divine help, I enjoy divine assistance, I enjoy grace.

❖ I cannot be lost, I cannot be killed, I cannot be stranded, and I cannot be put to shame. There are always opportunities for me, there is always an escape way for me. There is always what I can do, through the ministry of angels, I will receive all my redemption benefits in full. Hallelujah!

PRAYER POINTS
PSALM 68

1. Lord, I thank You because You are slow to anger and great in mercy (Ps.145:8).

2. Sing great song of praise to God of mercy with (Ps.89:1).

3. My Father, my Father, give me the servant Spirit of Jesus Christ so I may serve others like He did.
4. My Father, my Father, teach my hand to war and my fingers to fight only the battles You want me to fight.
5. Lord, open my eyes to where I have missed it, and help me to retrace my steps back to You.
6. Lord, give me grace to follow You in spirit and in truth.
7. Angel of the Lord, reconnect me to my place of destiny.
8. Shout, God of Mercy 21 times, send Your angel of connection ahead of me to connect me with my spouse (Gen.24:7).
9. Angel of help, appear to me in all my dreams (Gen.31:11).
10. Angel of deliverance, appear to me (Exod.32).
11. Angel of revelation appear to me (Eccl.1:9).
12. Angel of good news appear to me (Luk.2:10).
13. Strengthening angel appear to me and minister to me (Luk.22-43).
14. Eyes that attract help is my portion today.
15. Every agenda of the enemies to frustrate me, scatter by fire, in Jesus' name.

16. Every helping hand I employ that turn demonic at night to deal with me, be wasted by fire.
17. Every strange voices manipulating my destiny helper be silent in Jesus' name.
18. Sing a worship song and exalt God for your answered prayers.

DAY FIVE
SOURCE OF HELP: THE PROPHETS
EXHORTATION

Following a Prophet can either earn you a MANTLE for LIFE or a BATTLE of LIFE. It depends on you or who you followed" - **Oluwafemi Alabi**

"...Believe in the LORD your God, and you will be able to stand firm. Believe in his prophets, and you will succeed." 2Chr.20:20

A prophet is anybody with the gifts of Prophecy. Prophecy is the human report of a divine revelation. Thus, prophecy is not based on a hunch, supposition, inference, educated guess, or even sanctified wisdom. A prophet's primary function in the Old Testament (OT) was to serve as God's representative or ambassador by communicating God's word to his people. True prophets never spoke on their own authority or shared their personal opinions, but rather delivered the message God himself gave them. Several texts make this explicit; God promised Moses, *"Now go; I will help you speak and will teach you what to say"* Exod.4:12. God assured Moses, *"I will raise up for [my people] a prophet like you . . . and I will put my* words in his mouth. He will tell them everything I command him" Deut. 18:18. The Lord said to Jeremiah, "I have put my words in your mouth" Jer.1:9. God commissioned Ezekiel by saying, "You must speak my words to them" Ezek.2:7. And many of the OT prophetic books begin with the words, "The word of the LORD that came to . . ." (Hos. 1:2; Joel 1:1; Micah 1:1; Zeph. 1:1; cf. Jonah 1:1). Amos claimed, "This is what the LORD says" (Amos 1:3).

God has made use of His prophets to send help all through the Bible. Prophets have been agents of deliverance, rescue, direction and preservation to God's people. It is so unfortunate that this office of the Prophet has been jeopardized by false prophets today. But if there exists a fake, there must be an original. Genuine prophets of God still abound even though we may not see them often. Remember, when Elijah thought he was the only true prophet alive, God told him otherwise.

Ezra talks about the prophets helping to make the Israelites rebuild the House of God which was demolished. Ezr.5:2 **Then Zerubbabel son of Shealtiel and Joshua son of Jozadak set to work to rebuild the house of God in Jerusalem. And the prophets of God were with them, supporting them.**

A prophet helped Jehoshaphat to win the war against his adversaries 2Chr.20:15. Jahaziel said, **"King Jehoshaphat, listen! All you who live in Judah and Jerusalem, listen! The Lord says to you, 'Do not be afraid. Do not lose hope because of this huge army. The battle is not yours. It is God's.**

PROPHETS AS SOURCES OF HELP
The following are ways by which prophets can be of help;

1. **DELIVERANCE:** Acts.7.34 - *You can be sure that I have seen the misery of my people in Egypt. I have heard their cries. So, I have come to rescue them. Now go, for I will send you to Egypt.'*
Hosea 12:13 - *And by a prophet the LORD brought Israel out of Egypt, and by a prophet was he preserved.*

A lot of souls are in captivity, many are imprisoned, oppressed and afflicted by the devil but God delivers these people through the ministry of the prophets.

2. **DIRECTION:** 1Sam.9.9 - *(In those days if people wanted a message from God, they would say, "Let's go and ask the seer," for prophets used to be called seers.)*

Saul was merely looking for his father's donkeys but he found a prophet and found a throne by prophetic leading. It's now evident in our contemporary world that everyone wants a word from God about their life situations. Though many seek the prophet of God, without interest in seeking the God of the prophet. However, prophets are carriers of God's message which is profitable to direct and reveal hidden mysteries about life situations.

3. **PROSPERITY**: *Believe in his prophets, and you will succeed."*2Chr.20.20

Prophets are carriers of divine instructions that can help you achieve breakthrough if you believe and obey. In 2Kings 4, The wife of the deceased son of the prophets who was owing before he died, sought Elisha and she was given instructions concerning selling the olive oil and she paid her debts. The Shunamite woman who built a house for Elisha also received her own son through prophecy.

4. **REVELATION**: *Thus says the LORD who made it, the LORD who formed it to establish it (the LORD is His name)* Jer.33:2

Prophets are custodians of revelations. When they operate in their office, deep mysteries, secrets, visions, trance, audible voice are ways by which they receive revelations.

5. **MANTLE/POWER**: 2Ki.2:9 *Elisha said, "Please let a double portion of your spirit be upon me."*

Prophets are carriers of power. The Bible gave records of great miracles wrought by Prophets both in the Old and New Testament. If you are a wise, obedient and faithful son of the prophet, you can carry the mantle of your prophet.

CONFESSIONS

❖ Prophets are God's mouth piece. My prophet speaks peace into my life, my prophet speaks life into me, my prophet speaks joy into my life, and my prophet speaks mercy into my life. When my prophet prays for me, God answers.

❖ Prophets are God's eye balls. Prophets see beyond the ordinary, prophets see when evil is coming, prophets see when good is coming, prophets know what to do per time. My prophet will tell me what to do.

❖ Prophets know the mind of God. Prophets give divine directions, prophets lead to the Promised Land, genuine prophets do not lead astray, my prophet will lead me to my Promised Land.

❖ I will not abuse my prophets, I will not get careless with my prophets, I will celebrate my prophets, I will enjoy the reward of the prophet, and I will receive help from my prophets.

❖ The source of my help will never dry, the source of my help will not be blocked, the enemies will not know my secret.

❖ My prophets will tell me what to do, my prophet will guide me by God's Spirit. Prophets opens closed doors through God's leading.

❖ Help will not be far from me, and help will not be missing in my life. I will not suffer shame and mockery.

❖ Help will break the yoke of delay in my life. Help will break the yoke of slavery in my life.

❖ Help will locate me from above, help will locate me from abroad, and help will become my daily experience.

❖ I will not be far from help, I will not be stranded, and I will not be missing where I would be blessed. My children will be helped, I will not miss the best of God. My head shall be lifted high. I will not eat crumbs, my prophet will intercede for me, I shall be helped.

PRAYER POINTS

2ki.3:1-21

1. Father, I thank You for Your servant that brings liberation to those whose lives are in bondage.
2. You spirit of pride and error, I bind You in Jesus' name.
3. Voice of darkness in my foundation be silent in Jesus' name.
4. Where is my prophet, appear to me by mercy (Hos.12:13).
5. Say, fire of the Holy Spirit 12 times, surround me and my children.
6. Every fire-extinguisher, your time is up!
7. God of our fathers, open the book of remembrance for me, in Jesus' name (Est.6:1-3).
8. Help of 'it can only be God' locate me by mercy (Mk.5:1-20).
9. Lord, turn my minimum to maximum by Your great mercy (Mk.51-20).
10. My ordained helpers in any nation of the world, locate me with divine urgency (ICor.12:1).
11. Lord, make me a candidate for sudden help (Ps.40:13).
12. Lord, help me to trust that You are with me even during the storm of life (Isai.43:2).

13. My colorful destiny tied to evil altars, I release you by prophetic instruction (Mk.11 :1-7).
14. Anointing of unity flow into our ministries in Jesus' name (Ps.133).
15. As I begin to pray in the Spirit, I receive fresh fire of the Holy Spirit to dominate my environment.
16. God of Mercy, change my story (Mk.10:36-42).
17. Terrifying noise from above, arise and pursue my pursuers in Jesus' name (2Ki.6:24; 7:6).
18. Worship Him with a song (Ps.149).

DAY SIX
SOURCE OF HELP: UNCOMMON HELP
EXHORTATION
"God in Cage is man's limitation - when you cage God with unbelief, you're only limiting yourself" - Oluwafemi Alabi

"And we know that God causes everything to work together for the good of those who love God and are called according to his purpose for them." Rom.8.28

God is a mysterious God, and often He reveals Himself to us in different forms. By making the donkey to help Balaam against the attack of the angel, it connotes that help can come from various sources. Num.22:33: *"The donkey saw me and turned away from me these three* times. *If it had not turned away, I would certainly have killed you by now, but I would have spared it."*

A raven came to the rescue of Elijah. 1 Ki.17:4 *"You shall drink from the brook, and I have commanded the ravens to feed you there."*

A dove brought good news to Noah concerning the flood. Gen.8:11 And behold, the dove returned to him in the evening with a freshly plucked olive leaf in her beak. So, Noah knew that the waters had receded from the earth.

The Sun and Moon helped Joshua win the war. Josh.10:13 *"So the sun stood still, and the moon stopped, till the nation avenged itself on its enemies, as it is written in the Book of Jashar. The sun stopped in the middle of the sky and delayed going down about a full day."*

A dragon wanted to eliminate a woman and her glorious pregnancy, and the Earth helped her. Rev.12:16 *"And the earth helped the woman, and the earth opened her mouth, and swallowed up the flood which the dragon cast out of his mouth."*

The forest helped David win a fierce battle. 2 Sam.18:8 *"The battle spread out over the whole countryside, and the forest swallowed up more men that day than the sword."*

The earth also helped Moses and swallowed up his enemies. Num.16:32 *"and the earth opened its mouth and swallowed them and their households, and all those associated with Korah, together with their possessions."*

The wind brought Quails for the Israelites to eat in the wilderness. Num.11.31 – *"Now the LORD sent a wind that brought quail from the sea and let them fall into the camp and all around it! For many miles in every direction from the camp there were quail flying about three feet above the ground."*

With God all things are possible. The supernatural or the miraculous still exists, it's just that our walk with God has dwindled and we are so far away. One of our fathers of faith was on a journey, suddenly the fuel was exhausted. He told his driver to go down the stream and fetch fuel (water) and pour it into the tank. The driver hesitated but obeyed. Behold the car started and worked on water back to their destination.

Every elements in the sight of God are LIVING THINGS. When God addresses both living and non-living things, He addresses them as if they were living and they obey him. With God all things have ears. As believers, our help source is not limited to human beings or angels, there are certain times whereby all the elements (sun, moon, star, wind, thunder, Earth, etc.) God created need to favour us. In spiritual warfare, it's called 'fighting from the heavenlies'

The diabolical ones understand this secret, so they alter the weather, send storm, hold still the rain or send thunder against their enemies. Such demonstration of power belongs originally to God and his children. I was praying with my first son at home in the midnight and the enemies sent thunder into the room, and I returned it back to the sender by the Holy Ghost. A man of God once had a crusade in a village, a very terrible herbalist was living there so he warned us to cancel the crusade or else he would send rain to disrupt us. The man of God was vexed and extended the days of the crusade instead. The herbalist sent the rain truly but the rain excluded only the crusade ground and fell everywhere. The man of God later sent back the rain to the house of the herbalist and it removed the entire roof of the herbalist's house.

When the battle you are facing as a child of God is fueled by human beings or diabolical people then fighting from the heavenlies' is one of the best weapons of warfare you can use. All human beings have lots of water in their body, you can command such body fluid to work against them or dry up, every human must walk on the ground, every unrepentant enemy of yours can be buried. The sun must shine daily, command your glory to shine as the sun shines throughout the world.

Engage in commanding the Morning early before the day rises, cancel every curse and evil satanic shot fired into the skies against your day. Command the wind from the Lord to blow into the nooks and crannies of the world and draw sales, customers, helpers to your business, and ministry. If your faith and walk with God is intact you will experience this kind of uncommon or unusual help.

CONFESSIONS

- ❖ My heavens are open, my voice is heard, my opportunities have multiplied, my help has come. I am not stranded and I am not isolated.
- ❖ Shame is not my portion, mockery is not my portion, I will not breakdown, and I will not miss my blessing. Help has arrived for me.
- ❖ I am blessed beyond the curse, I am too connected to be frustrated, breakthrough is my portion. No more loss.
- ❖ My morning has arrived, the night is gone, my joy has multiplied, the joy of the Lord is my strength.

- Grace is multiplied for me, peace is multiplied for me, and favour is multiplied for me. I am not an outcast, and I am not a loser.
- God has sent help to me, what belongs to me will not go to another person. My God can do all things. I rise above limitations, help has arrived for me. It is well with my soul.
- I receive help, I receive uncommon help, I receive unusual help, I receive irreversible help, I receive significant help.
- I am not alone, God is on my side, I cannot die in battle, the enemies cannot overcome, greater is He that is in me, my help has come, my helper is near, I cannot be frustrated.
- There is always a package for me. God is my shepherd, I shall not lack help. The children of lion may suffer hunger, God will supply my needs, I serve a God of abundance.
- Life will not pass me by. Life will not be bitter for me neither will life be hard for me, I will get to my Promised Land, I will renew my strength in the Lord. No good thing shall be withdrawn from me. Hallelujah!

PRAYER POINTS

PSALM 84

1. Sing a song to the King of kings and Lord of lords.
2. Let us praise the name of the Lord, for at His command we were created (Ps.148:5).
3. Help of the Lord, show up to me in unexpected places (Jon.20:14).
4. Holy Spirit, I know that I am powerless in myself to resist temptation I need You, help me.
5. Help me oh Lord to follow Your lead (Isai.42:16).
6. Messenger of uncommon help locate me and my children in Jesus' name.
7. Generational secrets which are God giving, expose them to me Lord.
8. Evil winds blowing against me, be reversed in Jesus' name.
9. Blood of Jesus, secure my portion and my destiny in Jesus' name.
10. Lord, make me a vessel capable of knowing the secrets of my uncommon help.
11. You power of my in-law's house holding my uncommon help captive, scatter by fire.

12. Every power converting my life into a war zone, be wasted in Jesus' name.
13. Every blockage to the flow of a new anointing be removed from my life in Jesus' name.
14. Lord, help me to co-operate with Your plans for my life.
15. Lord, open the eyes of my uncommon helpers to see me.
16. My Father, my Father connect me to the source of my uncommon help.
17. Every barrier between me and my uncommon helpers be dismantled in Jesus' name.
18. Pray in the Holy Ghost for 10 minutes.

DAY SEVEN
SOURCE OF HELP: GOD'S MERCY
EXHORTATION

If heaven is where God lives, and Mercy is higher than the heavens, then Mercy is higher than God- Olaitan Aranmolaran

"And when He came near the gate of the city, behold, a dead man was being carried out, the only son of his mother; and she was a widow. And a large crowd from the city was with her.
When the Lord saw her, He had compassion on her and said to her, "Do not weep." (Luk.7:12,13)

The Mercy of God is a great source of help we should ask for. When mercy is at work, no judgment can stand. James 2:13 says, **"Mercy triumphs over judgment.'** Mercy is the greatest currency that can birth help for any man. Favour is a function of Mercy. Mercy qualifies the unqualified, Mercy speaks for the voiceless, Mercy makes worthy the unworthy, Mercy makes the unfit fit. Mercy breaks protocols. The last can become the first when it comes to Mercy.

Saul was from the tribe of Benjamites which is the least and smallest of all tribes in Israel, yet Mercy left Judah and picked Saul to become a King. Certificates do not certify when mercy is at play. You would wonder how it happened when a miracle is delivered via Mercy, you can't just fathom it. Two thieves were crucified alongside Jesus, yet Mercy rescued one and he got a free passport to paradise no efforts. No prayer life, no fasted life, no church going, no theological certificate etc. except by acknowledging that he was a sinner and accepting Christ as Lord, he made it to heaven! Wow! Mercy is great and extremely powerful.

I wonder how God considered people like me for salvation, yet in my own self-righteousness as human being, I still wonder how God could save the likes of a former armed robber and assassin and transform him to a powerful Minister of God.

Mercy is the greatest source of help. Mercy saved the soul of a persecutor and killer Saul and made him Paul who later wrote two-thirds of the new testament. Mercy rescued an accused prostitute ready to be judged and Mercy discharged and acquitted her.

The widow of Nain benefited from this source. She was not asking for help but mercy spoke for her and she was helped. Isa.65.1 - The LORD says, **"People who never** *before inquired about me are now asking about me. I am being found by people who were not looking for me. To them I have said, `I am here!'*

Sometimes, we do not ask for help but we get it anyway because of God's sure mercies. The man at the pool of Bethesda is also a good point. While he did not ask for help, mercy located him and gave him help.

HOW TO ACTIVATE MERCY IN ORDER TO RECEIVE HELP

1. ACKNOWLEDGE YOU ARE A SINNER - 1 Joh.1:8-10 *"If we say that we have no sin, we deceive ourselves, and the truth is not in us... If we say that we have not sinned, we make him a liar, and his word is not in us."*

2. CONFESS YOUR SINS - 1 Joh.1:9. *"If we confess our sins, he is faithful and just to forgive us our sins, and to cleanse us from all unrighteousness."*

3. ACCEPT JESUS CHRIST AS LORD AND SAVIOR - Joh.14.6 – *"Jesus told him, 'I am the way, the truth, and the life. No one can come to the Father except through me.'"*

4. SERVE GOD IN HIS VINEYARD WHOLEHEARTEDLY - Exod.23.25-26 - *"You must serve only the LORD your God. If you do, I will bless you with food and water, and I will keep you healthy. There will be no miscarriages or infertility among your people, and I will give you long, full lives."*

5. BE MERCIFUL TO OTHERS AND FORGIVE QUICKLY – Matt.5:7 **"Blessed are the merciful, for they will be shown mercy."**

6. CRY OUT TO GOD FOR MERCY IN PRAYERS - Luk.18:38 *"And he cried out, "Jesus, Son of David, have mercy on me!"*

7. SOW SEEDS OR SACRIFICIAL GIVING. Acts 10.31 – **"He told me, 'Cornelius, your prayers have been heard, and your gifts to the poor have been noticed by God!'"**

CONFESSIONS

- ❖ I am a product of grace, a candidate of mercy, I am the outcome of favour, I am the example of God goodness, I am the Lord's chosen, I am a vessel of honour.
- ❖ Grace has swallowed disgrace in my life, honour has swallowed shame in my life, glory has covered my destiny, mercy has covered my errors, favour has coloured my efforts. It is well with me.
- ❖ Mercy is not far from me, I have a goodly heritage, I have a living covenant of mercy. God cannot lie, God has said it, and I believe it. Therefore, my case is settled.
- ❖ There is always a way out, no matter the situation, God knows what to do, David recovered again, Esther won her battles, the lion was too small for Samson, Moses conquered Egypt.
- ❖ Wherever I am in the center of the universe, God's mercy can reach me. Failure is not my portion, I will not breakdown.
- ❖ The valley of the shadow of death is not my last bus stop, I will survive, I shall not die, God will have mercy on me, God will send help, my story will change for the better.
- ❖ I will not live in regrets, I will not lament over anything, what is making me happy will not cause me sorrow, God will not

allow me to take the wrong step, I will not fall into a pit.

❖ Mercy will speak for me, mercy will silence judgments, antagonists, and all condemnations. Mercy will follow and overtake me.

❖ Mercy will turn my bitter water to sweet water, mercy will speak peace into my life, chaos is not my portion, calamity is not my portion.

❖ I receive the key of help, I open the doors of help. Hallelujah!

PRAYER POINTS

PSALMS 30

1. Lord, I thank You for You are merciful and gracious.

2. My Father, I thank You for Your mercy will see me through in the battle of life.

3. Every spirit that causes me to indulge in any act of unfaithfulness be destroyed, in Jesus' name.

4. Lord, forgive all my unrighteousness in Jesus' name.

5. Every threatening of the devil around my family stop now in Jesus' name.

6. Mercy of God, bind my wounds and heal the pains I have got as a result of my carelessness in Jesus' name.

7. The discipline I need to tarry in Your presence Lord, give it to me in Jesus' name.

8. God of mercy arise and fight my battles of helplessness.

9. All you midnight caterers, your time is up now, be wasted in Jesus' name.

10. Announcements that will favour me, come forth now in Jesus' name.

11. Lord, instruct my children and teach them in the way they should go (Ps.32:8).

12. I withdraw my name from the register of frustrated people in Jesus' name.

13 God of mercy, give me help in unusual places in Jesus' name.

14. God of mercy, give me help in unusual times in Jesus' name.

15. God of mercy, give me help from unusual people in Jesus' name.

16. My Father, my Father, help me to finish strong.

17. The wonder of 'it can only be God' cause it to happen in my life in Jesus name.

18. I thank You Lord for answered prayer in Jesus' name.

DAY EIGHT
THE PURPOSE/BENEFIT OF HELP

EXHORTATION

HELP IS THE BRIDGE BETWEEN POTENTIALS AND ACTUALIZATION

P A OLOWOPOROKU

The LORD is my shepherd; I have everything I need. (Ps.23:1, NLT)

Help is a mechanism instituted by God to render assistance to man and his labour on earth. Endeavour of great value is always in need of assistance either physically or spiritually. We could see the angel coming to Jesus' aid when He needed it. We saw an angel coming to the assistance of another angel in the Book of Daniel and we could see men arising to the occasion when their fellow brethren were in need. Our lives overlap with one another. The way God program life, nothing can subsist on its own; we all need one another to function.

On a lighter note, even the devil needs humans to be relevant. If there were no humans for him to torment, I believe he will become redundant. When Adam was created in the Garden of Eden, God came to the conclusion after having observed Adam's labour that he needed assistance and to solve that problem, He extracted from Adam, his assistant — the woman. Contrary to popular belief, a woman is not created to serve a man but rather to 'assist' the man. That is why it is imperative for you to marry a woman ordained by God for you. If you do not, it will complicate your life as you will not get the needed assistance.

Help as we all know has its purpose and benefits. Anyways, we shall be examining some of them today. What are my gains when I obtain help?

- **HELP – THE CATALYST FOR DESTINY FULFILMENT (GEN.2:20-22)**

  When you obtain help, you will fulfill your destiny with ease. There is a reason we have been placed where we are, so identifying and doing what is expected of us is what is called DESTINY FULFILMENT. Many people were unable to fulfill their destiny because they were unable to get help. The scripture is replete with examples of many people whose fulfilment of destiny came through helpers. Some of them include:

  - **MOSES** (cf. Exod.2; Act7) He was sent to deliver the Israelites in Egypt in a period of persecution. Moses would have died as a baby when the evil king wanted to thwart his destiny but God sent a helper in the person of the King's daughter to aid Moses in fulfilling his destiny.
  - **DAVID** (cf.1Sam.18). It was David's destiny to be the king of Israel but king Saul would not allow it. However, Jonathan was sent by God to help him fulfill that destiny. Without him, he would have been killed. Do you know how many people they have killed for them not to fulfill their purpose? Think about that!
  - **SOLOMON** (cf. 1Ki.1) Solomon ageing father has promised him the throne but there was a coup to overthrow that plan if not for a Prophet Nathan. He roused Solomon's mother and compelled her to confront king David concerning the issue.

- **HELP – THE CATALYST FOR DIVINE LIFTING (PS.116:6)**

110

We all need help when our lives are at its lowest. There are periods in life when we find ourselves in situations where we know that without divine lifting, our lives will remain where they are.

- **JOSEPH:** If God had not been with Joseph and eventually lifted him up, how could he have become the Prime Minister in a strange land. His story is highly motivating and encouraging; from a nobody to a great person all because he was helped.
- **GIDEON**: He saw himself as the lowest of the low yet God called him a 'mighty man of valour.'
- **SAUL**: The man that hid among the stuff. He had low self-confidence yet God chose him to lead Israel. When you are helped, your background will no longer be relevant.

- **HELP – THE CATALYST FOR DIVINE SPEED**
Achieving one's purpose in life is one thing; achieving it on time is another. Of course, there is time for everything, thus having a grip on timing is pertinent. If you are lackadaisical or being drawn back, it will affect your destiny. There is the need for correct timing in order to be appreciated. That is why there is need for help if you want to achieve your purpose on time.
- **DAUGHTERS OF REUEL**: They were able to accomplish great things in a short while due to help received. Have you not seen some people around you who were able to achieve great feats in a short while? Their secret is the help they obtained.

- **EZRA AND THE HOUSE OF GOD**: Ezra had gathered some people with king Artaxerxes's blessing to rebuild the Temple of God in Jerusalem but some enemies in disguise offered to assist. When their offer was rejected, they decided to stop the project. They succeeded for two years until the prophets came and prophesied; strengthening them to continue. With the Prophets' help, they were able finish the project on time.

- **HELP – THE CATALYST FOR DIVINE BREAKTHROUGH (ROM.8:26)**

If you are experiencing delay and setbacks in your life, there is the need for help.

DANIEL AND THE PRINCE OF PERSIA: Although Daniel was set to do God's will, he was encumbered by spiritual attacks but when help came, he had breakthrough.

CONFESSIONS

❖ I cannot do it alone, I need help God, God will help me, God will not delay.

❖ I reject evil help, I reject satanic help, I reject ritualist help, I reject manipulations, I reject selfish help, I choose divine help.

❖ Help will speed up my journey, help will relief my heavy burden, help will multiple my success; help will simplify what is hard.

❖ I receive timely help, I receive uncommon help, I receive suitable help, I receive comfortable help, I will receive help without stress, I receive help without committee, I will receive help without regrets.

- ❖ Help is not far from me, and help is not missing in my life, my careers receive timely help, my promotion is a product of help.
- ❖ My help comes from the Lord, the doors of help are open to me, the gates of help are open to me, I am not to be pitied, i am to be envied, I am to be supported, I am to be assisted, I am to be recommended, I am endorsed.
- ❖ I receive the crown of help, I receive the anointing of help, I receive the mandate of help, I receive the commandment of help, help is not scarce in my life, help is available for me.
- ❖ The language of help is constantly on my lips, I receive generational help, I receive global help, I receive national help.
- ❖ I receive nearby help, I receive help from above, I receive distant help, I receive help from abroad, I receive regular help, I receive help from strangers.
- ❖ I receive physical help, I receive spiritual help, I receive financial help, I receive help in abundance, I receive help to go to the next level, I receive help to become a great person.

PRAYER POINTS

PSALMS 46

1. Father, I thank You for You alone are worthy of my praise in Jesus' name.
2. Father, I praise Your name, for the season of my divine help has started today in Jesus' name.
3. Giant of error, jump out of my life in the name of Jesus.
4. Anointing of overcomer possess me.
5. Uninvited help, appear in my life now by mercy.
6. A heart that accurately judges situations and people possess me.
7. Help that swallows shame, possess me now in Jesus' name.
8. Help that terminate evil and frustration, possess me now, in Jesus' name.
9. God of mercy, connect me to my domain of help.
10. My original life what are you doing in captivity come forth by fire.
11. Strange help, come to me suddenly by mercy.
12. Lord, help me to be strong and wait for You (Ps.27:14)
13. Help that will make me go far, possess me now in Jesus' name.

14. Spirit of prayer and supplication, rest upon my life in Jesus' name.
15. Holy Spirit, incubate my prayer life.
16. Thou river of help, flow into my life in Jesus name.
17. Help that I don't merit, fall on me by mercy.
18. Pray in the Spirit for 10 minutes.

DAY NINE
DIMENSION OF HELP: THE WORD OF GOD
EXHORTATION

Study this Book of the Law continually. Meditate on it day and night so you may be sure to obey all that is written in it. Only then will you succeed. (Josh..1.8)

Your Word is a lamp to my feet and a light to my path. (Ps.119:105)

The Word of God is another sure way of getting God's help. Knowing His Word and utilizing it guarantees sure success at all time. Our greatest adversary tempted Jesus by quoting some scriptures, Jesus our Lord in return replied and overcame him by the Word "*It is written*".

The reason there are so many immature Christians or Christians who are not all that different from unbelievers in the church is not because they never came out for altar call or surrendered their lives to Jesus, but they did so and yet refuse to become Bible students.

If you gained admission to study Medicine at the University, for seven years you would be trained as an intern. Then you would eventually graduate to become a certified Medical Doctor; after having undergone practical pieces of training. Same way with Christianity. It's high time we stopped deceiving ourselves by attending Church alone. There is the need to practice what we have learnt. Studying the Bible and putting it to practice is the height of Spiritual Maturity (Joh.8:31). You cannot mature to become a man of God from being a child of God if you don't eat strong meat (Heb.5:12,14).

WHY BELIEVERS NEED FOUNDATION IN THE WORD

1. **We are God's Building.** 1Pet.2.5 - *Present yourselves as building stones for the construction of a sanctuary vibrant with life, in which you'll serve as holy priests offering Christ-approved lives up to God.*

2. **It has all it takes to uphold us.** 2Tim.3.17 - *Through the Word we are put together and shaped up for the tasks God has for us.* 2Pet.1.3 - *as His divine power has given to us all things that pertain to life and godliness, through the knowledge of Him who called us by glory and virtue,'*

3. **The Word has the final authority.** 2Cor.1.20 – *'For all the promises of God in Him are Yes, and in Him Amen, to the glory of God through us.'*

BENEFITS OF THE WORD TO US ALL

1. **Make wise unto Salvation.** 2Tim.3.15 – *"and that from childhood you have known the Holy Scriptures, which are able to make you wise for salvation through faith which is in Christ Jesus."*

2. **Producing Faith.** Rom.10.17 – *"So then faith comes by hearing, and hearing by the word of God."*

3. **Reveals Jesus**. John.5.39 – *"You search the Scriptures, for in them you think you have eternal life; and these are they which testify of Me."*

4. **Builds up**. Acts.20.32 – *"So now, brethren, I commend you to God and to the word of His grace, which is able to*

build you up and give you an inheritance among all those who are sanctified."

5. **Produce Profit**. 1Tim.4.15 – *"Meditate on these things; give yourself entirely to them, that your progress may be evident to all."*

6. **Makes you Complete.** 2Tim.3.17 – *"that the man of God may be complete, thoroughly equipped for every good work."*

HOW TO KNOW THE WORD

1. Read it; Josh 1:8, Study it; 2 Tim 2:15, Cram or memorize it; Heb 10:16, Speak it; Job 22:28, Pray it; Matt 4:4, Listen to it; Romans 10:17, Play Bible computer games, Watch Bible stories as films.

WHAT HAPPENS WHEN A BELIEVER NEGLECTS THE WORD

1. He will fall out of Christ: To fall out of the Word is to fall out of Christ... John 15:4 REMAIN IN ME... Dwell... Live... Stay... and this will lead to spiritual weakness; 1Pet.2.2 – *"as newborn babes, desire the pure milk of the word, that you may grow thereby,"*

3. He will lose the Life of God... e.g. love of God, zeal for God's house, the fear of God...Ps.119.11 – *"Your Word I have hidden in my heart, That I might not sin against You."* And his heart will be corrupted... Rom.12.2 – *"And do not be conformed to this world, but be transformed by the renewing of your mind, that you may prove what is that good and acceptable and perfect will of God."* Eph.5.26 – *"that He might sanctify and cleanse her with the washing of water by the word,..."*

5. He will backslide... 2Tim.4.10 – *"for Demas has forsaken me, having loved this present world, and has departed for Thessalonica--Crescens for Galatia, Titus for Dalmatia."*

6. He won't prosper... Josh.1.8 – *"This Book of the Law shall not depart from your mouth, but you shall meditate in it day and night, that you may observe to do according*

to all that is written in it. For then you will make your way prosperous, and then you will have good success."

CONFESSIONS

- ❖ I found restoration in the Word of God, I found hope in the Word of God, I found help in the Word of God, I found prosperity in the Word of God, I found deliverance in the Word of God.
- ❖ When I hear "thus saith the Lord" my hope is kindled, I know something is about to happen, I know there is a divine intervention. Whenever I hear "fear not" I know my case is settled.
- ❖ Shame is not my portion, mockery is not my portion, the Lord is on my side. Great peace have they that keep Your Word, nothing shall offend them.
- ❖ Your Word is a lamp unto my feet, Your Word is a light unto my path; with your Word I cannot be lost, the word of man may fail, but the Word of God cannot fail. I hope in Your Word.
- ❖ The Word of God contains power, the Word of God contains blessing, the Word of God contains glory, the word of God gives direction.
- ❖ The Word of God opens the eyes of the blind, the Word of God carries weight, the

Word of God is my confidence, the Word of God is my boundary.

❖ Like the snake of Moses that swallowed the snake of Pharaoh, the Word of God in my life swallows the words of enemies. David's word overcame the boastful words of Goliath, my enemies are not powerful than my God.

❖ The Word of God never disappoints, the Word of God never loses power, the Word of God never falls to the ground, the Word of God upholds me.

❖ The Word of God shapes my world, the Word of God inspires my faith, the Word of God crumbles my mountains, the Word of God bring dignity.

❖ I will honour the Word of God, I will apply the Word of God, I will believe the Word of God, I will celebrate the Word of God, I will give the Word of God first place in my life, the Word of God is established forever, Hallelujah!

PRAYER POINTS
PSALM 119

1. Father, I thank You for Your word will work wonders in my life today.

2. Help me oh Lord to confidently rest in the assurance that You are always with me.
3. My Father, my Father, give me grace of second chance in Jesus' name.
4. Help me become more like You day by day in Jesus' name.
5. Jesus, fill my ordinary life with the power of Your spirit in Jesus' name.
6. Help me to overcome my fear of telling others about You, in Jesus' name.
7. Lord, let Your word increase me and I decrease in Jesus' name.
8. Every agent of shame working against me be paralyzed in Jesus' name.
9. Power of maximum achievement possess me in Jesus' name.
10. I break every curse of failure upon my life in Jesus' name.
11. Lord, make me a proof producer through Your word in Jesus' name.
12. Lord, hasten Your word to perform miracles in every areas of my life, in Jesus' name.
13. Power prolonging my help be wasted in Jesus' name.
14. Oh lord, purge my tongue by Your fire.
15. Anyone in custody of my help within 24hours come and drop it for me in Jesus' name.

16. Voice of critics be silent around me in Jesus' name.
17. I receive grace to offer profitable service for my maximum lifting in Jesus' name.
18. Pray in the Holy Ghost for 15 minutes.

DAY TEN
DIMENSION OF HELP: CONNECTING HELPER
EXHORTATION

Now Naaman, captain of the host of the king of Syria, was a great man with his master, and honourable, because by him the Lord had given deliverance unto Syria: he was also a mighty man in valour, but he was a leper. And the Syrians had gone out by companies and had brought away captive out of the land of Israel a little maid; and she waited on Naaman's wife. And she said unto her mistress, Would God my Lord were with the prophet that is in Samaria! for he would recover him of his leprosy.
2 Kings 5:1-3

Divine connectors are the missing link between who you are and who you are designed to be. Most of the time they look insignificant because they don't have what you are looking for. They look very ordinary but the strange thing about them is that they can connect you to what you are looking for. That is why only the humble can receive help. When you are pompous, proud and arrogant, you might miss a connecting helper. When you are only kind to the elites or people of your caliber, you might miss a connecting helper.

Do you know as ordinary as your house help, gatemen, laundry men, store keepers, and other people who are of low status to you, they can be your connecting helper.

Naaman was healed of leprosy because there was a maid in his house who became a divine connector. The entrance of divine connectors into your life links you to your future.

An encounter with them causes doors to be opened. Connecting helpers are people who might not be able to help you but they direct you to where you can get help. Pastor Olukoya told us that a security personnel helped him to take his documents to the appropriate quarters when he did not have the opportunity of doing so himself.

Many maltreat their maids or cleaners yet treat their own children well. You are only ignorant of the future. The slave today can become a king tomorrow. He or she might be at a position to help you tomorrow. Be kind to everyone even those lower to you in status.

Connecting helpers are different from gossips, they are good referrers. They may not be buoyant enough to buy your products but they can link you up to someone who can. They may not have anything they sell but they know where to buy quality products good enough for you. Andrew did not have food, but he knew who had and he brought him to Jesus.

Same Andrew brought Peter to Jesus who became instrumental in the early Church. King Saul was possessed with evil spirits. He was tortured occasionally, and one of his cabinet members remembered there was a boy in the wilderness who was skillful in playing harp. He was the one who referred David to the king and David became an official musician to the king. Imagine if someone were to connect you to become personnel in the office of the president?

When the multitude were with Jesus and He needed to feed them, Andrew, one of the disciples brought a little boy with the two fish and five loaves that was instrumental in feeding everyone (cf. Joh.6). We can never do away with these kinds of people. They might not need the help themselves but will be willing to give it to you if you need it. The maid did not need the assistance of Elisha but Naaman did. Naaman did not know of Elisha but she did and was able to orchestrate the meeting of the two. That is how connecting helpers operate.

Many people whose lives are stagnated would not have been there if there had been someone to connect them. Naaman might have died a leper if not for the young maid. That is how essential these people can be. Do not look down on anyone. God has created everyone with one capacity or the other so we can have need of one another. Do not let ignorance and arrogance kill you. While you are up there, take time to look down once in a while. The secret of your remaining up there might be down here.

My prayer for you is this: at every juncture where you have need of a connecting helper, the Lord would provide them for you speedily in Jesus' name.

CONFESSIONS

❖ I cannot be frustrated. I am connected to the source of help, I cannot be stranded. I am connected to the source of help, I cannot be confused. I am connected to the source of help.

❖ Help is available for me, I receive help in high places, and unusual places. I receive angelic help, I receive human help, helping hands are stretched out towards me.

- ❖ I am not in a lock down, I am not in a cage, I am not in bondage, there is help for me in God, God has opened the heaven for me, my helper is nearer to me, my helper has located me.
- ❖ Doors of help are opened for me, I walk into a new level of help, windows of help are opened for me, all who will help me shall see me, help in every forms are available for me.
- ❖ I receive timely help, I receive godly help, I receive available help, I receive sufficient help, I receive comfortable help.
- ❖ God will make a way for me, where there is no way, I am not lost, I am helped, I am not at a disadvantage, I am helped.
- ❖ My burdens are lighter, because my helper has supported me, my limitations are broken, because my helper has supported me, my mountains have been moved, because my helper has supported me.
- ❖ Help is the favour that makes life easy, my life shall not be difficult; help is the support that brings speed, my life shall not be slow, and I shall move forward in life, I shall be highly favoured.
- ❖ Shame on those who mock me, shame on those who had written me off, shame on those who closes a door, God has opened multiple doors for me; I have multiple advantages, Hallelujah!

❖ It is well with my soul, I am the head and not the tail, I am connected to the living. I am helped!

PRAYER POINTS
PSALMS 89

1. Sing a song to unquestionable God.
2. Lord, help me to recognize Your presence and Your touch in the midst of things that frightens me.
3. Oh Lord, accelerate the timetable of my destiny in Jesus' name.
4. Oh God, convert every ridicule in my destiny in Jesus' name.
5. Oh God, order my steps and guide every move I make in Jesus' name.
6. Let Your glory over shadow my children in Jesus' name.
7. Every child of the devil occupying my children's position, somersault and die.
8. My Father, my Father baptize me with the spirit of uncommon favour in Jesus' name.
9. Oh Lord, let all my entitlement in my work place locate me, in Jesus' name.
10. Oh Lord, convert the wisdom of my antagonist to foolishness in Jesus' name.
11. My divine promotion, locate me by mercy.

12. I receive grace to find favour before my boos in Jesus' name.
13. My Father, my Father, reveal Your divine plan for my life in Jesus' name.
14. Help of God that swallows rejection, fall on me in Jesus' name.
15. I bind every spirit of fear in me in Jesus' name.
16. Lord, bring me into great favour with all those who will decide my matter in Jesus' name.
17. Lord, open my eyes to know how to deal with any weakness working against my destiny in Jesus' name.
18. Pray in the Spirit of 10 minutes.

DAY ELEVEN
DIMENSION OF HELP: CONSISTENT HELP
EXHORTATION
The three shades of Help are 'HelpFULLness', 'HelpLESSness' or 'HelpNOness' the difference is clear. - Oluwafemi Alabi

For at that time men came to David day after day to help him, until he had a great army, like the army of God. 1 Chr.12:22

A consistent help is a continuous and steady help over a period of time. For instance; God can connect you with someone who would take delight in your child and offer to pay his or her school fees every term till he/she graduates from the University.

Multiple and constant inflow of help will lead you to abundance. The rich are known for their constant inflow of cash. When your inflow supersedes your outflow, you will be buoyant. It is same with Help. One of the reasons many are stranded in life is because there is little or no help. 'Helpfulness' is a stage where you have help in abundance, whether it comes bigger than your problems, it comes even in a bit but constantly or daily or it comes when you are in need of not.

'Helplessness' is the second stage of Help. At this stage, help comes but lesser than expected. For example, a person who is in need of N100,000 but receives N20,000. Help can be said to have been received help but lesser than the needs required.

'HelpNoness' of course is not a dictionary word but permit me to use the slang to mean NO HELP! It is the worst scenario any man can encounter. You'll hear situations where people exclaimed that a certain minutest amount was all they needed at a point to balance up the hospital bill needed to rescue their loved one but were unable to get it.

Help could be consistent like the one David enjoyed till he became great. The plans of God for His children are well stipulated in Jer.29:11 – *"For I know the plans I have for you, 'says the LORD. "They are plans for good and not for disaster, to give you a future and a hope."*

So, our God doesn't have it in mind to leave any of His children stranded in life without hope or help. God makes provision for daily benefits for those who fear and trust Him.

The Psalmist in 68:19 says, *'Blessed be the Lord, who daily loadeth us with benefits, even the God of our salvation.'*

A one-off kind of help is a type of help that comes just once or for a particular season and then stops. An example is the one-time event like we had in the case of Elijah and the raven bird. The Bible says after a while the river dried up and God made another helper for Elijah. 1Kgs.17:7 -9, *But after a while the brook dried up, for there was no rainfall anywhere in the land. Then the LORD said to Elijah, Go and live in the village of Zarephath, near the city of Sidon. There is a widow there who will feed you. I have given her my instructions."*

We must be able to discern between consistent and one-off help which we've received so as to avoid wasting our time and resources on places where there is no help. A one-off help is as crucial as a consistent help. It can set one up for life so let us not trivialize it. In our pursuit for help, the ability to discern between the two will go a long way in preventing heart ache. For instance, someone that has been sent to you to help you once would render the help and go his own way while you will still pursue him to help again. He might feel overwhelmed by your burden because he has not been sent to do more. On the other hand, a consistent helper will be on your neck demanding you come for more. Even when saturated, they will still be bother you to help.

So, you see, both of them are important but they have different seasons in your life. While human help might be considered consistent, the most consistent help of all is from God. He is our all-time Helper that can never be weary of our demands. Unto Him must our hopes and aspirations be. Man, at his best is still a man with limitations but God transcends limitations.

You need Him for those daily benefits (Ps.68:19)!

CONFESSIONS

- ❖ My God is unlimited, I cannot break down, my God is sufficient, I cannot lack, my God is abundant, therefore, scarcity is not my portion, my God is able, I cannot lose what is best.
- ❖ I am a candidate of help, I am available to be helped, I can always see someone to help me, I have seen the seed of help, I cannot lack what is good, my harvest is ripe, I am ready for blessing.
- ❖ I will not be missing where I am needed, I will not be lost where I am useful, I will not be covered where I should be seen, my heavens are open.
- ❖ Nothing can stop my testimony, I am the head, I am not a debtor, I will not disappear, I will not lose my place, I will not die.
- ❖ My celebration shall increase, my breakthroughs shall be many, my songs of praises shall be louder, nothing will scatter all that I have gathered, I am under the shadow of the Almighty.
- ❖ I am available for help, I am within the reach of my helper, my helper will not be blind, my helper will not die suddenly.
- ❖ I will be helped in the morning, I will be helped in the afternoon, I will be helped in the night, I will be helped daily.
- ❖ God will silence my antagonists, my helper will not meet my enemies, nobody will

oppose my help packages, today is the day of grace.

❖ What is difficult for man is possible with God, what is lost can be found by the power of God. I enjoy the power of help, I enjoy the availability of help, I will not be disappointed. Hallelujah!

❖ Help will speak for me, help will open new doors, help will take me to the next level, help will cover my errors, mistakes will not ruin my career, help will give me another chance. Hallelujah!

PRAYER POINTS
PSALMS 118:1

1. Father, I thank You because You are God and Your mercies endures forever (Ps. 118:1).
2. Sing a song to worship the Root of Jesse.
3. Lord, reign in my heart so others can see You in me.
4. Help me to pray faithfully for those who do not yet know You.
5. Lord, deliver me from the dominion of the flesh.
6. My name shall not be erased from the Book of Life in Jesus' name.
7. Every arrow of distraction in the place of prayer, backfire, in the name of Jesus.

8. Lord, make all areas of concerns in my life become area of testimony (Ps. 2:1-5)
9. Lord, cancel all appointment with death in my life (Jon.8:1-10).
10. Raise a voice to defend me where my case is being decided in Jesus' name (Acts 5:33-40).
11. My Father, my Father, surround my life with helpers of destiny (Luk.8:1-3).
12. Lord, equip me with what will make me acceptable before my helpers (ISam.16:18).
13. Any power using my face to attack my helpers be wasted in Jesus' name.
14. Every opposition against my helpers, scatter in Jesus' name.
15. I reject fragmented help in Jesus' name.
16. Any evil done against me on my naming ceremony day that is now affecting my moving forward, be terminated in Jesus' name.
17. Every hinderance to my consistent help be scattered in the name of Jesus
18. Pray in the Holy Ghost for 15 minutes.

DAY TWELVE

DIMENSION OF HELP: NEGATIVE HELP EXHORTATION

My son, if sinners entice thee, consent thou not. (Prov.1:10)

But Amnon had a friend, whose name was Jonadab, the son of Shimeah David's brother: and Jonadab was a very subtle man. And Jonadab said unto him, Lay thee down on thy bed, and make thyself sick: and when thy father cometh to see thee, say unto him, I pray thee, let my sister Tamar come, and give me meat, and dress the meat in my sight, that I may see it, and eat it at her hand. (2Sam.13:3,5)

In our quest to get help, we tend to seek help where it is not helpful. You see, man's yearning to fulfill his purpose whether positively or negatively will make him take some measures to get it done either positively or negatively. Life consists of things and places we can never get to ourselves unless we are assisted, negatively or positively.

Just as there is positive help, there is also negative help. Of all the negative help mentioned in the Bible, the most bizarre of them all might arguably be the one rendered to Amnon by his cousin Jonadab. Amnon had been lusting after his step-sister Tamar and while it was incestuous, he persisted in pursing it until he got ill. In order to 'assist' his cousin friend to get better, Jonadab proffered a solution albeit evil. Amnon took the help and a cankerworm was opened in the house of David.

This seemingly innocent action almost destroyed the household of David. After the evil act, Amnon hated Tamar with passion. Tamar never got married. Absalom (the brother of Tamar) eventually killed Amnon when he saw the nonchalant attitude of David their father to the act. Absalom went into exile. Joab encouraged a woman to lie to the king. Absalom became rebellious and set Joab's farm on fire. He eventually grew bold and chased his father David away from the throne; defiled his father's concubine; and divided the kingdom into two factions. He succeeded in rendering his father the king homeless and eventually died a shameful death; all because of negative help!

While we might be musing about the failings of Amnon, let us take the time to consider our own lives. In which area are we accepting negative help? A young lady having marital delay took the advice of her friend to seek 'help' from a native witchdoctor. The witchdoctor seeing how beautiful she was, charmed her into marrying him. She did and bore him many children. A day came when the charm wore out and she learnt what happened. This grieved her so much that she ran away from that house. Till today, nobody knows what became of her.

Another Christian lady seeking the fruit of the womb left the living God and went to seek the 'help' of a fake prophet. The man convinced her to sleep with him in order to 'open' her womb. She did and that one-day decision gave her HIV which led to her death.

Negative help always brings death and loads of misfortune. Run away from it. Young fellow, your friends might be luring you to join fraudster gang in order to render help, run! Sir, your friends might be advising you to join the occult in order to get what you need, run!

The devil wanted to 'help' Jesus when he was in dire circumstances but He refused (cf. Mt.4). Child of God, you can do it too. Reject, refuse, run away from negative help.

These are some of the effects of Negative help:
- Negative helps do not take anyone far in life. *(Jer.17:5)*
- It causes of many people's sorrows and death. *(2Sam.13:23)*
- Negative helps make us to look away from the Lord and what He can do for us. *(Ps.20:7)*
- It is a self-life of seeking personal independence from depending upon the Lord. *(Rom.8:1-5)*
- It leads to chain of catastrophes in homes, churches and the society at large. *(Job 15:31)*
- Negative help makes us enemies of God and thereby truncating our divine purpose. *(Isai.48:22)*

In order not to fall victim of all these, we must then take the following steps to save our lives, souls and homes:
- Sound relationship with God and maintenance. *(Mt.11:28-30)*
- Rely on godly counsel and godly counsellors. *(Prov.20:18)*
- Repose to wait and hear the voice of the Lord before taking any decision in life. (Isai.30:21)
- Refrain from people with ungodly ways of help. *(Ps.1:1-3)*

- Reposition your heart to God to be your absolute source of help always. *(Ps. 121:1-4)*

CONFESSIONS

- ❖ David killed Uriah because he thought he could help himself, Sarah ask Abram to help God and got into trouble, Rebekah helped Jacob to deceive Isaac and robbed Esau. Negative help is no help, negative help will bring condemnation, negative help will bring damnation, negative help have no future.
- ❖ I reject satanic help, I reject demonic help, I reject help that is not from God, I reject evil suggestions, I reject help that brings trouble, nothing will ruin my career, nothing will ruin my calling.
- ❖ I will wait upon the Lord, He will help me. Woe to those who go to Egypt for help, for their horses are not sprint, I will not seek help from negative places, I will wait upon the Lord.
- ❖ Saul went to the witch of Endor, he returned condemned, the small prophet that accepted the help of the old prophet got eaten by a lion, any help that is not from God is a curse.

- ❖ I reject forbidden help, God has enough power to help me, whatever God will not do for me should remain undone, I prefer the "NO" of God to the "YES" of Satan, I cannot lose my privilege.
- ❖ My help cometh from the Lord, the maker of heaven and earth, my God is never late. Lazarus was dead for four days, but when his friend, Jesus, showed up, his fame shook the city.
- ❖ There is nothing to be ashamed when you are delayed, God is teaching me patience and long suffering, it is well with my soul, I reject negative help.
- ❖ I will not forfeit my chances of divine intervention, Adam and Eve later regretted their actions, the satanic help left them empty, they lost what they cannot regain.
- ❖ Help of God is available for me, I will wait for my time. Like Job, I will rise again.

PRAYER POINTS
ISAIAH 31

1. Sing at least seven songs of praise to the Lord.
2. Thank You Father for touching my eyes to see the new height You are taking me to.

3. Every project which I have abandoned before now, be resumed by mercy in Jesus' name.
4. Lord, I thank You for the ability to face the future without fear.
5. I receive grace to walk in wisdom with all men.
6. Every snare in form of help around my children Blood of Jesus, swallow it in Jesus' name (Isai.18:21).
7. Every wrong association that connects me with diabolic help I disconnect myself by the power of resurrection in Jesus' name.
8. Thou spirit of ignorance and spiritual deafness loose Your hold over my life in the name of Jesus.
9. I receive divine assistance and connection that will influence my life for good in Jesus' name.
10. I disconnect myself from every source of negative help in Jesus' name.
11. Every power contending with me over my possession be destroyed in Jesus' name.
12. Lord, teach my hands to war and my finger to fight that I may possess my possessions in Jesus' name.
13. Every padlock of the power of darkness that has tied me down to the same spot, break by fire in Jesus' name.

14. Every strange magnet magnetizing me to wrong help and helpers, be neutralized by the Blood of Jesus.
15. I command the earth and all the elements to cooperate with me in Jesus' name.
16. Let every satanic gate that has locked me out of my inheritance open now in Jesus' name.
17. Power to prevail in battle of destiny possess me in Jesus' name.
18. Begin to pray in the Spirit for 15 minutes.

DAY THIRTEEN

DIMENSION OF HELP: SPEEDY HELP/ ELEVENTH HOUR (LAST MINUTE) HELP
EXHORTATION
"GOD is our refuge and strength; a very present help in trouble." (Ps.46:1)
"And about the eleventh hour he went out, and found others standing idle, and saith unto them, Why stand ye here all the day idle?" Mt.20:6

There are circumstances in our earthly journey that have need of speedy or eleventh-hour help. If this help is not gotten, all might be lost.

Take the case of the widow of Nain as an example. She was a few miles to the burying ground of her only child. If Jesus had not taken charge that day, her story would have ended differently. What about the labourers in the parable told by Jesus, if that master had not found them at the eleventh-hour, their stories might have ended negatively.

At one point or the other we often pray and cry unto God for speedy help or what the Bible refers to as early help (Ps.90:14), *Delayed help can break the bones and weary the soul (Prov.13:12).* The reason why people lament, cry and shout is because help seems to be delayed. I trust God this season that as we all lift up our voices to God in prayer of faith we shall receive and enjoy speedy help from above in Jesus' name. We should not lose hope but keep our focus on Jesus as the all secured and guaranteed giver of eleventh-hour help.

Hagar and her son were thirsty and dying in the wilderness but an angel appeared and gave her guidance to the well of water. That was a speedy help for her (Gen.*16:7-16),* If not for the speedy help, Hagar could have died with her son, Ishmael. Our God is a specialist in rendering speedy help to the sons of men and He can do or employ anything including nature to bring speedy or eleventh-hour help.

Speedy/eleventh hour help comes when you least expect or have given up hope, they are interventions to sustain and succor us in times of challenges.

Jesus was walking on the sea and Peter requested Jesus to invite him if He were Jesus. Jesus asked him to come and he moved by faith. But suddenly he started sinking when he looked away from Jesus and concentrated on the storm. He cried and shouted for help, from Jesus and Jesus speedily stretched his hand to rescue him from sinking. *(Mt.14:22-31)*

The Israelites at the Red Sea enjoyed the same speedy mercy and help of God as the host of Egypt raged after them. Moses prayed and God speedily made a way for them in the Red Sea and thereafter, buried their enemies' therein *(Exod.14:13-22)*.

He also rescued Daniel from the paws of the lions in the den where he was thrown into. Likewise, Shedrach, Meshack and Abednego *(Dan.3:6),* were all delivered from the fiery burning furnace of King Nebuchadnezzar.
Jesus has always come handy to deliver His own people from the hands of death, sickness and sorrows
In this season of waiting upon the Lord, you shall experience and enjoy this speedy help beyond your expectation in Jesus name.

Men and women who enjoyed and partook in the speedy help from God had it in this form:

- Guidance voice from the Lord e.g. Hagar. *(Gen.16)*
- Angelic visitation leading to intervention e.g. Peter in prison. *(Act.12)*
- God overruling the element of nature e.g. the Red Sea. *(Exod.14)*
- He used the created elements to send help e.g. Raven feeding Elijah. *(1Ki.17)*
- Speedy help shows the supremacy of God over creation.
- It reveals God is never late as men terms it. *(Joh.11:20-25)*
- Speedy helps and interventions tell us that God is able and available to do what he wants to do. *(Luk.1:37)*

Speedy help can be provoked through the following means:
- Sound relationship with God. *(Joh.1:12)*
- Consecration and dedication to the service of the Master.
- Dedication to hearing the voice of the Lord and being led by same. *(Rom.8:14-16)*
- Holiness provokes speedy help. *(Dan.6:1-10)*

- Lifestyle of worship, praise and thanksgiving. e.g. Jehoshaphat *(2chr 20:15-22)*
- Sacrificial giving to the Lord and his cause. e.g. Solomon *(1Ki.3:3-12)*

CONFESSIONS

❖ Help is available for me, heaven of help is open to me, I have significant help, my needs cannot consume me, my helper is close to me.

❖ I am not delayed, I am not denied, I am not limited, I am not stranded, I am not frustrated, I am not left behind.

❖ The oil of help flows over me, that mountain of impossibilities is conquered, every enemy of progress are ashamed, my case is not the worst, I receive quick help, I receive speedy help.

❖ David received speedy help, he did not die in the battle even though he was tired, Solomon almost lost the throne, but Nathan helped him, Mordecai could have been killed, but Esther helped him, help is my portion.

❖ Help is not far from me, He is near that helps me, my lines are falling to me in pleasant places, I have a goodly heritage.

❖ I receive speedy financial help, I receive speedy counsel, I receive speedy emotional help. My helper, where are you? Locate me today!
❖ Every invincible hands holding up my speedy help, catch fire. Every invincible rope holding up my speedy help catch fire.
❖ The Lord has mentioned my name, help will not be far from me, I am a candidate to be helped, I am available for help.
❖ I will not miss my timely help, I refuse to lament, I refuse to miss my opportunities, I cannot lose what is valuable to me.
❖ Help will cover my errors, help will colour my efforts, the little I have shall be multiplied, God will make a way for me. I have no reason to mourn, help is available for me, the heaven of help is open for me. Hallelujah!

PRAYER POINTS
PSALM 94

1. Lord, I thank You for counting me worthy to be a carrier of Your divine power.
2. Lord, I thank You because Your master plan for my life exceed my own dream.
3. Favour of supernatural addition in everything I do possess me now in Jesus' name.

4. Unusual insight and continuous leading of the Holy Spirit possess me now in Jesus' name.
5. The secret of darkness in my place of work be revealed by mercy in Jesus' name.
6. God of Mercy Rain, do not allow the enemy to kill my children in order to silence me in Jesus' name.
7. You robbers in the dream, Holy Ghost fire waste you in Jesus' name.
8. Everything within me that is pushing me into error, Blood of Jesus push it out.
9. Call God of mercy nine times and say, 'send the angel of the eleventh-hour to me in Jesus' name'.
10. You gate and wall of my Jericho, fall down for me to enter in to my eleventh-hour help in Jesus' name.
11. My feet hear the voice of the God, you will not lead me into destructions in Jesus' name.
12. Lord, awake Your church from spiritual slumber in Jesus' name.
13. Earth, oh Earth, yield Your increase unto me in Jesus' name.
14. Authority for speedy help enter into my life.
15. Lord, let me excel in Jesus' name.

16. Every mark of rejection inscribed on my forehead, be blotted out now in Jesus' name.
17. Pray in the Holy Ghost for 10 minutes.

DAY FOURTEEN
DIMENSION OF HELP: FUTILE HELP
EXHORTATION

"He who is surety for a stranger will suffer, But one who hates being surety is secure." (Prov.11:15 ESV)
At that time did king Ahaz send unto the kings of Assyria to help him... And Tilgathpilneser king of Assyria came unto him, and distressed him, but strengthened him not." (2Chro.16,20)

Another important dimension of help is that some help could be futile. This might seem strange because while we keep emphasizing the importance of help, it needs be stressed too that if want our help to be rewarded there is the need for discernment.

Help can become futile if rendered in some circumstances. This means that the help will be useless and thus of no value. Remember that we have earlier mentioned that the essence of help is value. If help will not yield any value either physically or spiritually, we might as well not render it. Pastor Kumuyi in one of his sermons told the story of a drunk begging for money to buy more booze. While it is good to help, it will be advisable not to give such drunk that money because the purpose is worthless. If he needs it for food that is another case but to buy what is hurting him, that is futile help.

Another example of futile help is when we try to help someone that God is angry with. A Yoruba proverb warns that we must not live close to someone that God is angry with. Jonah was on the wrong side of God and God decided to discipline him. When the storm got fierce and the other seafarers tried to help Jonah, they encountered more trouble. Their ordeal ceased when they stopped trying to help Jonah.

Making an attempt to help someone who is not in right standing with God will lead one to trouble. Jesus did not bother to help the Pharisees and the Sadducees of His time because they felt they 'knew' better. He rather went to the common man who was hungry and thirsty for more of God. Concerning that situation, Jesus said, *"They that are whole have no need of the physician, but they that are sick: I came not to call the righteous, but sinners to repentance."* (Mk.2:17)

While we are compelled to render help, we are also cautioned to be discerning. Before we render help, let us ask God for help. Let me share this story to emphasize my point.

A man of God (a prominent Prophet), stood surety for one of the relatives of his Church Member. The young man had come to him for attestation necessary to gain employment with a prestigious bank. Without checking with God in prayer, he took his member's word at face value and signed the necessary document thereby unwittingly accepting full responsibility for misdemeanor on the man's part.

Few years later, the banker duped his bank of millions of naira and fled, and the bank arrested all his guarantors. The prophet's case got worse as his surety was major. The bank asked him to refund the money or face jail time; he could not pay the money so he was jailed. To cut the long story short, the prophet died a shameful death in the prison. He might have escaped unnecessary reproach and death if he had asked for God's help. Helping that young man was a futile help. He was an unrepentant crook looking for opportunity. The Writer of the Book of Proverbs under godly inspiration warned against this (Prov.11:15; 17:18).

King Ahaz (King of Judah) was a man who had set his heart against God. When God started dealing with him, he ran to and fro for help. He reached out to King Tilgathpilneser of Assyria but he refused to help him knowing that God was against him. Instead of helping him, the king of Assyria further *distressed him*! (cf. *2Chr 28*).

Learn that what works for someone might not work for you. Because someone helped the homeless and they were greatly rewarded does not mean you are to do same. Before you embark on that help journey, get down on your knees first. God might be angry with that person. Do not attract the wrath of God in your bid to help.

CONFESSIONS

- ❖ I reject miserable comforters, I reject empty sympathy, I reject shallow support, I reject fake promises, I reject un-committed committee.
- ❖ I receive help from above, I receive help from abroad, I receive local help, I receive global help, I receive national help, I receive international help, I receive physical help, I receive spiritual help, help is available for me – Hallelujah!
- ❖ What is difficult for man is possible with God, my case is not the worst. There is hope for me, God is good to me, God has made adequate provisions for me.
- ❖ You can always see the help of God, God has opened houses of help, I shall pray for

help, I shall seek help, I shall not be disappointed.

❖ The oil of help is upon me, I shall sow the seed of help. I shall reap the harvest of help.

❖ Nothing is wrong with my destiny, nothing is wrong with my country, my helper is not missing, my head is not empty, I reject futile help.

❖ God is everywhere, therefore help is everywhere, I shall not lack help, anytime I call for help, I shall receive it, before I make the requests the door is opened.

❖ Hatred may close the door, help will open the door, envy may close the door, help will open it, gossip may close the door, help will open it. I shall not lack available help.

❖ I am a product of help, I am in the plan of God for help, I cannot be at a disadvantage, I cannot lose what is valuable.

❖ Shame is not my portion, mockery is not my portion, I cannot disappear, I cannot be swallowed, failure is not my portion, I will not struggle to live, my enemies shame on you, I am the apple of God's eye. Hallelujah!

PRAYER POINTS
PSALM 107

1. Lord, I thank You for allowing me to be a part of Your work on earth.
2. Lord, give me the courage to live for what matters most in Jesus' name.
3. Lord, help me to trust the truth of Your Word when it is hard for me to feel Your presence.
4. My Father, give me the spiritual strength to resist sinning and damaging my relationship with You and others in Jesus' name.
5. Situation of no hope, no helper, vacate my life in Jesus' name.
6. Arrow of failure fired against me, backfire in Jesus' name.
7. My spirit, what are you doing in the prison of the enemy, come forth by mercy.
8. Racial or tribal sentiment that can cause me to lose my helper, expire now in Jesus' name.
9. Arrow of failure fired against me, backfire in Jesus' name.
10. Blackmailers working hard to destroy my image before my helpers meet double failure in Jesus' name.
11. Oh Lord, let joy replace tears assigned for me in Jesus' name.
12. Spirit of fruitless efforts assigned against me, be wasted in Jesus' name.
13. Far away helpers, my life is available, locate me now in Jesus' name.

14. Angel of God, compel my helpers to run towards me now in Jesus' name.
15. Fake help from wrong people, scatter by fire in Jesus' name.
16. Every help that will end in sorrow be nullified in Jesus' name.
17. Any power diverting the steps of my helpers elsewhere be wasted in Jesus' name.
18. Pray in tongues for 15 minutes.

DAY FIFTEEN
HELPING GOD
EXHORTATION

"And when Aaron and his sons have finished covering the sanctuary and all the furnishings of the sanctuary, when the camp is set to go, then the sons of Kohath shall come to carry them; but they shall not touch any holy thing, lest they die.
But unto the sons of Kohath he gave none: because the service of the sanctuary belonging unto them was that they should bear upon their shoulders.
And they set the ark of God upon a new cart,...
And when they came to Nachon's threshing floor, Uzzah put forth his hand to the ark of God, and took hold of it; for the oxen shook it. And the anger of the LORD was kindled against Uzzah; and God smote him there for his error; and there he died by the ark of God." (Num.4:15; 7:9; 2Sam.6:3,6,7)

Who help can God? Well, unfortunately, some people tried to help Him and the story ended badly. Our God is all sufficient. He is capable of doing anything. If He requires our help, He usually makes His intention known. When we disregard His intention in foolish piety, we will have ourselves to blame.

The wise man in the Book of Ecclesiastes exposed us to God's intention concerning His creation of man. He wrote, *"Let us hear the conclusion of the whole matter: Fear God and keep his commandments: for this is the whole duty of man"* (Eccl.12:13). Children of God, your role is clear, obey His commandment; do not deduct from it neither must you add to it. This pleases God more than our supposed input.

Some people in the Bible tried to help God and while one paid immediately with his life, the other placed the rest of us in perpetual problem.

In the Scripture quoted above, the instruction was clearly given concerning the Ark of Covenant; men of certain tribe and clan (Kohathites, Levites) are to bear it on their shoulders and must never touch it. When David became happy, he decided to bend the rules by ordering new carts to be made (1st sin). When the oxen stumbled because the presence of God was not with it, Uzzah (the son of Abinadab, not a Levite) tried to prevent the ark from falling by touching it (2nd sin). This angered God and Uzzah had to die. Blatantly disobeying God in a bid to help Him is unacceptable. Do not do it. Whatever God's instruction is, let us follow it and avoid additions. Familiarity breeds contempt.

Another person who tried to do God's work was Mummy Sarah herself. Having waited patiently for years for the promise of an heir from God and not getting it, she decided to 'help God' by sending her maid, Hagar, to her husband. The union produced a child (albeit not the heir) with grave consequences. Today, the result of Sarah's decision is a thorn in the flesh of Christians. Whatever God promise, let us patiently wait for it and try not to add to it. Today's action will eventually yield fruits.

There is another area where we try to help God do His work and this is prevalent in the House of God. When ministers of God do things that seem not to please us, we tend to sit in judgment. This is none of our business. Do you know what our business is? Praying for them, yes! Pray for them in their weaknesses, and not condemn, judge or gossip about them. God already knows about their failings. Miriam learnt this the hard way when she and Aaron tried to condemn the actions of Moses. God was displeased with her and struck her with leprosy (cf. Num.12).

We must ask ourselves today in what ways am I trying to help God accomplish His tasks? Many ministers have gone into syncretic practices in order to perfect the work of God. They utilize diabolical means to build and generate wealth, pull crowd and mesmerize the unsuspecting.

In our world today, we have a new term Paternity Fraud whereby a wife whose husband is challenged in a sexual way gets pregnant by another man while she claims it is the husband's.

A job applicant may falsify his or her age to get a job with an age restrictionin but introducing BVN which contains the correct date of applicant, may likely expose the person.

On no account are we to do God's work. If God needs your assistance, like Gideon, He would call you. Before then, just relax and watch things play out.

CONFESSIONS

❖ I will not ruin my career, I will not ruin my calling, I will not ruin my chances of getting divine help, Abram tried to help God, he was not justified afterward.

❖ I will wait upon the Lord, the Lord shall renew my strength, I will receive the best

152

God had reserved for me, I shall be encouraged. I shall not lose hope, I reject strange help.

- ❖ God is a warrior, God is a fighter, God is the Almighty. God is the wisest, there is no end to His might, I rest on God.
- ❖ I will not run ahead of God, I will not miss my timing, my children will come at God's best time, my marriage will come at God's best time, my letter of promotion shall arrive.
- ❖ God's time is the best, there is no regrets in my life, there will be no sorrow for waiting period, when I wait on God, my life will be better for it.
- ❖ My journey will not end prematurely, I will run my race patiently, I will not take a shortcut, I will not look for evil assistance, I will not accept unholy assistance, what God will do for me will be beautiful.
- ❖ Those who tried to help God multiplied sorrows for themselves, waiting time is not a wasted time, the period of waiting is period of preparation.
- ❖ God is wiser than me, I will humble myself before Him, He will help me.
- ❖ Some people help their gods, their gods are powerless, their gods needs them, they carry their gods, they fight for their gods, their gods are useless, stranded and irrelevant.

❖ My God is alive; He helps me; my God is powerful, He carries me; my God is useful; my God is relevant; my God is wise; God never lie; my God is never late; my God increase me more and more. Hallelujah!

PRAYER POINTS

PSALM 115

1.Lord, I thank You for the unspeakable peace given to me.

2. Sing a new song to the Most-High God.

3. Take authority over the presence of violence, drugs, robbery and other evil manifestation in your neighborhood in Jesus' name.

4. I reject and refuse every negative confession made over my children in Jesus' name.

5.Holy Spirit disconnect my children from time wasters in Jesus' name.

6. From every fear of the future, I deliver my children by the blood of Jesus.

7. Holy Spirit, help me not to end in the flesh the race I began in the spirit.

8. Every agent of shame working against my children be paralyzed in Jesus' name.

9.I handover the destiny of my children, Lord, take over in Jesus' name.

10. Every trap set for me in my place of work catch your owner in Jesus' name.

11. Holy Ghost fire accelerate my prophecies by fire in the name of Jesus.

12. Anointing of an intercessor, my life is available possess me now in Jesus' name.

13 Holy Ghost fire purge my life in Jesus' name.

14.I withdraw all my blessings kept in any satanic storehouse in Jesus' name.

15. I forgive everyone that has offended me one way or the other, in Jesus' name.

16.I receive grace to be rooted and grounded in Christ in Jesus' name.

17.Lord, give me a servant heart in Jesus' name.

18.Pray in the Spirit for 15 minutes.

DAY SIXTEEN
HELP BEYOND THE PHYSICAL / SUPERNATURAL HELP
EXHORTATION

For God speaketh once, yea twice, yet man perceiveth it not.
In a dream, in a vision of the night, when deep sleep falleth upon men, in slumberings upon the bed
Then he openeth the ears of men, and sealeth their instruction
Job 33: 14

And a vision appeared to Paul in the night; There stood a man of Macedonia, and prayed him, saying, come over into Macedonia, and help us. Acts 16:9

One unique way through which we get help but which is not commonly acknowledged is the help we get from our dreams or vision. How many times have we escaped from or fallen into trouble depending on our ability to rightly interpret a dream? This means that there are times that we escape trouble when we listen to our dreams and there are moments when we fall into trouble because we ignore instructions gotten from our dreams.

As believers, we are not to limit our scope of help because help can come from any channel. God is a dynamic God and as such can utilize any medium to express His will. In the Scripture quoted above, Apostle Paul was directed in his dream (vision) to go to Macedonia because some people there were in need. Apostle Paul could help but did not know that the Macedonians needed help. The Macedonians too did not know Paul nor knew that he could be of help but God came to the rescue for the two of them. In this case, God was the connecting helper.

When Apostle Paul awoke from his dream, he knew what to do and he went to do it. If God had not sealed his instruction, he might not have gone that way and the Macedonians would languish for lack of help.

If we are discerning, we will know that help can come to us through our dreams. God can give us a way out of our predicaments through our dream life. For instance, a lady shared her testimony sometimes ago. She had surgery but developed complications. The doctors tried their best but could not find solution to the problems. Being a believer, she took the matter to God in prayer. Before long, she dreamt that her mother who was a nurse before her death

156

was walking towards her, she ran to her crying and explaining her plight. She narrated all that the doctors said and how they were contemplating another surgery. The mother told her not to worry and, in the dream, called on the elder sister who was also a nurse and the two of them whispered somethings between themselves.

When she woke up, she knew her prayers had been answered. She called her elder sister and asked her if she knew the solution to her issue. The sister said why not and went to purchase some drugs. She used the drugs and the medical issue was resolved! The Doctors were mystified about the sudden turnaround and asked what she used. She told them it was God's doing.

Another incidence was a young man who came to me for counselling. He narrated how the elder brother usurped their parent's properties after their death. He and the other siblings were thrown out on the streets while their brother lived an extravagant life. He only took care of his immediate family.

This situation made me give the young man and the other siblings prayer instructions, and I also prayed for them. Not too long after, the elder brother came looking for them and started asking for forgiveness. He narrated how their late mother came to threaten him with death in his dream, from that moment, he gave them their share of the properties.

Our dream life is a powerful medium through which we can obtain help from God. Endeavor to listen to your dreams. Our dream life is our Alternate Reality. This means that whatever wants to happen in the physical must have first fine expression in the spiritual. Our dream life is synonymous to our real life. It is the other side of the same coin. Our ability to harness this existence will determine the success of our endeavors.

When Joseph interpreted the dream of Pharaoh, although Pharaoh was a pagan God, he was still discerning. Many Christians fail here. When God is sealing their instructions in their dream life, they fail to notice. They simply tag it as one of those things. Pharaoh, understanding the principles of Alternate Reality quickly sought the needed help to avert the looming calamity. Many of us would have also averted some certain calamities if only we had been discerning. I pray for you today, the grace to be spiritually discerning, may the Lord release it upon you in the name of Jesus.

The needed solution to Jacob's predicament was released to him in the spiritual world where he battled an angel. Although his father had released the blessings on him, he could not benefit from it because he was operating under closed heavens due to his name JACOB (SUPPLANTER). When he wrestled with the angel and prevailed (by wrestling we supposed Jacob must have fervently prayed and taken into the spiritual realm as established in Hosea 12:4 and not just fighting a physical being) his name was changed to ISRAEL (THE PRINCE THAT PREVAILED WITH GOD. This transported him into the fulfillment of his destiny because he then carried the presence of God which dissuaded his brother from killing him as previously determined. What we are trying to explain here is that Esau would have killed Jacob if Jacob had not had supernatural help (cf.Gen.32).

There are many battles of life that are constantly confronting us but if we can seek supernatural help, we will surely overcome.

CONFESSIONS

- ❖ I am born of the Spirit, I am born of incorruptible seed, I am born of the Word of God, I am born of Eternal Spirit.
- ❖ The power of God does not lose energy, the power of God works in my life, I am protected by God's power, I am precious to God
- ❖ I am a jewel in the hand of God, I am relevant in the program of God, I am settled in the heart of God, I am inscribed in the palm of God, nothing shakes me, I am born in glory.
- ❖ I am a very important person, I am hidden in Christ Jesus, I am not dead, I am alive in God, the life of God works through me, I am above destructions, Hallelujah!
- ❖ New thing will happen to me, old things have passed away, I know who I am, I am the apple of God's eye, I am a beautiful bride (of Christ), I am an Army of the Lord, I am His body.
- ❖ Help is not far from me, help in one form or the other is available for me, I cannot be stranded, I cannot be lost.
- ❖ God can make a way where there is no way, God can make a living out of a dead bone, my case is not over.
- ❖ There is hope for a tree that is cut down, when it's root is in the ground. At the scent of water, it shall spring forth, I have a living hope, I am alive.

- ❖ A living dog is better than a dead lion, my enemies cannot triumph over me, I have a goodly heritage.
- ❖ What is working for me is bigger than what is working against me, I am privilege in God, I am on a bigger platform, Hallelujah!

PRAYER POINTS
PSALM 121

1. I thank You for counting me worthy to be a carrier of Your divine power.
2. Thank God for the privilege and power to become a child of God.
3. Thank You for Your healing work sent to me.
4. I receive grace to promote peace in the body of Christ.
5. Lord, teach me how to yield to the Holy Spirit.
6. God, guide my step towards someone who needs the hope that only comes from me.
7. Lord, help me to move from childish things to dept of the Spirit.
8. Lord, Open my eyes to deeper things around me in Jesus' name.
9. I receive grace to rest like an eagle over every situation of life in Jesus' name.

10. Every relationship that will not help me to fulfil my destiny be terminated in Jesus' name.
11. My Father, my Father, let Your presence guide me throughout this year.
12. Help from above locate me and my children in Jesus' name.
13. You Spirit of the ancestors sitting on my breakthrough be dismantled by fire.
14. Lord, turn all my self-imposed curses into blessings, in Jesus' name.
15. The devil will never write the last chapter of my children's life in Jesus' name.
16. I receive help from above to execute all project that God has ordained for my life in Jesus' name.
17. Please, pray in the Spirit for 20 minutes.

DAY SEVENTEEN
DEMONIC HELP
EXHORTATION

"Then was Jesus led up of the Spirit into the wilderness to be tempted of the devil...

*And saith unto him, All these things **will I give thee,** if thou wilt fall down and worship me."* (Mt.4:1-11 emphasis mine)
'The blessing of the LORD, it maketh rich, and he addeth no sorrow with it.' – Prov.10:22

The time was high noon; the sun shining down mercilessly upon everything unfortunate to be on its path. The young man journeyed along, weak, tired and starving. He had just finished his forty days of fasting and prayer and would give anything to have a piece of bread and a gourd of cool water to quench his pangs of hunger but he was not fortunate to have it.

His mind started wandering to places of comfort and before long he started yearning for his needs. Enough, he said to his mind. He was on a mission and must not lose focus. To allow his mind to wander is to be distracted and distraction leads to temptation and temptation leads to death. All of these thoughts were swirling in his mind when he heard a strange eerie voice calling him.

"Who are you?", the young man asked.

"It does not matter who I am." was the sly response. "I could see that you are in need of help and I have come to help you." "Do you know that the hunger could be done away with just a piece of bread?" he asked.

"Of course, I know," said the young man.

"Well then, those stones are perfectly shaped in the form of bread, why don't you just command them to turn to bread?" the voice ordered.

Something flashed in his mind and he knew. Without missing a beat, the young man said, "It *is written, Man shall not live by bread alone, but by every word that proceedeth out of the mouth of God."* And eventually, *"Get thee hence, Satan!"*

The drama above played out between Jesus Christ and the devil. The devil knows even before you know that you have need of help and he would try his best to render it. Knowing the challenges of Jesus after fasting, he thought to trap Him with food. When that failed, he tried to trap Him with power. When he lost, he tried to get Jesus to worship him in promise of worldly kingdom. This is evil and unacceptable. Jesus quickly understood the tactics and triumphed with the Word of God.

Demonic help is simply the help rendered by the devil or his agents. Jesus was able to disregard demonic help glory be to God! The same help tactics was rendered to Eve and Adam in the Garden of Eden and they fell for it. God had told them what to do yet the devil came to circumvent their resistance to the instruction. This led to their expulsion from their comfort zone.

Accepting help from the devil is an affront to the Almighty God. What does the devil have to offer that is not in God? Did God not know that Jesus was hungry? Could He not have provided for Him? Of course, He could as He eventually did when the angels came to minister to Jesus! He just wanted the devil to know that it is not everyone that is susceptible to his wiles. The first Adam could fall but the second Adam will rise. Jesus knew who He was so nobody could tell Him otherwise. If you know who you are in Christ, no one will tempt you with transient help and you will fall. God has already made provisions for all your needs (Ps.23:1; 1Cor.3:21).

The devil and his agents could render help but we must never ever go to them for help as it negates the Scriptures and demands of God for us..., God Himself said, *"For I the LORD thy God will hold thy right hand, saying unto thee, Fear not; I will help thee."* – Isai.41:13

Beloved, with such an assertive statement, what else are you seeking? Why are you like king Saul seeking the help of the witch of Endor? There is nothing good with the devil. To every penny he gives you, he will collect millions. If he gives you a child, he will take the child back when you need him/her the most. If you collect wealth from him, he will ensure you suffer greatly to maintain it and eventually turn you to a beggar.

Any help he renders accompanies a great condition but hear the Word of God, *"The blessing of the LORD, it maketh rich, and he addeth no sorrow with it."* – Prov.10:22 When God helps you, you will be at ease. Whatever He gives, He will maintain. Listen to this, *"The LORD is the portion of mine inheritance and of my cup: thou maintainest my lot"* – Ps.16:5. If God gives you a child, He will ensure no evil happens to the child. An example is the child of the Shunamite's woman.

Be wise and discerning, that innocent help could lead you to the path of destruction. Rely on God and you will never regret (Ps.34:5).

CONFESSIONS

- ❖ I reject demonic help, I reject strange help, I reject help that is a trap. It is those who helped Absalom that ruin him at last.
- ❖ My God is sufficient to help me, my God is a capable God, my God is readily available, my God has promised to help my cases.
- ❖ I cannot deny my God when I am in need, even if He says "NO" that is good for me. The "NO" of God is better than the "YES" of devils, I will wait upon the Lord, I reject satanic help.
- ❖ Saul visited a witch for help he returned depressed and confused, at last he lost his throne and his life.
- ❖ Whatever God gives a man is good; the blessings of the Lord adds no sorrow; the blessings of God gives peace.
- ❖ Woe to those who put their trust in man, the best of a man is still man at his best, I shall be great.
- ❖ God has reserved the best for me, God has settled my case before the foundation of the world.
- ❖ I shall know the salvation of the Lord, I shall see the goodness of God in the land of the living.

- God will not suffer his righteous ones to see corruption. There is hope for me, there is help for me.
- God can make a way where there is no way, what is difficult for men is possible with God, I shall wait on God, blessed are they that wait, for they shall not be disappointed. Hallelujah!

PRAYER POINTS
PSALM 116

1. Sing a song of worship.
2. Lord, forgive me for my impatience before You.
3. Lord, forgive me for not serving You as I have vowed to.
4. Everything inside me pushing me to commit error disappear in Jesus' name.
5. Every gift of the Spirit that is dormant within me, be revived now in Jesus' name.
6. Every demonic help that robs me of my glory, I disconnect from you by mercy.
7. From every battle that have a legal hold on me, deliver me oh God of mercy.
8. The secret of a traitor posing as a friend around my children be exposed in Jesus' name.

9. Shout, God of mercy 21 times and say; rescue me from demonic help in Jesus' name.

10. The prayer which my destiny needs, Lord, reveal it to me by mercy.

11. Covenant of mercy, blow away every cloud of shame over my life.

12. Bad season shall not take over good season in my life in Jesus' name.

13. From the trap of demonic help, God of mercy deliver me in Jesus' name.

14. I command the original plan of God to be established in the life of my children Jesus name.

15. My foundation receive healing for God's testimonies in Jesus' name.

16. For the next 25minutes pray in the Spirit.

DAY EIGHTEEN
CRYING OUT FOR HELP
EXHORTATION

Then they cry unto the Lord of hosts in their trouble,and he saveth them out of their distress (Ps. 107:19)

"...Then the children of Israel groaned because of the bondage, and they cried out; and their cry came up to God because of the bondage. So God heard their groaning,... And God looked upon the children of Israel, and God acknowledged them. (Exod.3:23-25)

Call unto me, and I will answer thee, and shew thee great and mighty things, which thou knowest not. (Jer.33:3)

It is often said that a closed mouth represents a closed destiny. God gave us mouths not just to eat only but to use in calling out / crying out to Him. Our mouth is an important part of our anatomy. When there is a dire need, it must be put to use. How? By calling unto God in prayer. The devil understands this mystery and that is why he tries his utmost power to ensure that believers do not pray (Luk.21:15). When you fail to use your mouth (i.e. pray) you are only helping the devil to deal with you brutally.

One man that gave us courage to keep calling unto the Lord until He answers is Bar-Timaeus. He was a blind beggar who had lost all human prestige. His condition had so eroded his humanity that even his name was lost in history. Just like the woman with the issue of blood, he no longer had a name as his situation had overwhelmed his name. Think about this: Bar-Timaeus the Blind. The name Timaeus was his father's name and the Bar means son. Put together, you have Son of Timaeus the Blind. Life happened to this young man but one day, his story changed. There was a great clamoring and upon his investigation, he was told that Jesus was passing by.

His heart leapt into his mouth. Could this be the day, he wondered? Without further hesitation, he shouted, *"Jesus, Son of David, have mercy on me!"* What followed was a case of man's inhumanity to man. The people that knew quite well that the man was blind and would love to gain his sight back tried to shut him down. You too might be experiencing this. Your neighbours might be angry that you pray too much and too loudly. Your family members might be complaining that your Church attendance is too much (are you responsible for Jesus' death?). Some might pull you aside to deter you from contributing to God's work while some might try to stop you from fellowshipping with God. My friend, do not be deceived. That is the devil at work. Be like Mr. Bar-Timaeus, the more people try to stop you from doing what you know is helpful, do it the more.

So, Bar-Timaeus cried out the more to the one who could help him and he was helped. Crying out is not a thing to be ashamed of. When you need help, just cry out to God. The Bible records that even Jesus cried out for help, *'who, in the days of His flesh, when He had offered up prayers and supplications, with vehement cries and tears to Him who was able to save Him from death, and was heard because of His godly fear,'* (Heb.5:7). If Jesus cried out for help, who are you fooling! My friend, cry out today. When you cry, call and pray for God has promised to hear and answer you (Jer.33:3).

What are you waiting for? Call upon Him today. He is your Father and He desires to help you. He is just like a caring mother who will never ignore the cries of her hurting child. God loves you and wants to hear from you. Seize this golden opportunity today. Call upon Him and you will be helped.

Thousands of men and women of all ages have cried unto Him and they were not disappointed. The Israelites cried out and were helped. Jonah in the belly of the whale cried and he was helped. Peter cried out when he was sinking and he was helped. Jehoshaphat, the king cried out and he was helped. The lepers cried out and they were helped. Paul and Silas cried out with Psalms and were helped. The Church cried out on behalf of Peter and he was helped. There is no one who cried out to God that was denied help.

Will you cry out to Him today?

CONFESSIONS

- ❖ My God is not a deaf God, He will hear any cry for help, the eyes of God goes to and fro the earth showing Himself strong for those whose heart are steadfast toward Him, I will not cry in vain.

- ❖ My help comes from the Lord, the maker of heaven and earth, why my cry reaches to heaven, my heaven will open.

- ❖ There is no shame in crying for help, when Peter cried for help, Jesus saved him from drowning, when Samson cried for help his hair grew again, when Elisha cried for help, he got the mantle, when I cry for help, I will possess my possession.

- ❖ Crying is a form of praying, crying is a sign of humility, crying is a form of submission, crying is a form of brokenness.
- ❖ God rewards the humble, God uses the broken vessels, God hears the destitute, whenever I cry, the Lord hears.
- ❖ My time is not over, my case is not the worst, my heaven is not closed. God is not angry with me, my faith will work for me.
- ❖ Barthemaeus cry was heard and he received his sight, the Syrophoenician woman cry was heard and her daughter got her healing, God cannot reject a sincere cry, God cannot ignore a genuine cry, my crying to God is a sign of legitimacy. Hallelujah!
- ❖ It is not a shame to cry for help, crying for help is an act of faith, and God honours faith. Faith cry is a force that shakes heaven.
- ❖ God loves children, the kingdom of God is for child-like people, children cries for help all the times. God does not ignore crying.
- ❖ God has the title of "THE GREAT HELPER OF ISRAEL", God is a Father, and God is my Father, when I cry for help my Almighty Father will respond.

PRAYER POINTS
PSALM 60

1. Worship Him with a song.
2. Oh Lord, purge my tongue by fire.
3. Oh Lord, make me a proof producer in Jesus' name.
4. Every power prolonging my breakthrough be wasted by fire in Jesus' name.
5. Oh Lord, let my request find favour before my benefactor.
6. Shout God of mercy 21 times connect me to those who have what I need and those who need what I have in Jesus' name.
7. Timely helpers locate me by mercy.
8. Chains of captivity fashioned against my children break by fire.
9. My open heaven of help, appear by mercy.
10. Oh God, let the habitation of my enemies become desolate in Jesus' name.
11. Lord, help me draw wisdom from every situation I face in life.
12. I receive grace to be rooted and grounded in Christ.
13. Lord, give me a servant heart.
14. After the order of Joseph, he was taken from prison to palace. Help that will take

me from prison to palace possess me in Jesus' name.

15. Evil destructive plan of the enemy against the Church of God, be frustrated in Jesus' name.

16. For the next 20 minutes pray in the Spirit.

DAY NINETEEN
HINDRANCE TO HELP: SIN
EXHORTATION

Behold, the LORD'S hand is not shortened, that it cannot save: neither his ear heavy that it cannot hear: But your iniquities have separated between you and your God, and your sins have hid his face from you, that he will not hear (Isa 59:1-2)

When I would have healed Israel, then the iniquity of Ephraim was discovered, and the wickedness of Samaria: for they commit falsehood; and the thief cometh in, and the troop of robbers spoileth without. – Hoses 7:1

Although we keep emphasizing that everyone of us needs help, it is unfortunate to remark that it is not everyone that will eventually obtain that help; God's help anyway. This is because of their attitude towards God's instruction.

When we live a life that negates the principles of God, it will be hard-pressed for God to help us. The Bible says, 'God does not listen to sinners and if He does not listen to you, how will He help you when you call unto Him? (Joh.9:31ᵃ). You see, sin is the major reason why we languish in helplessness.

For the sake of our aspiring and new converts, let us quickly explore the world of sin. The Bible tells us that everything that God created is good (Gen.1:31) but with the expulsion of devil into our world (cf. Rev.12), he brought with him the attitude which led to his expulsion – pride and treason (Isai.14:12-14). When he disguised (he can disguise so don't let him fool you – 2Cor.11:14) as he fooled and tricked Eve and Adam, into doing what God disallowed and thereby succeeding in creating mayhem in the world.

So, basically, sin is simply DISOBEDIENCE TO GOD. When we do things that God has expressly warned us not to do, then we have sinned. How do we know what God wants us to do? Start with the Word of God. It will point you to the right direction (Ps.119:11)

Sin is a killer of destiny, joy, peace and relationship with God. It is a killer of revival, good health, mental dignity, conscience and eternal life. It has brought many down. The Bible warns, '*The wages of sin is death (Rom.6:23), it cuts short our glory (Rom.3:23)*. Mighty men like Samson were cut down in their prime by sin. Sin unchecked successfully ravaged and destroyed the family and kingdom of king David. Adam and Eve mortgaged the lives of unborn generation due to sin.

Jonah paid a costly price for his disobedience to the voice of God until he cried to God for mercy in the belly of the Whale. *(cf. Jonah)*

Samson paid dearly with his life for his sinful lifestyle eventually, life having first served his adversary which contradicts the plans of God for his life. *(cf. Judges 16)*

The Israelites having experienced the first-hand mercy, glory and power of God still went ahead to disobey Him. They also experienced the first-hand other side of God.

Sin is a killer of divine help. Many are suffering today because of sin. The way of the transgressor is hard *(Prov.13:15)*. It shall be well with the righteous but the wicked... *(Isa.3:10)*. God is angry with the wicked every day *(Ps.7:11)*, the sacrifice of the wicked is an abomination to God *(Prov.15:8)*. From all sides we see God not being happy or excited by the lifestyle of the wicked. This means that when the wicked cries unto God for help and assistance, God will not be willing to help. Sin separates us from God; it creates a chasm between God and man – God cannot come to man as vice-versa *(Isai.59:1,2)*.

My friend, if you are in this predicament, do not lose hope because there is a way out. That is why God in His infinite mercy has given us this topic for this season. The only way to reconnect back to God's help is by genuine repentance and the desire to forsake the old ways (Ps.51).

We must run away from sin and have righteous and Holy standing with God so that our prayers and cry for help can receive divine attention from the throne of mercy. *(Heb.4:16)*. Come to the Lord today and repent of your sins so that you can obtain help from the Lord.

STEPS TO REPENTANCE

- Acknowledge your sinful life *(Ps.51:3)*
- Confess and forsake your sins. *(Prov.28:13)*
- Receive Jesus as your personal Lord and Saviour. *(Joh.:12)*
- Pray in faith and believe you have been forgiven. *(1Joh.1:9)*

CONFESSIONS

- ❖ Righteousness exalts a nation but sin is a reproach to any nation.
- ❖ I will not allow sin to ruin my career, I will not follow the multitude to do evil, I will not stand in the company of mockers.
- ❖ I will wait on the lord for my breakthrough, I will follow the steps of God for my victory, God has promised not to abandon me.
- ❖ I will not explain my sin, I will not justify my wrong doing I will not hide my sin, I will not deceive myself.
- ❖ I will confess my sin, I will forsake my sin, I will receive forgiveness, I will be renewed, I

will be washed with the Holy Water of the Word of God.

- ❖ My garment shall be white, my head shall not lack oil, sin causes spiritual blindness, I will not sin.
- ❖ Sin causes a man to fall short of the glory of God, sin makes holiness impossible, sin brings shame and nakedness, I will not commit sin.
- ❖ I will follow the footsteps of Christ, I follow the example of godly mentors, I will be wise.
- ❖ Sin shall not block my heaven, sin shall not stain my white garment, sin shall not ruin my life.
- ❖ I am not a sinner, I am not a transgressor, I am not a mocker, I am not a stranger to God, sin shall not change my identity, I reject the garment stained by sin.

PRAYER POINTS

1. Worship the God of mercy with a song.
2. I receive grace to be totally sold into the will of God.
3. I pray daily for the grace to work in purity before the Lord.
4. Lord, cleanse me from all unrighteousness.
5. Ability to discern the strategies of the enemies, possess me in Jesus' name.

6. Every seed of hell in my life, be uprooted by mercy in Jesus' name.
7. Every wrong step I have taken that robbed me of divine help, God of mercy restore me.
8. Holy Spirit help me to see my faults and to change in Jesus' name.
9. Anti-help voices, I silence You over my life.
10. Every association robbing my children of their inheritance be disconnected in Jesus' name.
11. Father, forgive me for depending on my own understanding rather than looking up to You for sustenance.
12. Anointing of conquering, possess me in Jesus' name.
13. What has no remedy do not permit it to get my destiny in Jesus' name.
14. God of mercy, don't allow my enemies to kill my children in order to silence me.
15. Every good thing that the power of darkness has stolen from my life, covenant of mercy, restore it, in Jesus' name.
16. Pray in the Holy Ghost.

DAY TWENTY
HINDRANCE TO HELP: NEGATIVE ATTITUDE
EXHORTATION
"And he did not many mighty works there because of their unbelief." (Mt.13:58)

"Then Elisha said, "Hear the word of the LORD. Thus says the LORD: 'Tomorrow about this time a seah of fine flour shall be sold for a shekel, and two seahs of barley for a shekel, at the gate of Samaria.'"

So an officer on whose hand the king leaned answered the man of God and said, "Look, if the LORD would make windows in heaven, could this thing be?" And he said, "In fact, you shall see it with your eyes, but you shall not eat of it." (2Ki.7:1,2)

When seeking for help, let us endeavor to put our attitude in check in order to get our hearts desire. Considering our overall attitude as humans, God ought to be frustrated by our actions. Indeed, He was frustrated. In the Book of Gen.6:6, the Bible laments, *'And it repented the LORD that he had made man on the earth, and it grieved him at his heart.'* This is antithetical to His demeanor in Genesis 1:31 where it is proudly stated that all of His creation is good. How could something good grieve one's heart? The answer lies in one of God's creation. Out of everything that God created, man only has consistently given Him sorrow. He created man good but he found a way to corrupt himself and that corruption is what vexed God.

Bear in mind that the Bible says that God loves man (Joh.3:16), yet there are times when God would have no option but to destroy that same man that He dearly loves. Destroying him is not something that He relishes but it is a necessity to curb further evil. Imagine the actions of Er and Onan that made God kill them (cf. Gen.38).

Instead of them to receive help from God, they were destroyed because of their attitude.

The Israelites were another case in point. Being a first-hand witness to God's mercy and lovingkindness, they repeatedly frustrated His efforts by turning away from Him. They not only turn away from Him they engaged in actions that are discordant to His will. Psalms 78 vividly captures their negative attitude towards their helper. At last, God had to do away with them.

Our attitude towards God is instrumental to whether we will receive help from Him or not. When our hearts are not right with Him, we cannot receive from Him. Attitude is key towards receiving God's help. When you maintain positive attitude towards Him, you will enjoy all time help. That is the case with David. It was never said that he exhibited negative attitude in regards to his relationship with God. David was a man of sorrow yet he learnt how to be positive. His positive approach to life and to the things of God gave him a great privilege to God's help.

There were times when Jesus chastised His disciples by calling them men of *little faith* (Mt.8:26; 14:31; 16:8). By pointing out their weakness, He was trying to help build their confidence in God. Despite having performed many wonders, they were still apt to doubt Him.

However, your attitude towards God must be rooted in *faith* in Him (Heb.11:6). Anything short of that will not work. Faith is a prerequisite for our walk with God. Before Jesus could help some people, He would first ask them, *'Believe ye that I am able to do this?'* (Mt.9:28). When your faith is not intact, God cannot help you.

Another set of people who cannot receive help from God are the arrogant. That man upon whose hand the king leans wasted his life because of arrogance and unbelief.

One other negative attitude that hinders us from being helped by God is fear. Do you know that unnecessary fear is a sin (Neh.6:14) which could lead one to hell fire (Rev.21:8)? Paul while encouraging young Timothy persuaded him that fear is not of God (2Tim.1:7) and anything that is not of God must be done away with.

Beloved, if your attitude is negative towards God, please change today while there is time. Attitude is of the mind and God searches our hearts (Ps.139:23; Heb.4:12). If our heart is not right, we cannot enjoy God's help.

CONFESSIONS

- ❖ I will not ruin my glorious chances, I will not ruin my opportunities, I will not miss the blessings of God.
- ❖ My attitude will not stop my rising, I will learn how to talk, I will learn how to behave, I will learn how to comport myself, I will learn humility and grace.

- Jesus likened a woman a dog, yet she was humble and then got her blessing, Rahab saved her household from the fall of Jericho because she behaved herself.
- The woman that fed Elisha got her dead son to live again because she confessed positively, I will not allow pressure to cause me to misbehave.
- I shall not die, I shall live, I shall see the goodness of the Lord in the land of the living.
- My well shall not dry up, my source of help shall not be choked up, I will find peace of mind, I will find rest for my soul, those who will help me shall not change their mind, it is well with my soul. Hallelujah!
- I will cross the finish line, nothing wills stop me, my antagonist will have nothing against me.
- Satan will not deceive me, I will not drive away my helper, I will not use my month to cause my downfall.
- Help will not be far from me. Negative prophecies shall not come to pass against my family, my angels shall not depart from me.
- Holy Spirit will not leave me. I will follow divine counsel, I will go to mentorship class, I will improve myself.

PRAYER POINTS
PSALM 42

1. Worship the faithful God.
2. Thou Spirit of ignorance and spiritual deafness lose your hold over my life in Jesus' name.
3. I arise and shine for my light has come.
4. My Father, my Father deliver me from the spirit of mediocrity and average performance.
5. I repent of every act of carelessness and slothfulness for not acting in God's expectation in my life.
6. Every strange arrow that has entered my life through the dream be wasted in Jesus' name.
7. You my environment cooperate with me by fire.
8. Any power terrorizing my environment be wasted by fire.
9. By fire by force I possess my portion in Jesus' name.
10. Every agenda of my enemy to kill me before my time, scatter by fire.
11. My miracles what are You doing in an evil cage jump out by fire.
12. Any power backing up my enemies surrender by fire in Jesus' name.

13. Every area of my life that I have suffered defeat oh God, repair it by fire.
14. Every means of leakage of the anointing in my life, be blocked in Jesus' name.
15. Lord, baptize me with the anointing of ease in Jesus' name.
16. Pray in the Spirit for 20 minutes.

DAY TWENTY-ONE

HINDRANCE TO HELP: IGNORANCE/FAILURE TO ASK

EXHORTATION
My people are destroyed for lack of knowledge: because thou hast rejected knowledge, (Hos.4:6)
Ye lust, and have not: ye kill, and desire to have, and cannot obtain: ye fight and war, yet ye have not, because ye ask not. (Jas.4:2 emphasis mine)
"Ask, and it shall be given you; ... For every one that asketh receiveth..." (Mt.7:7,8)

One of the most unfortunate people in the Bible is the elder brother of the Prodigal Son. He was hard working and committed. He does what was expected of him with clinical precision yet he was lacking in fundamental area. He lacked in the area of wisdom, knowledge and understanding. Unlike his younger brother, he did not know the kind of father he had (knowledge), so he did not know that he could ask his father for something (understanding) and thereby became very angry when his younger brother who although was not very wise but he knew who his father was and was able to ask for something (wisdom).

In Luk.15 (the Lost Chapter), Jesus in His parables wanted to discredit the thought process of the Pharisees and Scribes concerning the sinners. He utilized the parables to explain God's love for the hopeless sinners who are so lost they could not find their way home. That is not where I am going today. Something worthy of note in the parable of the Prodigal Son is that there were two sons of a wealthy man. One of them having thought it through decided to *ask* their father for a portion that belongs to him. The emphasis here is ask. I am not here to condemn the young man but to stress his courage in going to meet their father to ask.

He had a knowledge of his father. He knew he had what he wanted and he knew he would be given if he would only ask. He tested his theory and he worked. Without wisdom of wealth multiplication, he squandered all and came back home into his loving father's arm destitute.

His elder brother on the other hand, was assiduous, diligent and committed but lacked the sense of asking. He might not have asked to squander like his brother but he might have asked for his own psychological well-being. He told his father, *'Lo, these many years do I serve thee, neither transgressed I at any time thy commandment: and yet thou never gavest me a kid, that I might make merry with my friends:'* He accused their father of not giving him something that will make him happy. Now hear his father's response, '*And he said unto him, Son, thou art ever with me, and all that I have is thine.* In essence, while the elder brother had access to all of the father's property, he had never asked and he never received (Mt.7:8). Those two key hindrances to help: IGNORANCE AND FAILURE TO ASK ensured that he got nothing (maybe he will inherit when the father dies).

The moral of the parable is that while some Christians profess their relationship with God, they stop short at the point of asking. When you refuse to pray, I wonder how God can help you. Ignorance will prevent you from asking because you might not even know you have a portion in God (1Cor.3:21). How do you deal with this ignorance?

By diligently studying the Word of God, Jesus Christ our Lord discovered His true purpose as He was studying the Word (Luk.4:16-21). If He had not studied and read the Scriptures, He would be ignorant of His calling and thus would have lived an unfulfilled life. But the knowledge of God's Word saved Him from that problem. While you and I might not specifically get our direct calling and purpose from the Scriptures (like Jesus), we can, by studying and meditating, and receiving inspiration of our purpose from the Holy Spirit. The Holy Spirit will breathe upon the Word in our hearts and release divine instructions on how to live our lives.

God told Hosea to tell us that His people perish because they are ignorant (Hos.12:13). Yes, ignorance can kill and many have died because they do not know what they are supposed to know. If they have known, they would have asked for help!

With all your getting beloved, get understanding (endeavor to understand this message)! If you do not understand, you cannot have knowledge and if you do not have knowledge, you cannot have wisdom. Wisdom is the right application of knowledge.

CONFESSIONS

- A closed mouth is a closed destiny, I will not close my mouth, I will call for help, I will get blessed.
- My help will not be delayed, my help will not be denied, my help will not be misplaced, I will not be stagnant, and I reject failure.
- God will give me beauty for ashes, God will shower his blessings on me, I will get

unlimited access, and my breakthrough is possible.

- I will seek knowledge, I will seek assistance, I will walk in dominion, I will walk with the wise, I will gain the upper hands.
- Failure is not my portion, opportunities shall not pass me by, my glory shall not turn to shame, I shall not labour in vain, I shall gain, I shall not loss.
- God will make a way for me, my God is a specialist in miracle, I serve a miracle working God, and there is abundant grace for me.
- Nothing can stop me, help is available for me, breakthrough is my portion, I will not breakdown, I will meet the right person.
- Open heaven is my portion, victory is my portion, the Cross is a turning point for me, I cannot be stranded, and there is help for me.
- My God is a miracle worker, the mountains cannot stand before Him, through the power of God, mountains melt like wax. I am blessed, I am privileged, I am a child of God.
- Jeremiah received help, he did not die in the dungeon. Peter received timely help, he did not die in prison. Shedrach, Meshach, and Abednego received timely help, they

did not die in the fire. I shall receive timely help. Hallelujah!

PRAYER POINTS

PSALM 38

1.Lord, I thank You that I can bring my needs to You. Sing a song to our Burden Bearer.

2. Abba, Father, help me to turn away from the sin in my life and make a new beginning with You today.

3. Help me to trust in the truth of Your word, when it is hard for me to sense Your presence.

4.Every grip of fear against me, expire in Jesus' name.

5. Every strong man assigned to monitor my children be paralyzed in Jesus' name.

6. Lord, make me an extension of Your power to liberate and deliver people from the power of darkness.

7. You giant of ignorance what are You doing in my life jump out by fire.

8.You power of failure at the edge of major help break, by fire.

9.Father, give me help from Your sanctuary in Jesus' name.

10.Lord, open the eyes of my helpers to see me in Jesus' name.

11. You dream invaders that weakens me spiritually receive the arrows of fire in Jesus' name.

12. Lord, strengthen my hands to fight and my fingers to war.

13. Circle of fire, surround my children.

14.Arrow of prayerlessness jump out of my life in Jesus' name.

15. I ask for forgiveness for not responding promptly to vital spiritual signals that You have shown me in Jesus' name.

16. Spirit of wisdom swallow the force of ignorance blocking my destiny in Jesus' name.

17. Pray in the Spirit for 25minutes.

DAY TWENTY-TWO
DEALING WITH ANTI-HELP SPIRITS
EXHORTATION

And he said unto him, Son, thou art ever with me, and all that I have is thine. 1Cor.16:9

Be not far from me; for trouble is near; for there is none to help. (Ps.22:11)

A rich man called his childhood friend who was passing through a tough time for assistance. When the man got there, the rich man rudely chased him away. He was surprised that his friend that called him would chase him away but after having gone through rigorous prayers, his friend called him, apologized. He explained that he saw a huge masquerade with that friend the other day he came and thought he had come to attack him.

Lots of people all over the world are frustrated because they could not find help. The principal reason why there is no help for them is because they have evil mark on them that is warding off potential helpers. Some ladies are experiencing marital delay because their potential suitors do not see them as women but rather as men or as old women.

ANTI-HELP FACTORS

1. **Curses:** Gen.49:4 Unstable as water, you shall not excel, because you went up to your father's bed; Then you defiled it— He went up to my couch. A curse is a solemn utterance intended to invoke a supernatural power to inflict harm or punishment on someone or something. To excel in life you need help, but when a curse has been placed on someone that he will not excel, then he can never be helped.

2. **Foundational battles**: Joh.7.52 - They answered him, Are you too from Galilee? Search [the Scriptures yourself], and you will see that no prophet comes (will rise to prominence) from Galilee. Your foundation is your source, your

family tree, your origin. Some family lineage does not receive help, because they've been sentenced to everlasting foundational poverty. So being helped has been a taboo to some family and such evil pattern has continued until it'll be broken.

3. **Sin:** Sin is a sinker, Isai.59.2 – *"But your iniquities have made a separation between you and your God, and your sins have hidden His face from you, so that He will not hear."* Help must first be endorsed by God before it can be given or received by any man on Earth. *"My help comes from the Lord."* Psalm 121. So, if we sin against this same God who is the ultimate source of help, this anti-help spirit will be empowered the more

4. **Filthy Garment**: *"Now Joshua was dressed in filthy clothes as he stood before the angel."* Zech.3:3. No one draws closer to a mad man in torn clothes to help him. Many may dress gorgeously in the physical but they are covered with filthy garment in the spiritual. The spiritual controls the physical so no matter the beautiful physical garment, people will not come closer to help him or her

5. **Evil mark of Rejection:** Gen.4.15 – *"And the Lord said to him, Therefore, if anyone kills Cain, vengeance shall be taken on him sevenfold. And the Lord set a mark or sign upon Cain, lest anyone finding him should kill him."* A lot happens in the spirit realms. This evil mark is never seen in the

physical but placed on someone in the spirit realm. Such persons will only just notice rejection and no help. Every witchcraft mark of rejection on you is cleansed now.

6. **Demonic Odour:** Eccl.10:1 *"As dead flies give perfume a bad smell, so a little folly outweighs wisdom and honor."* When you carry about demonic smells through demonic oppression and possessions, then it sends your helpers away. No matter how expensive your perfume, it can't quench such smell apart from the blood of Jesus.

For ways out of this predicament, check the topic: **ATTACKING ANTI-HELP SPIRITS IN THE ARTICLE PART OF THIS PRAYER MANUAL.**

CONFESSIONS

- Help is not far from me, my foundation cannot stop me, negative sentences cannot stop me, I cannot loss good things.
- God will give me beauty for ashes, wasters of destiny cannot waste my destiny there can only be survival with God.
- God will send help where there is no help, what nobody knows God knows. I am within the reach of divine help.
- I see a new day, I see a new opportunity, grace is at work for me, my God is a reliable

advocate my God will make a way, I have a goodly heritage.

- There is no hindrance on my way, there is no shame for me, there is no loss of valuable things for me. My case is settle, nothing bad has happen to me.
- My helper shall not die, my helper shall not be sick, my helper shall not be misled, my helper shall not change his mind, I shall get what belongs to me.
- I am valuable, I am worthy, I am precious, I am relevant, God has anointed me, God has shown me the way, I am blessed.
- Anti-help spirit, get out! I cannot be denied, I cannot be delayed, there is a new way for me, there are opportunities for me.
- I shall sing the songs of victory, I shall not be the tail, I shall not become a nobody, I shall see the goodness of God.
- My time is now, my help has come, it is my turn to shine. Hallelujah!

PRAYER POINTS
PSALM 22

1. Oh Lord, I thank You for the salvation of my soul, sing a song to Your saviour.
2. Lord, make me wiser than my enemies.
3. In every collective captivity where my destiny is locked come out by fire in Jesus' name.
4. Terrifying noise from above, arise and purse my pursers in Jesus' name.
5. Anointing of unity flow into the body of Christ in Jesus' name.
6. The prayer altar of my ministry, receive fresh fire in Jesus' name.
7. Arrows of error get out of my life and the life of my children in Jesus' name.
8. Oh God, help me from doubt in Jesus' name.
9. Oil of discerning Spirit come upon me in Jesus' name.
10. I will see my children's children and also live to witness their season of glory.
11. Ever spy in our midst working for the enemy be exposed and disgraced in Jesus' name.
12. Lord, teach me to pray a prevailing prayer.

13. Rain of mercy fall upon me for unusual victory.
14. The sword of my enemies shall not kill my children in Jesus' name.
15. Lord, visit our ministry with signs and wonders in Jesus' name.
16. Every sick person in the hospital receive healing in Jesus' name.
17. Pray in the Spirit for 25 minutes.

DAY TWENTY-THREE
HELP ACTIVATOR: PRAYER/FASTING
EXHORTATION

"Ask, and it shall be given you; seek and ye shall find; knock, and it shall be opened unto you". Matt.7:7
"Help, LORD; for the godly man ceaseth; for the faithful fail from among the children of men." Ps.12:1

Our relationship with the Lord Jesus will help us to stand firm in Him when we pray. Most times when I need to figure things out on my computer and keep all the programs in it running, I need help. It is just too complicated for me. I don't really understand how it works. When I try working it out, I still struggle with it over and over again, so instead of wallowing in frustration, I simply call out for help. Can you relate with that?

It is natural and easy for most of us to talk to a person we can see. It depends on the level of our desperation for answer. We can still talk to a person we cannot see as long as we can hear an audible voice that provides solution as in a telephone conversation.

However, in a situation like this, we cannot see God. He can seem so silent and distant when it comes to communication but we still need to adhere to His Word. According to Matthew 7:7, ask when you are in need of help. You are free to look out for help and you can knock doors that are barricading your help.

It was not too difficult for Jabez to discover that he needed help when he kept on congratulating his age mates for their accomplishments while his own life was stagnated. Have you put in efforts to your advancement without result too? You can act like Jabez who decided to call for a personal retreat, that is, prayer and fasting. He cried out aloud to God for help and God answered his prayer. His story was re-written and people are reading his testimony today. Are you experiencing such? It is not difficult for God to harken to your voice and change your story.

Prayer works! Fasting also comes with amazing answers. What then is prayer? According to Francis Thompson *"Prayer is the very sword of the saints"*. If that is true, why do we often keep the sword in its sheath?

Lee Roberson called prayer *"the Christians secret weapon, forged in the realms of glory"*. The question is, why then do we not use it more effectively? Why are people still helpless? The answer lies in the fact that they refused to pray and fast.

Abraham did and he got answers to his long-awaited miracle. Elijah prayed with passion to restore rain back to the land and God harkened to his voice. He was helped. The Israelites prayed and fasted and God turned his wrath away from them. You too can pray your way out till your testimony shows forth.

Hannah prayed to God for help concerning her reproach in childlessness. Today she is one of the Biblical women that got help. Her story changed from barreness to fruitfulness (1Sam.1, 2).

The current situation of the world of places a demand on prayer for help. There are lots of obstacles and problems everywhere that have need of help in order to be overcome. If we do not seek the face of the Lord in prayer like Esther, we just might be swallowed by the circumstances of life.

Beloved, fasting and prayer can never be overrated!

CONFESSIONS

- I shall not pray in vain, my prayers shall enter heaven, my prayer shall move mountains, my prayers shall bring blessings.
- I shall not pray amiss, I shall not pray to a deaf God, I know my redeemer liveth, whenever I cry, He will answer
- Prayer is a blessing to move the hand of God, I will pray and I will fast, I will take steps of faith, God will be glorified.
- I will pray when it is convenient, I will pray when it is not convenient, I will pray until it is convenient, my prayers are not wasted, God shall notice my prayers.
- I will fast when it is convenient, I will fast when it is not convenient, I will fast until it is convenient, I will not hunger in vain, fasting is a sacrifice.
- My prayer and fasting will bring help my way, God will reward my fasting, God will acknowledge my fasting, like Cornelius God shall reward my fasting and prayer.
- Prayer and fasting works, prayer and fasting changes things, prayer and fasting make all the different, I will not be lazy.
- Heaven always respond to prayer and fasting, there is always a renewal of

strength when I fast, I will fast my way out of problems, I will move mountains with my prayers.

- Joshua stopped the sun and the moon. Elijah called down fire, Moses parted the Red Sea, Deborah defeated an army.
- Prayer is an official invitation for divine intervention, I shall pray, I shall fast, I shall employ the heavenly host, things shall change for me. Hallelujah!

PRAYER POINTS
PSALM 30

1.Celebrate the Lord that gives us victory at all times-sing a new song to Jesus.

2. You arrow of no helper in my destiny, come out by fire (Jon.5:7)

3. Mercy rain fall upon me, for unbelievable help.

4. Holy Spirit refrain my destiny helpers from sleeping, compel them to help me.

5. The step I need to take to over-come the battle of helplessness, Holy Spirit, reveal it to me in Jesus' name.

6. Angel of revelation, visit my dream life.

7.Every error of my parent that is manifesting in my life be swallowed by the Blood of Jesus.

8. Fresh fire of the Holy ghost fall upon my altar/ prayer for the next level of glory in Jesus' name.

9. Fresh fire possess my environment in Jesus' name.

10. Ever satanic wind that is blowing away my opportunities, be still in Jesus' name.

11.Every evil pattern that I inherited from my lineage be wasted in Jesus' name.

12.Reigning King over my territory I dethrone You by fire in Jesus' name.

13. Silent killer arrow in my blood waiting for my day of celebration come out by force.

14. I shall not sleep the sleep of death in Jesus' name.

15. Rain of mercy fall upon my life for healing.

16. Lord, turn my weeping into laughter (Ps.30:5).

17. Pray in the Spirit for 20 minutes.

DAY TWENTY-FOUR
HELP ACTIVATOR: GIVING/SACRIFICE/SOWING
EXHORTATION

There is that scattereth, and yet increaseth; and there is that withholdeth more than it meet, but it tendeth to poverty (Prov.11:24)
Give, and it shall be given unto you; good measure, pressed down, and shaken together, and running over, shall men give into your bosom. For with the same measure that ye mete withal it shall be measured to you again. (Luk.6:38)

If there is a man that can quickly get help from God, it will be a man who is a good helper, giver, sower. Helping others is a great way of activating help. The Bible mentioned a man and woman whose helping hands opened the gate of heaven and shut the gate of death.

CORNELIUS: He was a Roman Centurion (a centurion is a Roman commanding officer with a hundred soldiers under him). He was the first gentile convert. That means he was the first gentile to become a Christian. Despite his sensitive post as a Roman soldier, he was convicted by the Holy Spirit to renounce his idolatry tendencies and embrace the grace of God. This he did wholeheartedly to warrant a place in Biblical history.

Cornelius stood out as an exemplary model because of these great qualities:

1. He had the fear of God in him and also encouraged his household to do the same.
2. He was a man of prayer and he was a giver. Do you know that God takes note when we are open-handed towards our fellow human

beings? When we are willing to be generous towards others, it pleases God. Cornelius' action so pleased God that an angel was sent by God to Cornelius to assure him that his deeds are noted. Note also that all of our actions are being recorded (the earthly book of records that elevated Mordecai should be seen as a prototype of the heavenly book of record). Everything we do is being recorded and there is reward accordingly.

The day came when Cornelius' *book of records* was opened and an angel from the Lord came with the good tidings. Observe what was said of him, **'Thy prayers and thine alms are come up for a memorial before God.'** Beloved, can your prayers and alms be remembered by God? Have you done enough to guarantee such? Be the judge!

Cornelius was specially remembered by God because of his prayer and giving habits. His actions so pleased God that He chastised Peter who did not feel too happy about the induction of Cornelius into the Christian Hall of Fame. Solomon the Wise quipped, *"When a man's ways please the LORD, he maketh even his enemies to be at peace with him."'* Cornelius was able to warm the heart of God through alms giving. (cf. Acts 10)

DORCAS (aka TABITHA): She was a Christian woman at Joppa whose helping hand saved her from death. She was a widow *fashion designer* who spent a great deal of her labour in tending to the needy around her. Hear what was said of her, *"this woman was full of good works and kind acts that she was doing;".* Friend, what will be said of you when you die? Will you be remembered as a helper or a destroyer? Note that if Dorcas had been selfish, neighbours would have been hard-pressed to seek restoration for her.

Our **Annual Women's Convention** is modeled after this gracious woman. The Program is called **DORCAS INITIATIVE** and it was instituted to assist the less privileged; helping them to find their footing through empowerment. Hundreds of widows are also empowered out of despondency caused by the death of their spouses.

Apostle Peter was entreated by her friends and neighbours to do something about her death because they felt she was helpful; he obliged them (by praying for Dorcas, he raised her back to life). Dorcas escaped death because of her habit of helping others. Have you learnt something today? What you sow today will germinate to become what you will reap tomorrow.

Alms giving is a sure help activator. You cannot live your life by helping other and fail. If you fail with people (which is certain – some people can be funny, the more you help them, the more they will hate you), you can never fail with God; He will repay.

An elderly woman took in a young boy who was brought in by one of her sons. Without knowing his origin, she took full responsibility of the child to the best of her ability. With time, her own son (who brought in the other boy) died. Later on, this young man became an accomplished professional in his field and went abroad. He became great there and being a grateful person helped all the other children of the elderly woman. In fact, he adopted the woman as his mother and ensured that she came over to wherever he was in the world every year. I imagine what would have happened to the woman if she had chased the boy away that fateful day she saw him.

CONFESSIONS

- My help comes from the Almighty. God is the most reliable source of help, Help from God does not bring sorrow, I am happy to wait upon the Lord, Help from God does not disappoint.
- The Law of saving and reaping shall favour me, I shall sow bountifully. I shall not be

overcome by greed, God shall show me the path of life.

- My heaven is not shut, my life is not at the mercy of my enemies. God can meet my needs, I cannot be stranded, my God is alive.
- I shall help others, I shall offer my shoulders, I shall be available for others, I shall sow kindness, I shall give money, I shall be the help somebody needs, I shall be the answer to someone.
- What my life needs is available, what I lack is abundant somewhere. I shall always meet those who need me, I shall not miss those I need, whatever I sow, I shall reap good harvest.
- My helper will arise and locate me, lack is not my portion, my vision shall not lack provisions, my mission shall not lack direction, my project shall not suffer setback, God will supply my needs according to his glory.
- I claim beauty for ashes, I choose life over death, I claim blessing over curses, my family is blessed, the works of my hands are blessed, I shall see the goodness of the Lord.

- My location is not hidden, my helper shall find me, my face is not lost in the crowd, my helper shall locate me.
- I am visible, I am available, I am within reach, I am identified, I am located, I am blessed, I am a blessing.
- Help is not far from me, my sowing and sacrifice shall work for me, God cannot lie, I am satisfied with God's goodness.

PRAYER POINTS

PSALM 63

1. Sing a song to the Most-High.
2. Lord, help me to follow Your example of service in Jesus' name.
3. Lord, break me down and remold me.
4. Lord, let this program be the beginning of new things in my life and family in Jesus' name.
5. You spirit of rejection turn to acceptance in Jesus' name.
6. Ever arrows of financial set back fired against me, backfire, in Jesus' name.
7. That which will make me great for others to emulate, fall upon me in Jesus' name.

8. Ideas that will attract great helpers to my life possess me in Jesus' name.
9. Every arrow of 'thou shall not succeed' fired against me, backfire in Jesus' name.
10. Every evil voice giving wrong commands, shut up in Jesus' name.
11. Every storm assigned to swallow me, be still in Jesus' name.
12. Every strange voice manipulating the destiny of this country be silenced in Jesus' name.
13. My Father, my Father, stir up my sacrifice to speak for me where necessary.
14. Every strange king enthroned from the pit of hell over the throne of my community, I dethroned You by fire in Jesus' name.
15. Voice of justification, swallow the voice of condemnation over my children.
16. The offering of Solomon connected him to generational blessing. God of mercy, let my

offerings connect me to my destiny helpers.

17. Pray in the Spirit for 25 minutes

DAY TWENTY-FIVE
HELP ACTIVATOR: RENDERING HELP
EXHORTATION

"Thou shalt not see thy brother's ass or his ox fall down by the way, and hide thyself from them: thou shalt surely help him to lift them up." (Deut.22:4).

"Be not deceived; God is not mocked: for whatsoever a man soweth, that shall he also reap." (Gal.6:7)

The Scripture affirms strongly that whatever we sow in life is what we will reap. If you sow help and kindness, you will reap same, and if you sow evil, you will reap it in abundance too (2Cor.9:6; Gal.6:7). Life is not a vacuum, it is what you so that you will harvest at the end.

The law of help and kindness attracts same in return. We live in a world where people's bowels of mercy have been shut up; people hardly ever care about the welfare of their neighbours. Instead of people emulating Christ, they have rather chosen to emulate the devil in perpetuating evil. The reason why evil abounds in the world today is because the evil we put in overwhelms the good that is being done.

What people seem to have forgotten is that in their quest to get the needed help in the fulfilment of destiny, they have a role to play and that is the role of being of assistance to someone. The way God configured the world, He has made us to be dependent on one another. The high will depend of the low while the low will lean on the mighty. If we fail to work concentrically, we will never be able to achieve our purpose in life.

In 1sam.30:1-17, the enemies invaded Ziklag and carried all that David and his servants had. It was a horrible moment in the life of David. It got to the point that even his soldiers planned to mutiny; their condition was that adverse.   But after encouraging himself and consulting with God, he was instructed to pursue the enemies. David was able to pursue, overtake and recover because of his 'help others' mentality.

Picture that scenario, you were pursuing an enemy to get back what he has taken from you, you met with someone who needed assistance, logic dictates that you mind your own business (even the priest and the Levite in the parable of the Good Samaritan 'minded their business') but David was a man of God and had God's Spirit in him so he did what Jesus would have done by stopping to help the afflicted.

The payback was that the wounded young man was able to point him to the right direction after been restored. What would have taken him considerable time and resources to locate was given to him free of charge because he paused to render help. Look around you today, is there someone you could be of assistance to even in your busy schedule?

The Shunamite Woman is another example. Having observed that Prophet Elisha is always passing by her domain intermittently, she determined to be of assistance to him. She in agreement with her husband built a resting place for the Prophet and she got a miracle baby she had been waiting for as a reward. And when the devil wanted to snatch the child from her, the Prophet was instrumental in restoring him back to life. (cf.2Ki.4)

Joseph was able to fulfill his dream-vision because of the assistance rendered. What is your problem? What are you passing through? Do you know that your situation is not an excuse to be stingy? Joseph, despite being in a dire situation, was still able to think about others. If it were another person, he or she would have been so self-absorbed and embittered to render help again. Joseph was able to put aside his problems to assist others. This seemingly ordinary aid was instrumental to giving him a top seat in Egyptian Government which culminated in the realization of his dream.

Nevertheless, there are doors that will not open except someone help you to open them. If you do not help them, how will they help you? You must be willing to render help in order to obtain help. Another important point is that you must not discriminate when it comes to rendering help. Do not overlook or downgrade anyone. The insignificant gateman may have access to the Director's heart. Endeavor to spread your love to everyone, it will come back to you in a bountiful harvest (Eccl.11:1).

CONFESSIONS

- I cannot be stranded, people will rise up for me. God shall send help to me, wherever I find myself, I shall be helped.
- My giving shall speak for me, my giving shall speak louder for me, my sacrificial giving shall speak up for me.
- My seed of help shall never be silent, anytime I need it, my space shall not be occupied.
- God shall support me, God shall assist me, God shall enlarge my coasts, help from above is available for me.
- Do not rejoice over me oh my enemies, I am a product of grace. Mercy shall speak for me, there is help for me in God.

- Silence oh mockers, shame is not my portion, I shall rise again, I shall be above, I shall not be below, God shall give me strength.
- Help will raise me up, help shall keep me up, help shall sustain me, help shall make a way for me, I shall be blessed
- I shall not cry in vain, I shall not expect in vain, I shall not lose hope, my faith in God shall work wonders.
- Where others have failed, I shall get results, the seed of help I have sown shall speak up for me, whenever I need help, I shall get help, my God is fair, my God is just, my God is good.
- I receive solution to my problems, I shall not be abandoned, I shall not lose my opportunities, the best of God is kept for me, I shall not lose. Hallelujah!

PRAYER POINTS
PSALM 27

1. Sing a new song to the Most-High God.
2. Lord, help me to prepare well that I may end well in Jesus' name.
3. Lord, open my Eyes to see how You want me to serve You in Jesus' name.
4. Father of miracles, soak me in Your mercy, grace and favour, in Jesus' name.

5. Anointing to be preferred above others possess me in Jesus' name.
6. Every evil tongue speaking evil against my children be glued to the root of your mouth in Jesus' name.
7. My destiny, arise and come out from the pot of shame, in the name of Jesus.
8. The magnetic force of the Lord, I will not miss my contact person, in Jesus' name.
9. Lord, God, of leadership, use the leaders in the Federal, State and Local Government to deliver this nation from hardship in Jesus' name.
10. Any spirit making me to be critical of others, be bound and be cast out in Jesus' name.
11. Oh, Lord, remove spiritual contact from my eyes in Jesus' name.
12. Oh Lord, reveal to me every secret behind my problem in Jesus' name.
13. Oh Lord, teach me deep and secret things.
14. Lord, give me power for maximum achievement in my next project in Jesus' name.
15. Lord, fortify my children with Your power.
16. Holy Spirit open my eyes and help me to make the right decision in Jesus' name.
17. Every power wasting my rendered help, be dismantled in Jesus' name.

18. Pray for in the least for at least 25 minutes.

DAY TWENTY-SIX
HELP ACTIVATOR: GRATITUDE
EXHORTATION

"Father, I thank thee that thou hast heard me". Joh.11:41b
"Although the fig tree shall not blossom, neither shall fruit be in the vines; the labour of the olive shall fail, and the fields shall yield no meat; the flock shall be cut off from the fold, and there shall be no herd in the stalls:
Yet I will rejoice in the LORD, I will joy in the God of my salvation". Hab.3:17-18

We acknowledge the boundless grace we have enjoyed from our help in ages past, our hope of victory, breakthroughs, healings and solutions to pandemic, kidnappings, child molestations and our shelter from the stormy blast as we begin to unleash the unlimited grace and mercy of God in this year **40DAYS APOSTOLIC MERCY RAIN ANNUAL PROGRAM**. *Title "Help from Above"*

On many occasions we have been enjoying the awesomeness of God's help from above in all we do, think and desire.

What is help from above? Help from above is a help that cannot be stopped by any mortal. It is a help that cannot be mixed with sorrow. It is a help that causes wonder to many. It is also a help that puts your enemy into confusion. We all are candidates of help.

Help from above can only be attained, when we obey the principle of God regarding praise, *"He inhabits the praises of His people"* (Ps.22:3).

Whatever prayers and fasting cannot handle, Praise will. The Psalmist exclaims in Psalm 19, **'the heavens declare the glory of God...'** over every circumstance of our lives. There is no challenge that prevails over the power of God, **'...the firmament showeth His handy work'.**

Why is it difficult for we Christians to praise God in advance for the testimonies we are trusting Him for? We always prefer to see the manifestations of all our requests before saying "Thank You" to God.

Christ, the power of God and the wisdom of God, honours praise. When you worship God for who He is it brings His glory down to wrought miracles, to heal, to save, deliver and defend us. No wonder, the Psalmist says; *"I will lift up my eyes unto the hills, from where my help comes from".*

Lazarus died for four days before his life was restored. He had been buried and was already decomposing when Christ the Anointed came to the scene. He said, *"Father, I thank thee that thou has heard me". (Joh.11:41b).* thereafter, amazing things happened when He praised God.

Jesus' encounter with Lazarus restored him back to life! If you are facing challenges in the area of sickness for some years/ months that's your own

Lazarus. Is it marital delay, is it the fruit of the womb, is it seeking a well-paid job that is your own Lazarus? Jesus has laid down an example for us when He praised God. You too can begin to praise God for all that you are trusting God for in this year's Mercy Rain, do not hesitate to begin to praise God for all dead issues of your life. Praise Him with all your being, give Him glory because God is greater than all our challenges. He will answer us all in Jesus' name.

Another example of gratitude opening the door of help is in the case of king Jehoshaphat. The children of Moab, Ammon and other enemies set ambushment against Jehoshaphat the King of Judah. Although he was afraid he went to God in prayer. The Spirit of the Lord came upon Jahaziel and he prophesied victory for the inhabitants of Judah. The king appointed Praise singer unto the Lord and as they were thanking the Lord for victory in advance, the Lord demolished their enemies (cf. 2Chr.20). The Lord will fight your battles when you praise/thank Him.

Many people are waiting for the Lord to help them before thanking Him. The Bible teaches otherwise. Apostle Paul writing to the Philippians exhorted, *'Be careful for nothing; but in everything by prayer and supplication with thanksgiving let your requests be made known unto God (Phil.4:6).* You can thank the Lord for what you have not gotten. Lord, I thank You for giving me a job (the jobless). Father, thank you for my baby (the barren). Lord, by Your stripes I am healed, I bless You (the sick) etc. Don't wait until your testimonies arrive before thanking Him. He already knows what you need. When you appreciate Him in advance, you are demonstrating uncommon faith and it is this faith that pulls His hand (Heb.11:6).

CONFESSIONS

- I am a grateful person. The Lord is good to me. The blessing of the Lord has made me rich and never adds sorrow.
- The Lord has blessed me, the Lord has made me a blessing, the Lord has given me beauty for ashes, there is glory for me.
- The Lord has anointed me, the Lord has turned my mourning into dancing, the Lord has the bars of iron.
- The Lord has opened my eyes, the Lord has pleaded my case, I have been justified, I have been glorified, I am alive.
- The Lord has forgiven me, the Lord had paid my debt, the Lord has fought my battles, the Lord has enlarged my coast.
- The Lord has increased me on all sides, the Lord has comforted me, the Lord has put my enemies to fight.

- I have no shame, I have no regrets, the Lord has done great thing, The Lord has opened my heaven.
- The Lord has put an end to my warfare, the Lord has leveled my mountains, the Lord has filled up my valley.
- The Lord has straightened my crooked paths, the Lord has raise me up above my enemies, the eyes of the Lord guided me everywhere, I have no regrets.
- The Lord has strengthened me, the Lord has magnified me, the Lord has taken my reproaches away. Glory be to God in the highest, I am extremely grateful.

PRAYER POINTS

PSALM 100

1. Sing a song to Jesus our helper.
2. Lord, I thank You for Your invisible hand that is upon my life in Jesus' name.
3. My Father, my Father, equip me with what will make me acceptable before helpers in Jesus' name.
4. Father, I thank You because You are greater than our wisdom can comprehend.

5. My Father, my Father, I thank You for the unbelievable testimonies You are rendering in our midst.
6. I thank You for counting me worthy to be a carrier of Your divine power.
7. Anything in my future waiting to disgrace me be reserved in Jesus' name.
8. I thank You for Your great deliverance from the power of the evil ones.
9. Enemies of my help, you shall not triumph over me in Jesus' name.
10. Every spiritual vails covering my face from recognizing my helpers, catch fire.
11. God of mercy give me help from all my troubles. For vain is the help from man.
12. God of mercy, make haste to help me (Ps.70:1).
13. Help that will terminate my need, locate me now (Ps.72:12).
14. God of mercy, You have laid help upon someone that is mighty, connect me to him (Ps.89).
15. The grace to trust You for my next help, I receive it in Jesus' name (Ps.115).
16. In my low estate and position, send help to raise me, in Jesus' name.
17. As I show my gratitude today, position me for help.

18. Pray in the Spirit for 25 minutes.

DAY TWENTY-SEVEN
HELP ACTIVATOR: FAITH
EXHORTATION

But without faith it is impossible to please him: for he that cometh to God must believe that he is, and that he is a rewarder of them that diligently seek him. (Heb.11:6)

When Jesus heard this, he was amazed and said to those following him, "Truly I tell you, I have not found anyone in Israel with such great faith. Mt.8:10

Do you know that the only time Jesus mentioned **great faith** in the Bible was when He was talking about a gentile (a name given by the Hebrews to all those that had not received the Law of Moses) – Mt.8:10; Luk.7:9? He marveled at how 'outsiders' can have more faith than the Israelites. He even alluded to the transaction between Elijah and the Widow as well as Elisha and Naaman to explain how 'outsiders' seemed to have higher faith than the Israelites (Luk.4:25). Whenever He encountered such situations – where gentiles come to Him, He was always willing assist. Even when He seemed to taunt the Syrophoenician woman, she still demonstrated great faith and Jesus helped her (Mk.7:26).

Our faith in God is the key to a locked door of help. Faith means I am helpless. Faith means I cannot do it. Faith means I need help. Faith means I need God. When we have faith in God, He will help us. Just as we never disappoint our children when they rely on us for assistance, so also does God never disappoint everyone that trusts Him for help (1Chr.5:20; Ps.34:5).

Looking unto God for help in prayers with your mind wandering on other sources you trust like your rich friend or relative may make God fold His hands. Men and women who received Jesus' help were people who displayed great faith. Some of them were not even the supposed Jews or belong to the house of Israel. A Centurion displayed a great faith by telling Jesus not to visit his home but to just send a word of healing to his sick servant and the boy was healed (cf. Mt.8).

A woman with the issue of blood displayed great faith in Jesus in other to get her healing. In Matthew 9:22,23. She said to herself, *"If I only touch his cloak, I will be healed.' Jesus turned and saw her. "Take heart, daughter," he said, 'your faith has healed you.' And the woman was healed at that moment."*

While Jesus greatly commended the gentiles for their faith, He chastised the Israelites for their apparent display of little or no faith. He deemed their faith as *little faith* (Mt.6:20; 8:26; 14:31; 16:8).

Many Christians today are so familiar with God that they demonstrate no faith when in Church while people of other religions who are in awe of the presence of God show great faith and thus receive great blessings. Truly, God is no respecter of persons (Act.10:34). He will deal with you at your level of faith. It does not matter the number of years in which you have been attending Church, if you refuse to grow your faith, you will continue to languish in Church.

7 REASONS FAITH IS IMPORTANT

1. **We Can't please God without it**. Heb.11:6 states, *'But without faith it is impossible to please Him, for he who comes to God must believe that He is, and that He is a rewarder of those who diligently seek Him.'*

2. **Jesus Notices our Faith**. Mt.14:31: *"And immediately Jesus stretched out His hand and caught him, and said to him, 'O you of little faith, why did you doubt?'"*

3. **Faith moves God to act and help us**. Mk.2:5 says, *"When Jesus saw [his friends'] faith, He said to the paralytic, 'Son, your sins are forgiven you.'"* The lame man got up, grabbed his mat, and went home

4. **Faith gives us strength during trials**. Jas.2:3 says that *"the testing of your faith produces patience.'*

5.**Faith Helps our Works**. Jas.2:26 states, *"For as the body without the spirit is dead, so faith without works is dead also."*

6. **Our Faith can encourage others**. Col.1:3-4 says, *"We give thanks to the God and Father of our Lord Jesus Christ, praying always for you, since we heard of your faith in Christ Jesus and of your love for all the saints."*

7. **Faith is the basis of our Salvation.** Eph.2:8-9 declares, *"For by grace you have been saved through faith, and that not of yourselves; it is the gift of God, not of works, lest anyone should boast."*

CONFESSIONS
- My faith is alive, my faith is growing, my faith is matured.
- My faith is great, my faith bears fruits, I have a gift of faith, I do faith works, I have faith to see good days, I have faith to change my life.
- I have faith to live, I shall not die, I have faith for healing, I shall not be sick, I have faith to be on top, I shall not breakdown, my faith works.

- My faith shall speak, my faith shall speak loudly, my faith shall move mountains, my faith shall get heaven's attention.
- My faith shall raise the dead, my faith shall heal the sick, my faith shall please the Lord, my faith shall work wonders, my faith shall bring blessings; miracle shall happen.
- Two are better than one, God will make a way for me, God shall answer my prayers, God shall send assistance to me, I shall see the goodness of the Lord in the land of the living.
- I shall pray in faith, I shall fast in faith, I shall sow the seed of faith, I shall stand on my faith.
- My faith shall not disappoint me, my faith shall be a key, my faith shall overcome my challenges, faith is help.
- There is hope for me, because I have faith. God cannot lie!
- My faith shall break the yoke of helplessness over me, I shall be helped.

PRAYER POINTS
PSALMS 119
1. Thank the Lord for blessing you with help you do not deserve or qualify for.
2. Sing a new song for God of mercy.
3. I cover my helpers with the blood of Jesus.

4. The position I will occupy to help others, appear in Jesus' name.
5. Holy Spirit help others through me so that You might be glorified in Jesus' name (Lev.19:18).
6. Lord, keep my feet from straying, in Jesus' name.
7. Help me to confidently rest in the assurance that You are always at Your post (Ps.12:14).
8. Help me to become more like You day by day as I leave the old self behind (Eph.17:4-24).
9. Show me how to help my enemies move closer to You (Luk.6:27).
10. Help me to turn to You when I am worn out in others to find sustenance (2Ki.19:5).
11. Lord, I thank You for the believers who helped shape my faith in You (2 Tim.1:5)
12. My Father, my Father, by faith I activate all inactive and dormant helpers assigned for my life and destiny.
13. As it is written, 'who through faith, subdue kingdoms, wrought righteousness, obtained promises...' Therefore, by faith, I obtain the needed help for my children (Heb.11:33-35).
14. It is written, 'only believe.' Therefore, I believe help is locating me this season (Luk.8:50).

15. My Father, my Father, it is written in Your word that the just shall live by his faith. By my faith, I declare that I am the next in line to experience help (Heb.10:38).
16. My help cometh from the Lord. By faith, I collect my help (Ps.12:1-2)
17. Pray in the Spirit for 25 minutes.

DAY TWENTY-EIGHT
HELP ACTIVATOR: DIVINE LOCATION
EXHORTATION

Divine Location is not about choice, it is about direction. – Anon.

And the LORD appeared unto him, and said, Go not down into Egypt; dwell in the land which I shall tell thee of:
Then Isaac sowed in that land, and received in the same year an hundredfold: and the LORD blessed him.
Gen.26:2,12

A profound help activator of all time which many hardly give credence to is **Divine Location**. God will only send help to a man who is where God wants him to be. Most times, it seems odd (Abram must have rolled his eyes when God said he should leave his comfort zone for unknown destination) to be rooted to a place but if God says that is where you need to be, please do not argue; just carry your bags and go there. Help is waiting for you there.

Many great Men of God of today have great testimonies of how God divinely placed them. Our Daddy in the Lord, Papa Adeboye reminisced on how God instructed him to move to the present-day Redemption Camp. When he got there, the place was an eyesore. It was an undeveloped thick forest but God said, "this is the place". Today, by the grace of God, they are a force to reckon with in that region.

Daddy Oyedepo also testified of how God instructed him to leave where he was in the north and move to Lagos. He tried to reason with the Lord that there were more than enough Churches in Lagos already but God said, go, and he went. Today by the grace of God, his ministry is massive.

Pastor David Ibiyeomie was struggling with his ministry in Lagos when God said he should move to Port-Harcourt. He heeded to the voice of God and today, the whole of Port-Harcout wait on him.

There are many instances in that regard but let me share this testimony with you. A young man went to England in the eighties for greener pastures. He labored for years but with nothing to show for it. It was after engaging in rigorous prayers for divine direction that God instructed him to move back to Lagos. It seemed antithetical to him; going back to where he ran from but by the grace of God he obeyed and moved back to his home town in Ekiti. While there, opportunities for forestry came to him and he seized it. Today, by His grace, he is sending people abroad on scholarship.

My friend, stop this rat race! Ask God for your Divine Location. There is always a place called Divine for every one of us. Once you are there, no evil will be permitted to befall you (Do you know that there are people in difficult places that are enjoying God's protection?) When you are in the right place, divinely directed by God, even while others are perishing around you every good thing will be struggling to locate you. Elijah only got refreshment when he got to the right locations (1Ki.17).

The character of our central text is Isaac. He had wanted to follow the pattern of his father Abraham who went down to Egypt when famine came (Gen.12:10). That is the problem of so many people today, they already have laid down patterns to follow. They would want to do things the way their predecessors did it but the Bible nullifies that (Prov.14:12). God is dynamic; He does things differently every time. He might want your father to do something one way while He determines for you to do it another way. If you are not sensitive to Him, you might be tempted to go the 'established' way which will be detrimental.

Concerning journeying on the path of life, Jesus said, 'I am the WAY' (Joh.14:6). The way to wherever you need to be in life is in Christ. If you don't know Him and do not walk with Him, you will get lost in life. Isaac would have gotten lost if he had not been sensitive to God. Following laid down rules are good but obeying God is better. If you want to succeed in life, please ask for Divine Location because that is where your help will be resident. Your provision is in your location. You can only get what you need when you are where God wants you to be. Stop living your life for others. Follow God and He will lead you to your Rehoboth.

BENEFITS OF DIVINE LOCATION

1. **Protection: Ps.91/1** If you obey God's instruction, He will preserve your life. Even when evil is befalling others, it will not touch you. The Israelites in Goshen is an apt example. God saving Elijah from Jezebel is another example.

2. **Provision: Ps.23/1** In the forty years sojourn of the Israelites in the wilderness, they had all that they needed because they were where God was their leader. Elijah had all that he needed when he

went to where God wanted him to be. The disciples had no lack when they went out for evangelism because they obeyed the directives of Jesus Christ.

3. **Expansion: Isai.54/2,3** All the aforementioned men of God were able to enjoy great expansion because they obeyed God and came to where He wanted them to be. Isaac waxed stronger and became great because he stayed back on God's instruction.

These three things are what we are all seeking in life. Once we are well protected, have adequate provision for survival and be able to expand our frontiers, then we are set in life. All these things are obtainable as long we are rooted in God's obedience. So, you see, as wisely quoted, divine location is not about choice (just as Lot looked and decided to choose what seems good) but about Divine Direction (Abram permitting God to direct him to the best place).

CONFESSIONS

- I shall not stand in the wrong place, I shall not follow the crowd, I will not miss my way, I shall be the head, I shall not be the tail

- The grace of God shall work for me, the grace of God shall speak for me, mercy is my portion, I am helped.

- I shall not blunder, I shall not live in the wrong place, my business shall not be wrongly located, my business shall not collapse, there shall be open doors for me, mercy is my portion, I am helped.

- Help shall locate me where I am, help shall not bypass me, my helper shall not change his mind, help is my privilege.
- I cannot be depressed, I cannot be stranded, I cannot be left behind, I shall always be relevant, help shall locate me.
- Help shall silence my mockers. Do not rejoice over me oh my enemies. I shall arise. I shall live. I shall not die. God will hear my cry.
- Moses received help in the desert. Ishmael received help in the wilderness. David received help when he was running from Saul.
- Help shall locate me, I am not far from help. I am not at the mercy of my enemies; my antagonist shall not have the final say.
- The glory of God is my covering, whenever I am, help is there, because God is with me, therefore help is available.
- Those who know me shall help me, strangers shall help me, man shall help me, women shall help me, I receive the garment of help, I receive the anointing of help. Hallelujah!

PRAYER POINTS

PSALMS 33

1. Lord, I thank You for the salvation of the multitude.
2. Sing a new song to Jesus the way maker.
3. Oh Lord, my God, cause me to be at the right place at the right time to meet the right people (Mk.10:46-62).
4. It is written, 'trust in the Lord with all your heart, in all your ways acknowledge Him and He shall direct your path.' Direct my path to my destiny helpers (Prov.3:5).
5. My Father, my Father, peradventure my current location is not available for divine help, by divine arrangement relocate me (2Sam.9: 1-13)
6. Hear the word of the Lord from my mouth, You angel who excel in strength, I activate your ministry of help in my life today (Ps.103:20).
7. As an heir of salvation, whom angels had been assigned to help, you ministering Spirit go into every satanic prison where my helpers are kept and release them, in Jesus' name (Heb.1:14).

8. Thou Spirit of the Lord move like a wind, locate and direct my ordained helpers to me, in Jesus' name (Jon.3:8).

9. Every secret I need to know about my environment be revealed in Jesus' name (Lev.18).

10. I reclaim all the ground I have lost to the enemy, in Jesus' name (Jon.3:8)

11. Lord, by a strong east wind, drive away all the darkness surrounding my help environment in Jesus' name.

12. Shout God of mercy 21 times, do a re-arrangement in my children's life and destiny in Jesus' name.

13. Holy Spirit guide my steps today to someone who needs the hope that only come from Jesus.

14. Light of Jesus expose and expel every darkness and dew of wickedness dominating my family.

15. Fountain of discomfort in my life, dry up now.

16. Pray in the Spirit for the next 25 minutes.

DAY TWENTY-NINE
HELP ACTIVATOR: DIVINE GUIDANCE

EXHORTATION

And when Moses' father-in-law saw all that he did to the people, he said, What is this thing that thou doest to the people?... And Moses said unto his father- in- law, Because the people come unto me to enquire of God:... And Moses' father in law said unto him, The thing that thou doest is not good.
Thou wilt surely wear away,... Hearken now unto my voice, I will give thee counsel, and God shall be with thee... So Moses hearkened to the voice of his father in law, and did all that he had said. EXOD.18:1-24 (PARAPHRASED)

The conversation above is between Moses and his father-in-law Jethro. Moses had been given the commission of overseeing the Israelites on their way to the Promised Land. Leading about two million plus people is a daunting task (no wonder King Solomon sought God's wisdom when it was his turn to lead the Israelites). Anyone that has ever led in any capacity will tell you how overwhelming it could be.

Leadership has always been one of the major areas of human development. Sociologists, psychologists, anthropologists and other professionals in the field of studying human behaviour will tell you how societies and individuals thrive better when they are under good leadership but fail to develop if the leadership is poor. Many great books have been written on the subject-matter of leadership but as children of God, the essential thing to note is that any leader that will not rely on God's guidance and directive will never do well and the fallout will be on the followers.

Starting from the Book of Romans, Apostle Paul told us that **there is no authority except from God** (Rom.13:1).

God Himself informed Prophet Jeremiah that He will, *'...will give you pastors according to mine heart, which shall feed you with knowledge and understanding.'* Jer.3:15.

So, all good leaders are appointed by God.

The next point is that leaders flourish when they obey godly counsel. Any leader that wants to be a lone ranger can never prosper. The people that God has sent you to lead are an eclectic bunch and there is no precise manual with which to successfully lead other than the leader to first surrender to God. By doing this, instruction will come and you will succeed.

Moses being appointed by God to lead the Israelites took his job seriously but while discharging his duties, he was physically, spiritually and emotionally drifting. Jethro, his father-in-law noticed this immediately he came across his ministration and proceeded to teach him one of the major principles of leadership - **DELEGATION.** Every responsible leader must cultivate the act of delegating or else, they will die untimely. No man has been called to do everything. Jesus Christ before starting His ministry employed others so He can disburse the responsibilities to them. The Apostles also had to appoint deacons in the early Churches so as to make their spiritual work less cumbersome. Every leader that wants to succeed must take Jethro's advice to heart.

Moses thought he could handle everything on his own but his wise father-in-law thought otherwise. He 'helped' him by guiding him on how to go about the business. Help can come your way if you take godly counsel. Note that Jethro did not impose his idea on Moses. He advised him to seek God's opinion on the matter and God must have ratified it because Moses put it to action.

This takes us to the next issue which is that every advice that is given to you must first be presented to God for approval. Imagine if Adam and Eve had sought God's advice before eating the fruit. How about if Amnon had asked God about the advice Jonadab gave him? It is not all counsel that is productive. The devil too can advise and if you dare listen to him, you will fail.

If you need help in life, please seek out godly counsellors. God has empowered them to give godly counsel. There are people like Ahithophel albeit on the positive side whose counsel God will approve. When I was struggling as a young minister and was at my wits end, in fact, I was at my breaking point, I had the opportunity to meet with Pastor E. A. Adeboye. I went to him for spiritual guidance and counselling. What he told me that day helped shape my life and has made me to be who I am today. What about if I had not gone? That is where I many make mistakes. This spirit of know it all is an affliction and if you are not careful, it will sink you. You cannot know everything. The Bible even says that we know in part (1Cor.13:9). The part you know is one but there is someone somewhere that knows the other part. You need to look for them so they can set you on the right path.

But on your journey to seek direction, endeavor to test the spirits (1Joh.4:1) because there are ravenous wolves in sheep's clothing (parading as prophets) who are looking for whom to devour. Many ministers out there are ungodly and if you go to them for guidance, they will mislead you. Let the Spirit of God direct you to the right path. If you want the Spirit of God to direct you then you need intervention of Christ in your life. If Christ is in your life, the Holy Spirit will be there to lead you (Isai.30:21).

Many people that come to us ministers for counselling do so because they believe God can use us to help them and many of them have been tremendously helped. Testimonies abound of how our counsels have wrought great deliverance. Seeking and taking divine guidance can activate help for you.

CONFESSIONS

- I shall not miss my way, I shall not make friend with those who hate me, I shall not miss the best of God for me.
- Great grace is my portion, the packages of God for me shall locate me, I will know what to do, I shall know who to meet, I shall know what to say.
- My steps are ordered by the Lord, I shall not miss my way, I shall not enter the wrong bus, I shall not enter the wrong house, my eyes shall see the way
- Darkness shall not cover me, confusion is not my portion. Arrows of confusion back to the sender, garments of heaviness back to the sender, garment of shame shall burn to ashes.
- The plan of God for me shall succeed, the agenda of evil for me shall fail, I shall not enter evil traps.
- Where there is no hope, help shall rise for me, where I am lost help shall rise up for

me, Where I am lost help shall find me, I shall not end in shame.

- There shall be new beginning for me, there shall be open door for me, there shall be new opportunities, there is glory for me, failure is not my portion, I am blessed.
- My helper is not blind. My helper is not lost. My helper shall not go to the wrong location. I shall increase.
- The best days are before me. Old things have passed away. Beauty shall be revealed. It is well with me.
- I will meet the right person, I will do the right thing. God is my guide. Hallelujah!

PRAYER POINTS
PSALM 124

1. Lord, I thank You for the mystery of guidance that is connecting me to my destiny helpers.
2. Sing a song of praise.
3. My Father, my Father, through the angel of guidance, guide me to the place where I can access help (Exod.2:20)
4. Oh Lord, my God, guide me with Your eyes and connect me with my helpers (Ps.32:8).

5. My Father, my Father, by Yourself guide both me and my helpers in life till we meet.

6. As it is written that as many as are led by the Spirit of God are the sons of God, Oh Lord, lead m by Your spirit to helpers ordained and attached my destiny (Rom.8:14).

7. My Father, my Father, grant me prophetic guidance that will open me up to help and helpers of divine assignment (Act.13:1-4).

8. My Father, my Father, where human help fails me, let our help take over (Gen.21:14-19).

9. My Lord, my God, You who helped Peter from sinking, help my marriage from sinking (Mt.28:31).

10. God of mercy, make me a candidate for help.

11. God of mercy, make me a beneficiary of unsolicited help. Let help that I never asked for, be the order of the day, in my life.

12. Every attitude inherent in me restricting the flow of help into my life be rooted out by the resurrection power in Jesus' name.

13. Oh Lord, teach me deep and secret things.

14. Oh Lord, reveal to me every strange secret in my family, in the name of Jesus.

15. Every great and divine prophecy hovering around my destiny manifest now by mercy in Jesus' name.

16. Oh Lord, baptize me with the Spirit of Prayer, In Jesus' name (Ps.119:164; 55:17).

17. Pray in the Spirit for 25 minutes.

DAY THIRTY
THE HELP FROM EGYPT
EXHORTATION

For my people have committed two evils; they have forsaken me the fountain of living waters, and hewed them out cisterns, broken cisterns, that can hold no water. JER.2:13

Woe to them that go down to Egypt for help; and stay on horses, and trust in chariots, because they are many; and in horsemen, because they are very strong; but they look not unto the Holy One of Israel, neither seek the LORD! ISAI.31:1

It is a known fact that many Christians who have once enjoyed the help of God later turn their back on Him to seek help elsewhere. One major problem that is confronting the Church today is that of members leaving the Church to look for solution to their problems elsewhere. When confronted, they have a ready excuse of not having all the time in the world because God is taking too long to help them. These are people that have testimonies of God's goodness. They have tasted and seen the goodness of God yet when confronted with new challenges, instead of running to God, they chose to seek help from *'egypt'*.

A popular 19th Century Hymn was one penned by James Montgomery. The title of the hymn is **IN THE HOUR OF TRIAL.** This hymn has greatly helped many believers in their spiritual journey. The first stanza reads:

In the hour of trial,
Jesus, pray for me!
Lest by base denial
I depart from Thee...

Every true believer will nod to the fact that no Christian is beyond the grips of the trials of life. In fact, a major part of Jesus' exhortation is to expose the disciples and followers to the trials of life and how to overcome them (Joh.16:33). At a point, He specifically prayed for Simon Peter that although the devil will afflict him but he has been strengthened (Luk.2:31,32). This buttresses the fact that believers/Christians will always encounter hard times (1Cor.10:13) but God will always be there to help.

Unfortunately, many Christians have denounced their faith in the face of adverse situations. Not only did they denounce the faith, they have also turned their back on God, clearly forsaking Him. Their argument is that God has not come to their rescue in their hour of need. Is this true though?

The fact remains that God will never allow the righteous to be afflicted unnecessarily. The stories of biblical heroes like Abraham, Joseph, Job, Daniel, The Three Hebrew Boys, Jeremiah, etc. confirm this. Every of our suffering has a purpose as noted in the account of Job. So, no trials should be strong enough to make us forsake our Helper (cf. Rom.8).

In the second stanza of our beloved hymn, Montgomery posits:

With its witching pleasures
Would this vain world charm,
Or its sordid treasures
Spread to work me harm...

This means that it is not only hard times that can make us forsake God. Pleasures of life too can also make us forsake our True Helper. In Deut. 32:15, the Bible laments, **'But Jeshurun waxed fat, and kicked: thou art waxen fat, thou art grown thick, thou art covered with fatness; then he forsook God which made him, and lightly esteemed the Rock of his salvation.'** Many people have left God because they have been blessed. This decision they have taken to their peril. The blessings we get from God are supposed to help us rely more on Him and to encourage others to come to Him (in John chapter 12 vs.9). Many people came to Jesus not because of Him but to marvel at Lazarus. Lazarus' testimony brought many to Him. So also, your blessings and testimonies that attend them are supposed to bring others to Christ). Leaving Him when we have been blessed is pure foolishness; the devil is just att the corner waiting to snatch the blessings away from us.

One major Biblical character who greatly enjoyed God's help but later defaulted was Asa. He was the King of Judah and much beloved. He instituted many reforms in Israel during his reign and God gave his land peace. He was greatly helped by God who gave him victory over the vast army of the Cushite King Zerah. His reign was peaceful until he was confronted by Baasha King of Israel who built Ramah to discomfit him. Instead of Asa to recourse back to God for help, he went to Benhadad king of Syria for help. When Hanani, the Seer, came to point out this error to him, he got angry and jailed him. At the end of his reign, he got infected with a foot disease but still insisted on not seeking the Lord for help but relied on physicians. He would have gone down in history as the next best King after David but alas, the title went to another all because he left his 'fountain of help'. His account can be found in the Books of 1Ki.15, 2Chr.15 & 16.

We can see how King Asa forfeited a coveted relationship with God by turning away from Him. This is a word of admonishment; do not ever contemplate forsaking the Lord. Whatever the case may be, there is no challenge that is bigger than our God. Every situation is within His control. He will definitely come through for you.

Also, notes of warning to those that receive blessings and run away. Remember that Lazarus would have been killed if he was not found with Jesus. If after having been restored back to life, he went away from the protective custody of Jesus, the people would have killed him. Their efforts failed because Lazarus did not leave His Helper (Joh.12:9,10). Do not leave your helper when the going gets good.

In the same vein, take note not to leave the people that have once helped you worse than before you met them. Many people have repaid evil for good. After having benefitted greatly from their helpers, they turn around to bite the fingers that have once fed them. The Bible has already judged such people. Read Proverbs 17:13.

When you spoil your 'place of rest' because you have gotten a 'better offer', you might never get help again.

CONFESSIONS

- I reject strange help, I reject help from the enemies, my problem can be solved by my God, I shall wait on the Lord my God. He is able.
- I shall not backslide, I shall not lose my light, I shall not be at the mercy of my enemies, there shall be no vacancy on my position, wonderful things shall happen to me.
- I reject help from strange places, I reject help from places God has not approved. There is no marriage between light and darkness.
- Dark cloud will not overwhelm me, my opportunities shall not miss me, my help shall come from the Lord, I reject miserable comforters.
- It is my turn to shine, it is my time to rise, I shall not be late, I shall not miss my turn, I shall not be replaced.
- My blessing shall not turn to curse, my breakthrough shall not be reversed, my heaven shall not be closed.
- Things shall not turn bad for me, what is working in my life shall not stop working, my laughter shall not turn to weeping.

- What is sweet in my life shall not turn sour, my glory shall not be in the reverse, I shall enjoy my days on earth.
- Sickness shall not cut me short, I shall not be in a trap, ambush is not my portion, loss is not my portion.
- Nothing is wrong with me, nothing is wrong with my destiny, I shall not regret my Life, the Lord is pleased with me. Hallelujah!

PRAYER POINTS
ISAIAH 31

1. Jesus, I thank You for Your sacrifice (Heb.2:18)
2. Sing a song to Jesus for His redemption package that He has made available to us.
3. Lord, help me to rearrange my priorities, so that I will value the need of others as well as my own (Phil.2:3-4).
4. Lord, help me keep my eyes on You when I feel upset by other people, in Jesus' name.
5. Lord, let me see the world the way You do, and let me join in Your eternal rescue mission (Luk.19:10).

6. Every diabolical 'egyptian help' in my possession, I lose it in totality, Holy Ghost take over from me.
7. Lord, give me a heart that accurately judges situation and people in Jesus' name.
8. Lord, forgive my wrong decisions to go down to Egypt and redeem me of its implication (Gen.12:10-20).
9. Father, it is written in Your Word that, 'strangers shall be my nursing mother'. Therefore, from today let total stranger help me (Act.28:1-2).
10. Oh Lord my God, cause me to access help from men of nations of different color and languages in Jesus' name (Mic.4:1-2).
11. Father, it is written that, 'the wealth of the gentiles shall come to me'. Therefore, let the help of gentiles locate me (Isai.61:6)
12. Power of intercession, fall upon me, in Jesus' name.
13. Every structure put in place in the spirit realm against my children be dismantled by fire.
14. I withdraw my name, from the register of failure and non-achievement in Jesus' name.

15. Just as You used Pharaoh to compensate Joseph for the evil of his brothers, You will use this kind on earth for me, in Jesus' name.

16. All that I have lost through the family of rejection, I regain them in Jesus' name.

17. Pray in the Spirit for the next 25 minutes.

DAY THIRTY-ONE

CONSEQUENCE OF NOT ASKING FOR HELP: DEATH

EXHORTATION

'And Ahab spake unto Naboth, saying, Give me thy vineyard, that I may have it for a garden of herbs, because it is near unto my house: and I will give thee for it a better vineyard than it; or, if it seem good to thee, I will give thee the worth of it in money.
And Naboth said to Ahab, The LORD forbid it me, that I should give the inheritance of my fathers unto thee.
Then they sent to Jezebel, saying, Naboth is stoned, and is dead'. (1Ki.21:2,3,14)

Help from above is a blank cheque that Christ gives to every child of God as a compensation for accepting Him as your Lord and Saviour. God offers help in very specific circumstances and rejecting some may just get an apathetic shrug from God. The circumstances I see God offer and give help to people most often is when the person that needs help is asking for it.

Can anyone reject God's help? Yes, it is possible. Christ has paid for all our infirmity and made our salvation to be free of charge. Some decided never to embrace this God given lifetime grace.

Naboth planted a flourishing vineyard near King Ahab's palace. The beauty of the vineyard attracted king Ahab, who sought for the owner and made a simple but dangerous demand, *"give me your vineyard"* and Naboth refused. While we might be quick to condemn Naboth's insolence in denying the king's desire, it will be good of us to have a little understanding of what an inheritance is. When Naboth told king Ahab that God forbids that he will do give away with his inheritance, he was subtly lecturing the king on land acquisition and distribution. Historically, each of the twelve tribes (except for the tribe of Levi) was allotted a parcel of land in the Promised Land - Canaan. That inheritance determines their destiny so giving it up means giving up his heritage. Of course, the king offered other incentives land but that particular portion is the heritage of the clan of Naboth so losing it is like losing their history. Each Israelite is identified by his land; so, if you lose your land, you might as well be dead.

Although Naboth was right in his decision, he did not think beyond reality. Gullibly, he felt the case was settled but unfortunately, he was unwittingly contending with king Ahab and by proxy his wicked wife Jezebel. The king, sad, embittered and angry about the refusal agreed to the wife's decision which was to kill Naboth.

While Naboth might have done well in not surrendering his heritage, he made the grave error of not reporting the case to a higher authority - **The King of Kings**. His nonchalant attitude towards the whole scenario eventually cost him his life. In life's battle, when someone is contending with you, you have need of a higher power in order to overcome. Naboth was flippant about the whole issue and when Jezebel assembled false witnesses against him, he could not win.

Naboth was an original stock of Israel, he could have prayed to God for assistance. He could have reported the case to the prophets. There is no excuse for ignorance because he must have heard about the wickedness of Jezebel the king's wife. She was not an Israelite (was from Tyre and Zidon) so might be unaware of the heritage but Naboth ought to be aware of her selfish acts and wickedness so he ought to have been prepared for eventuality.

There is a lesson to learn here. When someone is contending your heritage with you, don't just think that shouting is enough. Go into your closet and report the case to God the impartial Judge. If Naboth had prayed about the issue, he would have been helped. How do we know this? Do you remember king Hezekiah? When the king of Assyria laid siege against Jerusalem, his messenger insulted both God and Hezekiah. Hezekiah, noting his weakness, took the case to God in the temple and sent for the prophet Isaiah. At the end, God helped him and the king of Assyria with his messengers were disgraced out of Judah (cf. 2Ki.18,19).

Naboth could have taken the case to God in prayer. Most people always act in ignorance like this, they believe God understands their plight and the struggles they are passing through. There is a need to pray and fast for divine help as a means of drawing God's attention to our urgent requests. Whenever we are confronted with challenges above our capacity and spiritual strength we need to pray! Jesus prayed all through His days on earth. He prayed at all times whether there were challenges or not.

God saw the injustice and sent a prophet to condemn the act of Ahab and his evil wife but it was too late for Naboth.

It is more profitable to be divinely helped while one is alive than getting help after one's demise.

I know of a young woman whose best friend was having an affair with her husband. She knew of the situation but as a Christian refused to seek God's help. She thought her friend and husband will weary of themselves and the husband will come back home. Wrong thinking! The friend was fetish so she killed this woman and forced the husband to chase away her children. She then set herself up as the Lady of the Manor. The children became useless as there was nobody to cater for them. These are well trained children that went to good schools but with the death of their mother and hostility from their father, they became area boys. Very pathetic. If only their mother had fought for her heritage!

Your vineyard might be your destiny /purpose in life but unlike Naboth you need to jealously protect it from the sight of the wicked ones.

When it comes to the issue of heritage, observe the following:

1. **Do not be over confident.** Naboth believed that the king will definitely understand the law that guides inheritance in Israel but he did not.

2. **Look for perfect protection that God can give to us**. No man can preserve your life and your inheritance, so give your life and your totality to God.

3. **Call out for help.** Help is not too far away. Call out for help in prayers and in fasting.

CONFESSIONS

- I will not die in silence, I will not lose my relevance, I will not become obsolete, I will cry out for help, I will not die in vain.
- I will not allow pride to ruin my chances of getting help, I will not overlook the opportunities to get help, I will not underrate who can help me, I will not bypass the person God has sent to me.
- Help is my birth right, I will seek help, I will knock the door for help, I will cry for help, I will ask for help, God will send help my way, I shall not die in silence.
- I reject unnecessary suffering, I refuse to stay in suffering, I reject prolonged pain and agony, God has solved my problems.
- I shall seek for help, the death of Jesus is not in vain in my life, Jesus's death and resurrection has purchased help for me.
- The Lord is my Shepherd, I know He loves me, I know He has my good interest at heart, whatever I need, He has supplied, I shall not miss my supplies, The Lord will lead me to where to get help: Amen.
- What is difficult for me is possible with God, my help is possible, my case is not finished, my matters shall end in praise. Hallelujah!
- I shall not die, I shall live, I shall see the goodness of the Lord, I shall sing the song of the triumphant, I shall rejoice at last.

- Help shall locate me, the veil of covering is burnt to ashes, I am visible to those who want to help me, my helper is not far, the place I am is the center of help. Hallelujah!
- I chose humility, I chose commitment, I choose service, I chose help, I choose assistance, I choose opportunities, I choose help. Amen!

PRAYER POINTS
PSALM 143

1. Sing a song to your Creator.
2. My Father, my Father, help me to pay the price of the high calling of God in Christ Jesus.
3. Lord, heal every broken home and dysfunction in my family and local Church.
4. My Father, my Father, increase my faith and help me to be completely dependent on You in all I do in Jesus' name.
5. I shall not be stranded in the network of help in Jesus' name.
6. Everything and anything that is dead in my life by the reason of not asking for help, come back to life in Jesus' name.
7. Every evil plantation in my life be rooted out in Jesus' name.
8. Wind of change of elevation, single my children out for good in Jesus' name.

9. Any power assigned to build walls of separation between me and my helpers, meet failure in Jesus' name.
10. Lord Jesus, equip my children with what will make them acceptable   before helpers in Jesus' name.
11. Spirit of pride, vacate my life by fire.
12. Spiritual darkness, vacate by life now in Jesus' name.
13. Power of healing and restoration, possess my life, in Jesus' name.
14. Arrow of death, I am not your candidate, backfire in Jesus' name.
15. Oh Lord, answer my helpers so they would remember me and help me in Jesus' name.
16. Power of death holding my children captive, release them by fire.
17. Pray in the Spirit for 20 minutes.

DAY THIRTY-TWO
CONSEQUENCE OF NOT ASKING FOR HELP: FALLING INTO TEMPTATION
EXHORTATION

"And lead us not into temptation, but deliver us from evil: For thine is the kingdom, and the power, and the glory, forever. Amen". Matt.6:13

"There hath no temptation taken you but such as is common to man: but God is faithful, who will not suffer you to be tempted above that ye are able; but will with the temptation also make a way to escape, that ye may be able to bear it." 1Cor.10:13

We have been learning about how to attract help from above. What qualifies us to be helped is the ability to be holy; for God will not answer insincere or selfish prayers that conflict with his nature and will. Our helper the Lord Jesus taught us to depend on Him implicitly for all our physical, emotional, social and spiritual needs and to seek the forgiveness of our sins.

You cannot be helped by who cannot trust you. Temptation is real. The most important thing is to avoid falling into temptation which will become a sin because sin is costly. Take for instance the story of Adam and Eve. The couple fell prey to temptation (consequently sinned) and the judgment did not stop with them. We all are paying the price of their sin until future generation.

What is Temptation?

Temptation is basically the inducement to sin. It means that you are at the border/crossroad of where you have been instructed not to go. An example is you know it is a sin to take what is not yours. When you got desperate, there was a purse belonging to someone just a little step away from you and there was nobody there to judge you. The next thing you knew, the purse was in your hand (how it got there even you cannot explain). Now, what do you plan to do? That is temptation. If you drop the purse and run away, you have overcome temptation but if you help yourself to the content of the purse, you have fallen into temptation. In order words, you have sinned.

Do you know that temptation really is not a sin? Falling into it makes you a sinner. You holding the purse might not signify that you plan to steal the content. You might want to return it to appropriate quarters. It is when we *decide* (note that word decide – we choose our destiny) to negate the principles of moral values that we err. God will not judge us at the border of temptation. When God gives instruction to His people, He expects total obedience. Unfortunately, the devil – sworn enemy of man- will start hassling us to disobey God. If we are not careful, we will fall prey to his wiles. At the point of temptation, we need God more than ever. That purse you are holding will either make or mar your relationship with God. Immediately your conscious mind notes the purse in your hand, the two spirits will start warring within you; one will say, 'drop it and run', the other will advise, 'take the money. Nobody will know'. It is the person you listen to that will become your master (Gal.5:17; Rom.6:16) and receive the reward accordingly.

Here are the Biblical examples of people that chose to fall into temptation.

SAMSON: He was born as a Nazarene. He violated some God's laws that he ate honey from the dead lion carcass. He married from a strange land. He also revealed his top-life secret to a strange woman that made it easy for his enemies to capture and mock him. He failed to call on God in prayer for help that could have defended him and made him prevail on the ugly situation.

JUDAS: Judas was one of the 12 disciples of Jesus Christ. He betrayed Jesus leading to enemies arresting, trying and crucifying Him. Jesus had warned His disciples to pray that they will not fall into temptation. Judas apparently must not have prayed because even when Jesus identified him as the one that will give Him up, he still fell into that temptation. Little sin of stealing that he was not able to overcome generated into a big sin of betrayal that later overcame him.

WHAT CAN WE DO TO RESIST FALLING INTO TEMPTATION TODAY?

1.   Identify your areas of weakness and surrender them to the power of Christ.

2.   Do not cover sin, expose it.

3.   Fast and pray over your areas of weakness.

4.   Do not expose yourself to your areas of weaknesses. If you know you are weak concerning the opposite sex, try your best not to be alone with them unnecessarily.

WHAT TO DO WHEN WE FALL INTO TEMPTATION TODAY

1. Do not run away from God. I repeat, do not run away from God. Run to Him!
2. Do not shift blame. Admit that you are responsible for your failings.
3. Seek the presence of God for forgiveness until the conviction turns to peace.
4. Seek grace to overcome the next time you find yourself in same circumstance.

CONFESSIONS

- I reject temptation, I am not powerless against temptation, the Power of God is available for me, I shall conquer my lust.
- With God all things are possible. I am baptized in the Holy Ghost, I shall meet the deeds of the flesh, I shall win the war against the world, I shall win the war against the flesh.
- I have the seed of God in me, therefore I cannot sin, the old man is crucified with his works, I am born again, I am a new creature.
- I shall not violate the laws of God, I shall not walk into the traps of the enemies, I shall not deny my weaknesses, I shall surrender to

the discipline of the spirit my weaknesses shall not ruin my destiny.

- I shall bear fruits of the spirit, I shall grow out of mediocrity, I shall be matured in the faith, I shall be an example for others.
- Temptations shall not blind my vision, temptations shall not ruin my chances, temptations shall not close the doors of glory against me.
- I am a soldier of the Lord, I am a building of the LORD, I am working under the grace of God, I cannot be put to shame.
- I am strong, I am rich, I am empowered, I have the strength of God, I have the anointing of God, I can do all things. Amen.
- God will not allow me to be tempted beyond my capacity, God will show me a way out of all my challenges.
- Arrow of temptations back to sender, I am a star, I shall shine, I am a seed of righteousness, I shall not see corruption/ The Lord is on my side. Hallelujah!

PRAYER POINTS
PSALM 28

1. Father, I thank you for you are good to me and my family.
2. Sing a new song to Jesus.

3. My Father, my Father, help me to see myself in how much You love me in Jesus' name.
4. Lord, help me to keep going with the work You have given me to do, no matter what the cost may be in Jesus' name.
5. I receive grace to be free from the temptation of self-evaluation, in Jesus name.
6. I confess and decree that my children will possess the gate of their enemies in Jesus' name.
7. Lord, I praise You for making a way for me in difficult times in Jesus' name.
8. Oh Lord, deliver me from the power of darkness.
9. Influencing grace that makes help available, possess me in Jesus' name.
10. Trap of temptation, release me by fire.
11. Destructive plans of the enemies projected against my children scatter by fire.
12. Evil harvesters of my labour, be wasted in Jesus' name.
13. Power diverting my virtues, your time is over, be wasted in Jesus' name
14. You serpent of temptation operating in my foundation, be exposed by fire and die in Jesus' name

15. Lord, give me the strength to overcome every temptation in Jesus' name.
16. Holy Spirit, renew and transform my mind in Jesus' name.
17. Pray in the Spirit for 25 minutes.

DAY THIRTY-THREE
CONSEQUENCE OF NOT ASKING FOR HELP: DISPOSSESSION
EXHORTATION

Then the five men departed, and came to Laish, and saw the people that were therein,... and they were far from the Zidonians, and had no business with any man... and came unto Laish, unto a people that were at quiet and secure: and they smote them with the edge of the sword, and burnt the city with fire.

And there was no deliverer, because it was far from Zidon, and they had no business with any man... Judg.18:7,27 (Paraphrased, emphasis mine)

Man is a being unto others. So said a wise man. When God created the first man, He came to the realization that there is a need of help for that man so He created a woman as a 'helpmate' (helper) for him. This eventually became a pattern as God created us to be a helper to one another.

Yes, I agree with the fact thatGod is the ultimate Helper but He still wants us to be a source of help to one another. You remember when the Israelites cried in their land of servitude and called unto the Lord, God said He would come down and help them yet He sent Moses (cf. Exod.3).

So, even though God can help us, He still prefers to use us as the source. All through the Scriptures, we could see how people were helping one another to achieve their purpose in life.

What then do you think would happen if a man thinks he does not need the help of others? One of the things that will happen to such person is that he will lose his properties and probably his life. This is the story of the inhabitants of Laish. In the Book of Judges Chapter 18, the story is told of a people who through careless living, and the thought that they had no need of other people's help eventually lost their land and their lives.

When Joshua distributed the land to the twelve tribes when they got to the Promised Land, the tribe of Dan (the second largest after Judah when entering Canaan) for an unknown reason got a small portion (comp. Num.26:54 / Josh.19:47) so some of them who were unable to get an inheritance went out in search of land (cf. Judg.18). They sent spies out to search out the land and they came upon certain inhabitants who although were part of the Zidonians cut themselves completely off from them and basked in a false sense of security.

In the Words of the Scriptures, they were quiet and secured, far from any other people, and had no business with other people. This false sense of security eventually led to their dispossession. When the Danites came to attack them, the Bible says there was none to deliver (help) them. Imagine if they had a form of alliance with some other people, the Danites might not have been able to prevail over them.

Don't be a loner. One tree cannot make a forest. You need others as much as they need you. What a man wants to carry that is too heavy for him, if four men were to carry it, it will become light. You need others to help you bear the burden of life. You cannot journey in life successfully alone. God Himself said that it is not good for a man to be alone (Gen.2:18). The Bible says two are better than one (Eccl.4:9). Help is dependent. It is not self-reliant. Some people not only think they don't need the help of others not to talk of God's help and that is more terrible. If you disdain the help of your Creator, then, there is no hope for you.

The people of Laish were dispossessed of their land because they felt they didn't need others (**had no business with any man**). They felt capable and self-sufficient in a land that was highly prosperous not knowing that some people were eying their possession. They failed to ask for help because they had disengaged themselves from the available help and were thus dispossessed of their possession.

Beloved, don't ever feel secured and safe except you are in Christ. If you do not have Christ, everything you have is not safe, your life inclusive. Marauders are everywhere seeking whom to conquer. If you bask in self-delusion of safety without a safety net, they will soon get you. It must have shocked the people of Laish that someone could come to attack them unaware. It will shock you too that day when trouble come and you are not in Christ - the very present help in times of trouble (Ps.46:1).

Beloved, don't be too proud to ask for help from others. Don't disengage yourself from others because you think you are better off than they are. There are things you have that are beneficial to others and there are things others have that are beneficial to you. It is your alliance with them that will provide the necessary fusion for success. The Bible says, 'ask and it shall be given' but how can you ask and be given when the people you are supposed to ask are far from you? Bring people close to you. Do not shut your heart from others.

Remember, man is a being unto others!

CONFESSIONS

- I will not lose what is valuable to me, I shall gain, I shall make profits, I shall not lose my relevance, God will show me His mercy.
- The enemy shall not get the upper hands against me. I shall receive all the help I can get, I will not suffer in silence.
- I reject prolonged sufferings, I reject affliction that has no reward, I reject unnecessary hardship, I embrace hardness.
- My possessions are under the Tabernacle of God, my treasured are stored where thieves cannot reach, I enjoy divine protection, I am under the wings of the Almighty.
- What is not working in my life shall start working again, I shall get the best packages of God, no weapons fashion against me shall prosper, I am under the canopy of God.
- Pride will not rub me, I refuse to be arrogant, I choose to be humble, no opposition can conquer me, and my help is assured.
- My Bible is a Book of help, my prophet is an agent of help, my friends shall help me, my family shall help me. Hallelujah!

- I have sown the seeds of help, I shall reap the harvest of help, there shall be an opportunity for me, my helper is available.
- What I cannot do shall not stop me, my weaknesses cannot stop me, I am moving forward, I am going higher, I am in the book of remembrance, I am not forgotten. Hallelujah!
- I receive the anointing to increase, I shall not decrease, I shall not miss my helper, I am invincible to those who want to rob me.

PRAYER POINTS
ISAIAH 41

1. Sing a song to the King of kings.
2. Father, grant me grace to live by your principle in the world and follow Your guidelines in all I do, in Jesus' name.
3. Lord, help my children never to partake in anything that will attract curses to their lives, in Jesus' name.
4. Giving is and act and a spirit. My Father, my Father, give me the Spirit of giving in Jesus' name.
5. Lord, grant me grace to identify things that are working against my ability to spend

time alone with You and grace to deal with them in Jesus' name.

6. Occult court set to de-robe me of divine assistance scatter by fire in Jesus' name.

7. Any power that wants to rob me of my birthright be wasted, in Jesus' name.

8. Every satanic throne established for the sake of my children, scatter by fire in Jesus' name.

9. All obstacles to my children academical breakthrough scatter by fire, in Jesus' name.

10. All obstacles to my calling, scatter by the Blood of Jesus.

11. Every power that is waiting or my un-guarded hour to attack me, be dismantled in Jesus' name.

12. Any power employing satanic tactics to eliminate me from my place of blessing, be wasted in Jesus' name.

13. You monitoring power in my environment programmed against my family, be wasted by fire in Jesus' name.

14. Holy Spirit uncover the secret of the enemy in my environment in Jesus' name.

15. Every of my dispossessed help, I receive you by mercy in Jesus' name.

16. Every parasite in my body causing sickness, come out by fire in Jesus' name.

17. Pray in the Spirit for 30 minutes.

DAY THIRTY-FOUR
CONSEQUENCE OF NOT ASKING FOR HELP: STAGNANCY
EXHORTATION

"I will utterly consume everything From the face of the land," Says the LORD;... Those who have turned back from following the LORD, And have not sought the LORD, nor inquired of Him."... And it shall come to pass at that time That I will search Jerusalem with lamps, And punish the men Who are settled in complacency, Who say in their heart, 'The LORD will not do good, Nor will He do evil.' (Zeph.2-12 NKJV emphasis mine)

Undoubtedly, when help is not intentionally demanded stagnancy is inevitable. Stagnation is a state of being grounded, stranded or tied to the same place or position. It is a state of life that is not flowing or moving. It is completely obstructing. The closest you can think of is like a rope limiting one's movement. Stagnation is like strongholds. It is like satanic embargo. It is a spiritual limit over your progress.

Eleven days stroll became forty years of wandering because of the spirit of error for the Israelites. Any such operation in my life or your life shall be destroyed by fire in Jesus' name. All they needed to do was to walk in eleven days of obedience and they failed. May we not fail in God's plan anymore in Jesus' name.

Stagnation is further illustrated below:

1. When one's life is static. The man at the pool of Bethesda was static for 38 years (Joh.5:1-11). He was on a spot in the same condition for such a long time without calling out for help (he said when he was about going down, someone else would go before him. Should he not have made arrangement with someone to help him?).
2. When one's life is oscillating. Activities without production. It can be called motion without movement. Luk.5: 1-11 unleashes the fruitless efforts of the men at the sea without catching any fish until they found help from God himself.

Causes of stagnation
1. **Satan and his agents:** Joh.10:10 The devil has only one ministry which is to kill, to steal and to destroy. The devil has no plan of progress for anyone.
2. **Lack of vision:** Prov.29:18; Gen.13:14, Jer.1:11,12. Vision is the mental picture of the designed future. A future you cannot picture is a future you can't venture to capture. Successful people are goal getters because they are goal setters. To live without a goal is to live a goalless life. Enough of running on a spot.
3. **Procrastination:** This is the act of leaving till tomorrow what can be done today. This attitude happens as a result of too much analysis that most time leads to paralysis (Joh. 4:35; 2Cor.6:2)
4. **Discouragement:** Ps.42:11; 1Sam.30:6; Mic.7:8. If you really want to go far in life you must learn to encourage yourself like David in 1sam.30:6. You must never give up like the lepers in (2ki.7:3-8).
5. **Fear:** (Isai.35:4; 2Tim.1:7; Josh.1:1-8). Fear is the lack of required courage to take positive steps toward a productive end. Twelve leaders from the tribes all saw

the goodness of the land but fear griped their hearts when they saw giants. Thank God for Caleb and Joshua who saw beyond the giants and affirmed their ability to conquer the land. Also remember the lepers in 2ki.7:3-8 who conquered the fear of death and stepped out. Your area of calling is not exempted. Not until you take a step, God will not step in.

6. **Pride:** Naaman who was a decorated war general needed help. He almost missed out of divine healing from leprously. The man of God simply said he should take a bath in River Jordan. Thank God for a good counsel that changed his life condition.

7. **Giant:** (1Sam.17) In the similitude of the Israelites' experience. A champion from the camp of the Philistines called Goliaths tormented the Israelites.

8. **Indecision:** In any way the enemy has trapped you with indecision, you're coming out in Jesus' name.

9. **Start but don't finish:** A lot of people are full of ideas and they always abandon prospective projects without any reasonable reason. An end has come to them all in Jesus' name.

10. **Negative mindset:** This spirit makes you to fail even before starting. It creates a mountain when there is none.

CONFESSIONS

- My life will be on the move, I shall move onward and forward, I shall not be under evil yoke, I shall grow from strength to strength

- Those who will lift me up shall appear to me, and I shall be visible to those who will help me, my situation shall improve.
- Stagnancy is not my portion, I shall seek help from those who can help me, I shall be at the right place at the right time.
- God heard Jonah from the belly of a fish. God heard David inside a cave. Help is not scarce in my life.
- My business shall move forward, my career shall move forward, my family shall move forward, my ministry shall move forward.
- I operate under an open heaven of help, I refuse to be stagnant, I choose life, I reject death, I choose speed, I reject stagnancy.
- Good things will happen to me, I will have joy in my soul, I will sing the song as triumphant winner, I will dance like a winner man.
- There are more people on my sides than those who are against me, the greater one is living inside of me, my difficult mountains are nowhere to be found, I am above, I am on top, I am alive.
- Everything I lay my hands upon shall prosper, where others have failed I shall succeed, the secret of God are with His prophets, I shall not be at the mercy of my enemies. Hallelujah!

- Happiness and Joy shall not be far from me, my house shall be a house of the Lord, Angels of help shall compass me about, I shall see the goodness of the Lord in the land of the living.

PRAYER POINTS
PSALM 44

1. Sing a song of worship to God of mercy.
2. Lord, help me to always shun the presence of evil and its agents in Jesus' name.
3. Jesus, help me to win souls for you on a daily basis.
4. Lord, help all our converts to manifest the fruits of repentance and fruits of the Spirit.
5. Lord, teach my heart to learn to cast all of my cares upon You in faith and not live in worry.
6. Lord, forgive me for all my past misdeeds, give me another chance to live my life for You.
7. My spirit, what are you doing in the camp of the enemy, come out by resurrection power in Jesus' name.
8. Any power using my face to attack helpers, release me by fire.

9. You, spirit of circular movement, release me and jump out by fire in Jesus' name.

10. Every generational strong man that is opposing my greatness, die by fire in Jesus' name.

11. Invisible chain that has tied me down, break by fire, in Jesus' name.

12. Let my fulltime enemies go on a journey of no return in Jesus' name.

13. Holy Spirit uncover the secret of the enemies in my environment in Jesus' name.

14. Strange altar harboring my family's help scatter by fire, in Jesus' name.

15. Shout Blood of Jesus 21 times, bring be out of generational prison in Jesus' name.

16. Shout Holy Ghost Fire 21 times, then say, witchcrafts bind in my neighbourhood, catch fire and die, in Jesus' name.

17. Pray in the Spirit for 30 minutes.

DAY THIRTY-FIVE
DELIVERANCE FROM HELPLESSNESS
EXHORTATION

" Likewise the Spirit also helpeth our infirmities: for we know not what we should pray for as we ought: but the Spirit itself maketh intercession for us with groanings which cannot be uttered.

And he that searcheth the hearts knoweth what is the mind of the Spirit, because he maketh intercession for the saints according to the will of God." (Rom.8:26,27)
Arise, Yahweh! God, lift up your hand! Don't forget the helpless. (Ps.10:12, WEB)

There are times in our lives when we will not be in a position to help ourselves. There are times when like the parable of the 100 hundred sheep, the shepherd will have to come look for us. There are times when we will feel totally helpless and hopeless. Have you ever experienced such a time? In all sincerity, every one of us have been there.

Jesus illustrated this state of helplessness in His parable of the lost sheep and lost coin. That sheep and coin are good example of helpless situations. They may know where they are but they cannot seek help for themselves, a force higher than them will have to locate them. At a time like this, before help comes, one might become discouraged, despondent and ready to give up.

We are not here to judge one another but rather to encourage ourselves. It is okay to experience discouragement. What is not okay is to refuse to rise above it. Diverse situations of life can surely render one helpless, and this will eventually birth discouragement (depression) but this is part of life. Discouragement comes most often when you do right things but experience wrong results. When you spend a great deal of time and effort to raise your children right but they rebel (so unfortunate). This could be depressing but in that depressive state, we have a glimmer of hope that God can still turn things around with prayer.

Hope is the major depression destroyer; the anchor of our soul (Heb.6:19). Jeremiah experienced lots of depression in his walk with God. Much of his tales of woes were rendered in the Book of Lamentation. But one thing was striking, while he started out helpless and hopeless, he ended his writings on a positive note because of the faith and hope he had in God that he will be delivered.

While reading and meditating on Jeremiah's experience, what comes straight to mind is Jesus' experience. Jeremiah's state of helplessness reminds us that even a faithful servant can become discouraged. Jesus lived above His feelings and fulfilled God's will. At the point of great depression, He beseeched God to roll away the burden from Him (Mt.26:39) but quickly located His hope **(Thy Will Be Done)**. We can also rise above discouragement by following these few steps:

1. **Be Sincere:** Let God know how you feel. God wants us to talk to Him even when we are angry, upset and frustrated

2. **Be Obedient**: Keep doing what God has called and ordained you to do. There are lists of challenges on our ways like Jeremiah. Our own challenges might be fear, financial, marital, health issues. The fire in him was hotter than the pressure of his own problems, God's message was like a fire in his bones.

3. **Be Focused:** Believe that He that calls you is with you. (Jer.20:11) *"But the Lord is with me like a violent warrior"*. Relax, fear not, though the pressure might be tough, the environment might be hostile, keep moving.

4. **Be a Worshipper:** Jeremiah, God's servant understood this principle. In his despondent state, he always worshipped God and He in time turned

his despair to joy. A major key that unlocks the door to victory is praise. No wonder he triumphantly proclaimed, *"... sing to the Lord! Praise the Lord"* (Jer.20:13). Yes, praise is more than just acknowledging, it is accepting from God all that comes our way, both the good and the bad.

DELIVERANCE IS MADE POSSIBLE FROM HELPLESSNESS WITH THE FOLLOWING:

1. **Praise recognize a provider:** When we praise God with all our mind and heart, He will eventually come through for us.
2. **Praise acknowledges a plan:** When we praise God, His plans for us will unravel (Jer.29:11).
3. **Praise accepts the present:** Not despising the days of little beginning is all about the total and joyful acceptance of the present as part of God's loving perfect will for us.
4. **Praise releases divine help:** Praise opens the door for God's power to move into our lives. The psalmist wrote... *"O thou that inhabits the praise of Israel"* (Ps.22:3). God resides in our praise. We unleash more of God's power when we praise.

CONFESSIONS

- I will not lose my life, I shall win the battles of life, I shall see my desire fulfilled, I shall see my vision prosper.
- I shall have the last laugh, my mockers shall be silenced, God will not allow evil prophecies come to pass against me.

- Shame and mockery are not my portion, mountains at impossibilities have become a valley, my rough roads are now smooth.
- God has spoken life into my destiny, God has blessed me beyond the curse, God has renewed my strength.
- I am not a target of those who want to destroy me, God shall justify me, every liar shall be exposed, every secret weapon shall not work against me, I shall be protected.
- Scarcity is not my portion, loneliness is not my portion, helplessness is not my portion, I reject garment at shame.
- Bad dreams shall not come to pass against me, nobody will pay me condolences, I shall never regret my life, I am helped.
- I am blessed, I am satisfied, I am fulfilled, I am justified, I am healed, I am alive, I am making progress, I am helped.
- I am not going backward, I am not a debtor, I am sick, I am not a prisoner, I am not poor, I am not condemned.
- My birthright in Christ is secured, I am accepted in the beloved, my mistakes shall be corrected, my God is able, My God shall turn my bitterness to sweetness. Hallelujah!

PRAYER POINTS
PSALM 94

1. Sing a song to Jesus.

2. Father, for every couple trusting You for the fruit of the womb in my local assembly, give them laughter today in Jesus' name.

3. My Father, my Father, deliver and set me free from every power making me lack needed help in Life.

4. Arrow of helplessness fired into my life, backfire in Jesus' name.

5. As You used Peter and John to perform miracles, use me and my children to perform spectacular miracles in this generation in Jesus' name.

6. God of all flesh, solve every of my problems and give me a new body in Jesus' name.

7. Lord, give me the servant spirit of Jesus that I may serve others just as You did, in Jesus' name.

8. Oh Lord my Father, let my life be characterized by uncommon help in Jesus' name.

9. Every addiction chasing help from me, expire in Jesus' name.

10. By the anointing of Jesus upon me, I shall be attracted like magnets to helpers in Jesus' name.

11. Oh Lord, let me enjoy strange attention that will favour me even in strange places, in Jesus' name.

12. Holy Spirit, trigger intercessors to intercede on my behalf, in Jesus' name.
13. Every evil eye monitoring my children for destruction, go blind in Jesus' name.
14. Every cloud of darkness holding my helpers captive, clear away in Jesus' name.
15. Keys of breakthrough, locate me by mercy in Jesus' name.
16. Shout God of Mercy 21 times, then say, release me and my children from the dungeon of helplessness, in Jesus' name.
17. Pray in the Spirit for 25 minutes.

DAY THIRTY-SIX
ENJOYING GOD'S HELP: DAVID
EXHORTATION

The LORD is my shepherd; I shall not want. (Ps.23:1)
And when he had removed him, he raised up unto them David to be their king; to whom also he gave testimony, and said, I have found David the son of Jesse, a man after mine own heart, which shall fulfil all my will. – Act.13:22

Looking through the lens of grace, one will surely agree that there is no other king who was *the apple of God's eye* but David. Their relationship is best understood as described by the Lord in (Act.13:22) *"A man after my heart, who will do all my will."* God's heart had a special affection for him.

David was not recorded in the scripture as a perfect man, but rather as a man who failed and sinned in many ways. Yet, despite these failings, David enjoyed God's help greatly. The question is, why did God help David so much? The answer can be deduced from the following:

GOD CHOSE DAVID (ROM.8:30)

Whoever God chooses, God will help. David greatly enjoyed divine help because he was chosen by God to become the king of Israel. God sees beyond the ordinary; He chose him because He knew David would represent His cause very well and he did.

GOD ANOINTED DAVID (PS.23:5^B)

Anointing plays a great role in the success of David's reign. He was greatly helped by God because God's anointing was upon Him. This anointing helped him to overcome the taunts of Goliath, build a great military following, transform the lives of his followers, write the Book of Psalms, plan for the building of the Temple and provide the lineage through which Jesus would be born. God's Love for David depended on God's Character, not David's character.

DAVID'S QUALITIES FOR HELP

DAVID'S SPIRITUALITY (PS.51, 139)

There is no denying that David truly loved what God loved. He was burdened by what burdens God. David's priority was living his life for God but he didn't just talk about living for God he put his faith into action as he tried to listen to and obey God in most areas of his life. When God confronted him with his sin, David took steps to change and repent of his sin.

Do you want to be described as "a man / woman after God's own heart?" Then give your heart completely to the Lord. Love what He loves, hate what He hates. Hurt when He hurts and rejoice over what He rejoices over. If you want to enjoy God's help too, you need to make God your first priority. Make Him your first love.

DAVID'S HUMILITY (PS.78:71)

Years of tending sheep and being the youngest in a family of boys, taught David to be humble. He was not Samuel's first choice but he was God's ultimate choice. In David, God saw an amazing young man who had a servant's heart. One who faithfully served in the fields tending few sheep, protecting them from danger. One who was willing to risk his life to bring fresh provision to his brothers in battle front. David faithfully served and never let success get to his head.

DAVID'S WISDOM (1SAM.18:14,15)

Wisdom is profitable to direct says the wise man, Solomon (Eccl.10:10). By making wise decisions and choices, David garnered more help from God.

When we display wisdom, we will attract more help. A foolish man will only attract punishment.

DAVID'S SKILLFULNESS (PS.78:72[B])

In the era where people do anyhow, David's skill in his work was recognized. It is very important to do whatever is expected from you very well. Any assignment must be given your best. Do not things because you want to do it, do them to the best of your abilities. Research, study, learn, ask questions, watch others in order to develop and perfect your skills.

DAVID'S INTEGRITY (PS.78:72[A])

Integrity means what we do when nobody is watching. David is described as having integrity of heart, it is worthy of note that God doesn't look at the outward appearance, he looks at our hearts (1Sam.16:17). David could have killed Saul in order to hasten his way to the throne but he never did. He allowed God to have His way.

CONFESSIONS

- My God is not a liar, He always do what He says, He has promised to help me, therefore, I shall enjoy Divine help.
- I shall testify to the goodness of God, there is no power that can deny me, I am above principalities and power.

- David enjoyed the help of God, Solomon enjoyed the help of God, they were able to do great exploits.
- By the help of God, I can scale a wall, by the help of God I can run through a troop, by the help of God I can pass through the Red Sea.
- Help of God is my birthright, help from God is my privilege, help through God is my daily benefits.
- I am among the Jewels of God, nobody can despise me, when I am under any pressure I will call for help.
- My helper is not lost, my helper is not blind, my helper is not powerless, my helper has not run out of resources.
- I serve a God of abundance, I am within the reach of His help, I am available for help, my helper shall not change his mind.
- New name is my portion, new level is my portion, new power is my portion, through the help of God, my life is better.
- My ministry is helped, my family is helped, my children is helped, glory is available for me, Honour is available for me, I am helped all the times. Hallelujah!

PRAYER POINTS

PSALM 146

1. Sing a song of worship to the Almighty God.
2. Lord, I thank You for who I am in Christ Jesus as revealed in IPet.2:9.
3. Lord, teach me Your ways, and lead me through the path of wisdom in Jesus' name.
4. God of mercy, may I never bring shame to Your name by my deeds in Jesus' name.
5. Lord, give me ears that hears your Spirit and a heart that follows your leadings in Jesus' name.
6. Lord, teach my hands to war and my fingers to fight only the battles You want me to fight in Jesus' name (Ps.114:1).
7. Lord, burden my daily helpers to connect me by mercy (IChr.12:22).
8. My Father, my Father, reject every of my competitors for me to be accepted, in Jesus' name.
9. Anointing to possess my God ordained inheritance, rest on me in Jesus' name.
10. Anointing to take testimonies, possess me in Jesus' name.
11. Every strange death in my family, loose your grip on me in Jesus' name.
12. I refuse to be deaf, dumb and blind spiritually.
13. The devil will not write the last chapter of my life.

14. Lord, help me never to miss my day of visitation, in Jesus' name.
15. Lord, show me those areas of my life where I am spiritually deficient.
16. Lord, raise a timely helper for me before my enemies prevail over me (2Sam.21:16,17).
17. Pray in the Spirit for 25 minutes.

DAY THIRTY-SEVEN
ENJOYING GOD'S HELP: JEHOSHAPHAT
EXHORTATION

'And the LORD was with Jehoshaphat, because he walked in the first ways of his father David, and sought not unto Baalim;
But sought to the LORD God of his father, and walked in his commandments, and not after the doings of Israel.
Therefore, the LORD stablished the kingdom in his hand; and all Judah brought to Jehoshaphat presents; and he had riches and honour in abundance
And his heart was lifted up in the ways of the LORD: moreover, he took away the high places and groves out of Judah.'
(2CHRO.17:3-6)

After David, another king that greatly enjoyed the help of God was king Asa of Judah and his son after him. At the beginning of his reign, he surrendered himself to the Lord. The Bible has this to say about him, *'And Asa did that which was right in the eyes of the LORD, as did David his father'* (1Ki.15:11). He made a lot of reforms in the land and his heart was right with God. Unfortunately, Asa was unable to seek the Lord till the end. The Bible warns that it is those that endured to the end that will be saved (Mt.10:22). The Bible also charges that the end of a thing is far better than its beginning (Eccl.7:8^b). although Asa started well, he ended up poorly.

What happened at that junction of his life, we will never know but what is said of him is that he stopped seeking the Lord for assistance. Although that is not our area of focus, I would like to sound a note of warning that it will be wise for every disciple of Christ to be ready to bear his/her Cross to the end. The Christian Race is a marathon and not a sprint so it is necessary to prepare oneself in the Holy Spirit for the journey. There is no excuse for falling by the way side. Some have made it, so we can make it too. What we need is the grace to persevere.

After Asa was his son and successor, Jehoshaphat. Jehoshaphat succeeded where his father failed. He was able to totally depend on the Lord for everything and God was with him all the way. Here are the outstanding things he did to be helped:
- Jehoshaphat did not seek Baals but sought the God of David and walked in His

commandments. Have you thought over this especially the way you need to walk in God's commandments and do away with every disobedient acts?

• He enjoyed God's help because God saw that he was a wise King that was so concerned about turning the hearts of the people back to the Him.

Jehoshaphat was a king with a difference and can be better described in the three **Ws** which are: **WORD, WORLD AND WORSHIP.** The Word was the foundation of his reign, the world was the great temptation of his reign, and worship was the great end, purpose of his reign.

THE WORD

It was clearly seen that he made the Word the foundation of his throne. The Levites and priests taught in the cities of Judah, having the book of the Law of the Lord with them. In our own era today, we have several platforms that we can use to reach out to the people. Jehoshaphat stole the heart of God by introducing the teaching of the Word of God which helped to eradicate idolatry from their hearts; unlike Asa's method that was in theory. So, the best way to teach people about God is not to just command but to correct using the Word of God.

THE WORLD

Jehoshaphat's frailty through an unwise alliance with the world was revealed when he associated with the wicked king of Israel – Ahab (cf.1Ki.22). This unwise decision would have cost him his life if not for the mercy of God. The world was a temptation for Jehoshaphat in the form of bad association which nearly corrupted his good manners (1Cor.15:33). Relating with this fact, no matter how rooted, strong, faithful a saint might be, the world is enticing. But as children of God, there is a need to beware of the association we join (Prov.1:10).

WORSHIP

Jehoshaphat enjoyed God's help as a worshipper. He emulated David and wanted to be a man after God's heart. He did not behave like Asa his father; when confronted with war from his enemy, he quickly retraced his steps and went back to the Lord. He proclaimed a fast throughout all Judah and they all assembled to seek help from the Lord.

Here is the core lesson to be learnt, life is full of challenges but we must be ready to always stand by God. Rely on Him. Trust Him and He will see you through.

CONFESSIONS

- No weapon fashioned against me shall prosper, all those who gather against me shall scatter; my God is the Almighty.
- Asa defeated over a million enemy soldiers, Jehoshaphat defeated three enemy nations, because God was behind their success.
- When God is behind you, you are safe. I am confident, I am stable, I am assured, I am satisfied.
- My God can do all things, my God can reverse the irreversible, my God can raise the dead, my God can change any bad situation to good, my God is a good God.
- My God can make all situation work for my good, I have no fear at what my enemies can do.
- My portion is to share testimonies, my portion is multiple breakthrough, my portion is victory over defeat.
- I shall enjoy the help of God, I shall receive the grace of God, I shall not miss the best of God.

- What is lesser than my God shall not glory over me, those who are lesser to me shall not take my place.
- I have a goodly heritage, help is my heritage, supernatural help is my birthright, I am helped.
- I shall not be on a dry ground, I shall be on the Mountain top, the beauty of God shall swallow my ashes. Hallelujah!

PRAYER POINTS
PSALM 108

1. Sing a song to Jesus.
2. Father, help my children never to partake in anything that would attract curses to their lives in Jesus' name.
3. Lord, grant me grace to restitute my ways in order to get a clear conscience before You and man, in Jesus' name.
4. Father, I thank You for all You do for me, particularly for all the battles You fight on my behalf which I know nothing about, in Jesus' name.
5. Lord, manifest Your power to set me free from every form of captivity I am experiencing today, in Jesus' name.
6. Lord, set my children apart for Your special encounter in Jesus' name.

7. Lord, help me to purge and purify myself so that I may be found suitable for your use in Jesus' name.

8. Lord, help me to love You as I ought to indeed and in truth in Jesus' name.

9. You are the Almighty, do Your mighty works in my family in Jesus' name.

10. My God, You said, "vain is the help of man," because true help comes from You. Lord, cause me to enjoy Your help.

11. It is written in Your Word that the people shall be willing in the days of Your power. Father, demonstrate Your power in my life and let people be willing to help me in Jesus' name (Ps.110:3).

12. I receive the Lord's protection from all forms of danger after the order of Jehoshaphat in Jesus' name (IKi.22:32,33).

13. Since the Spirit of Him that raised up Jesus from the death dwells in me, Lord, quicken and overtake my mortal body in Jesus' name.

14. You spirit of infirmity, get out of my body in Jesus' name.

15. I disconnect myself from every wrong relationship that is sinking the boat of my destiny in Jesus' name.

16. Since I pay my tithe regularly, I refuse to waste my money on hospital bills in Jesus' name.
17. Pray in the Spirit for 25 minutes.

DAY THIRTY-EIGHT
ENJOYING GOD'S HELP: RUTH, ESTHER
EXHORTATION

And Ruth said, Intreat me not to leave thee, or to return from following after thee: for whither thou goest, I will go; and where thou lodgest, I will lodge: thy people shall be my people, and thy God my God: (Rut.1:16)

Go, gather together all the Jews that are present in Shushan, and fast ye for me, and neither eat nor drink three days, night or day: I also and my maidens will fast likewise; and so will I go in unto the king, which is not according to the law: and if I perish, I perish. (Est.4:16)

It is amazing, that of all the notable women in the Bible, only two women have books written in their honour. They also have the reserved honour of being one of the few women in the genealogy of Christ. How did they get to this level? How were they able to enjoy the Lord's help in such an unwavering manner and even in a strange land? Their secret is rooted in their **devotion** to God, the people of God and the things of God.

HOW OUR DEVOTION CAN ATTRACT THE HELP OF GOD: A BRIEF INSIGHT INTO THE LIVES OF RUTH AND ESTHER

RUTH

She was a simple Moabite widow who was fortunate to benefit from God's help based on her decision to devote her life to the God of Israel. She became an essential character in the powerful story of Salvation woven through the Bible.

Naomi, the Israelite, with her family, left Israel when there was famine in the land. They sojourned in the land of Moab where her two sons and husband perished.

MORAL: Do not leave your divine location when there is trouble. Isaac sowed in his destined land during the period of famine and he became successful. Seek divine Instruction before moving.

With the death of her husband and children, she decided to go back home. But now, she has her daughters-in-law in tow. She entreated them to go back to their families and after much persuasion, Orpha went back but Ruth was adamant. The Bible said she was, *'steadfastly minded...' (Rut.1:18).* Her devotion to Naomi and her God compelled her to want to stay with her.

MORAL: Live an exemplary life that will attract people to you. Apostle Paul challenged Timothy to train the elderly women to be of good example to the younger women. Pass Jesus on to them not witchcraft. Pass godly values to them not worldly values. Let others see Jesus in you.

God honours devotion. He loves commitment. He loves loyalty. He loves constancy. That is why God helped Ruth. A foreigner from a land that even God despised (Ps.60:8) was able to receive God's help due to her devotion and loyalty.

ESTHER

An orphan (of the tribe of Benjamin) and one of the captives who refused to go back to Judea after the permission given by Cyrus to go back to Israel. Her father's brother Mordecai, trained her in the way she should go and she never departed from it (Prov.22:6). She was a composed, obedient young lady who trusted the God of her uncle. When she got to the palace, her devotion and loyalty to her uncle remained.

MORAL: Obedience is a major key to attracting God's help. Esther was obedient to her uncle when convenient and otherwise. If you want to enjoy God's help, obey God and godly men. Help is never far from obedience.

When the time came for Esther to prove herself, she was not found wanting. Confronting death, she chose to pay with her life. That is selflessness of the highest order. Jesus eventually died for mankind. Esther was willing to die for the captives.

Esther enjoyed God's mercy and help beyond her imagination in the following ways:

(1). No place of privilege can ever exempt a person from responsibility to respond to God's call. Mind you, God promotes you for a purpose. He wants you to serve Him with your position, grace, wealth, influence etc.

(2). No matter how helpless a situation might be, God is never helpless. God is help personified. He has a way of helping us to sail through every troubled waters of life. Ps.46:1 says, *"The Lord is our refuge, a very present help in time of trouble."*

CONFESSIONS

- I operate under the covenant of help, help is my birthright, help is not far from me, help makes life easy for me.
- I enjoy the benefits of help, I receive the packages of help, I connect with help that cannot be denied, help is my portion.

- I am the candidate to be helped, I am endorsed for help, I am available for help, I am connected to help.
- The source of my help cannot dry, the fountain of help is open to me, I receive the key to the doors of help.
- I shall receive help in difficult places. Like Esther, I shall receive help against all odds, my God shall send timely help, my God shall help me overcome great obstacles.
- What my enemies wish against me shall not come to pass through the grace of God. I shall overcome.
- I am getting better, I am going higher, I am the head, I am above, I am moving to the next level. I am helped.
- Like Ruth, I shall find grace for help, my case is not over. There is light after my tunnel.
- My call for help shall be heard, my cry for help shall receive speedy response where I am, help shall locate me, the doors of help is open to me.
- Where nobody is helped, I shall be helped before who do not help others, I shall be helped. Amen!

PRAYER POINTS
PSALM 70

1. Sing a song to Jesus.
2. Oh Lord, do not let the flesh, the world and the devil rob me of the benefit of my redemption in Christ. Let the people know that I am Your child.
3. Lord, grant me the grace to easily manifest Your mind in humility every day.
4. The Son of Man had no place to lay His head so that we would always have a roof over our Head. Where is mine? Lord by mercy I receive it.
5. Lord, grant me grace to align my life to conform with Your Word, in Jesus name.
6. Lord, let the Spirit of Holiness begin to manifest in the name of Jesus.
7. Oh Lord my God, as one whom You have chosen and formed like Esther, whenever I desire help, let help arise for me in Jesus' name.
8. It is written that all things are Yours. Therefore, my Father, from today and beyond, let help continually be mine to enjoy in Jesus' name.
9. It is written, *"I send you into the labour of others to reap where you have not*

bestowed labour..." Oh Lord, cause me to enjoy help in places I never labored in Jesus name (Joh.4:38).

10. Heavenly Father, the God of all flesh, enhance and establish my life with grace for timely help, in Jesus' name.
11. Lord, pour upon me grace that will cause me to be divinely connected in Jesus' name.
12. Lord, after the order of Ruth, connect me to the work that will favour me in Jesus' name (Rut.2:2).
13. My Father, my Father, after the order of Esther, let favour distinguish me and give me my throne in Jesus name (Est.2:15-18).
14. Every help destroyers around me, go and destroy yourself in Jesus' name.
15. Just as the glory of the sun cannot be hidden, so, my glory will not be hidden in Jesus' name.
16. Every calendar of evil proposed against my children be burnt into ashes in Jesus' name.
17. Pray in the Spirit for 20 minutes.

DAY THIRTY-NINE
ENJOYING GOD'S HELP: DANIEL, NEHEMIAH
EXHORTATION

'But Daniel purposed in his heart that he would not defile himself with the portion of the king's meat, nor with the wine

which he drank: therefore he requested of the prince of the eunuchs that he might not defile himself.' DAN.1:8
'And it came to pass, when I heard these words, that I sat down and wept, and mourned certain days, and fasted, and prayed before the God of heaven.' (NEH.1:4)

One thing that stood Daniel and Nehemiah out as men that enjoyed God's help is that they were Men of Prayer. They were self-trained to pray to God in difficult circumstances. Their unwavering attitude towards adversity made them enjoy God's help. Not only were they men of prayer, they also possessed good character traits that stood them out: they were courageous (during hardship), loyal (to their masters), and discerning (knew what to do per time).

DANIEL

Daniel was one of the captives taken to Babylon. Aside the fact that his life is worthy of emulation because he was able to distinguish himself just as the Bible warned (2Cor.6:14), there are other dynamics we need to take into consideration.

FIRST: WHY WAS DANIEL IN CAPTIVITY? Daniel was one of the 'unfortunate' righteous ones taken into captivity when the whole of Israel displeased the Lord. Remember, the prophets warned the Israelites (the northern and southern kingdoms) of the impending doom if they did not repent of their idolatrous ways but they rebuffed them. Eventually, they were taken into captivity and not only the disobedient ones but the righteous ones too.

Note that it is possible for the righteous to suffer the same fate as the unrighteous. You might be in similar circumstance right now (suffering for what you know nothing about) but be assured that God will be with you as long as you remain faithful just like Daniel. He never complained nor murmured. He simply trusted the Lord. Do the same. Trust God's purpose.

SECOND: TRAIN A CHILD IN THE WAY HE SHOULD GO: The wise man's advice in Prov.22:6 worked faithfully for Daniel. He must have had a solid home-training. His parents must have exposed him to God and His ways and embedded in him the importance of right living. You can see that Daniel displayed good character in a strange land; he comported himself well and dealt wisely everywhere he went. As he grew older, he kept on building on that good foundation and never compromised. God was never far away from him because of that.

Parent, what are you teaching your children? Are you instilling in them godly principles or are you trying to just 'help' buy their way out of everything? The morals of today will speak tomorrow. The grandmother and mother of Timothy were commended for training Timothy in the ways of the Lord (2Tim.1:5).

NEHEMIAH

Also, a captive in Babylon but unlike Daniel was not taken into captivity but rather born in captivity. One thing you should learn in the life of Nehemiah is to never allow your circumstance to define who you are or become. Although he was born in captivity, he never allowed the fact that he was a slave to hold him down. Many people in the same circumstance would never have amount to much in life. Instead of them to look for opportunities to maximize their potentials at that particular junction of their lives, they would rather sit back and watch life pass them by.

Nehemiah was in a place of opportunity and he made good use of it. He was diligent in his work to have been given such a sensitive position (king's cup bearer). He was able to seize the opportunity of the king's offer because he was on the lookout. Do not permit your circumstance in life to determine your future. Look for God. He will help turn your life around.

Another lesson learnt concerning Nehemiah is that he was compassionate. He was in a position of honour and thus should be less concerned about the remnants and the broken walls of

Jerusalem but like Esther, he had the heart of God. They did not care about themselves alone. They were not selfish. My friend, can such be said of you? Are you a selfless Christian? Do you think about others in your decision making? Do you worry about other peoples' lives? Are you concerned about God's projects? Do you pray to God to use you for others? Are you ready to leave your comfort zones for service to God and humanity?

Another lesson to be treasured in the life of Nehemiah is his faithfulness to his life assignment. Nehemiah's purpose was to rebuild the broken walls of Jerusalem, as insignificant as that might seem to some people, Nehemiah was ready to die doing it. When confronted with adversities, he did not allow them to weigh him down. He found ways around these obstacles to get the job done.

Are you serious about your life assignment? Are you a go-getter or an excuse-giver? Do you see your job as service to God which must not fail or do you see your job as inconsequential? Do you just go to work to pass time and not to add value? Are you ready to make sacrifice for your life assignment?

Also, Nehemiah's life has an added bonus of someone who was born outside of his homeland and who had not lived there till adulthood to still be filled with the kind of patriotic zeal for the homeland. As we can see in Nehemiah, this is an indication of the fact that the environment we find ourselves should not be a barrier for us to inculcate godly and moral principles we have learnt in our childhood. Nehemiah's parents must have done the good work of making Nehemiah imbibe not only godly attributes but also an undying passion for his homestead. Wherever we find ourselves in any part of the world, we should not forget who we are and where we are coming from. We should pass same to our children. Nehemiah, though he had not been to Israel since birth, he knew who he was and never forgot his roots.

As you can see, Daniel and Nehemiah both enjoyed God's help not only because they prayed their way through but because their hearts were also right with God.

CONFESSIONS

- I overcome all antagonist, I conquer all haters of goodness in my life, whoever hate me, shall not be there whenever I call for help.
- My God shall lock up those who hate me, before they could stop my help, I would have escaped.

- Nothing shall block my help, nothing shall block my helper. My helper will not change his mind.
- My documents shall be favored, my letters shall be favored, my requests for help shall be granted, help shall work out for me. Amen.
- I shall respect the principles of help, I shall follow the due process of help, where help is hidden I shall get help, help is my birthright, therefore help is not far from me.
- Angels of help shall visit me today, messenger of help shall deliver to me, help is my portion, help is my heritage.
- I cannot be denied, I cannot be stranded, I cannot be turned back, help is reserved for me.
- I have been recommended for help, I have been raised through help, my work shall receive recognitions.
- Help shall be abundant for me, help shall be sufficient for me, help shall be very close to me, Hallelujah!
- Weeping is not my portion, what is sweet in my life shall never become bitter, help is available for me. Hallelujah!

PRAYER POINTS
PSALM 54

1. Give God worship in Spirit and understanding.
2. My Father, my Father, grant me the grace to honour You in all I do, all the days of my life.
3. My Lord, grant me grace to study Jesus lifestyle and help me to respond to situation the way He did in Jesus' name.
4. Lord, keep genuine Christian leaders across the globe from falling in Jesus' name.
5. Lord, open my eyes to severity of eternal hell.
6. My Father, my Father, do all You need to do in me to present me faultless before Your throne in Jesus' name.
7. My Father, my Father, the Father of mercy, from today and beyond let my life become a rallying point for helpers in Jesus' name.
8. Oh Lord, my God, put men under serious pressure to arise for my help in Jesus' name.
9. Daniel was relevant in the reign of many kings, cause me oh Lord to be relevant by Your help all through my life, in Jesus' name.

10. Lord, give me burden for Your people and the house of God like Nehemiah.
11. Every stronghold of darkness standing between me and my helpers of destiny, dismantle them by Your power in Jesus' name (Dan.10: 10-13).
12. Grant me grace to understand the move of God from now in Jesus' name (Dan.9:1).
13. My Father, my Father, stir up the kings on earth to support my God given vision with all their influence and possessions in Jesus' name.
14. After the order of Daniel, let the craftiness of my enemies become their destructions in Jesus' name (Dan.6:22-24).
15. Oh Lord, cloth my life with a new grace and glory in Jesus' name.
16. Pray with in the Spirit for 30 minutes.

DAY FORTY
GOD - THE CREATOR OF HELP
EXHORTATION

*"And when the king of Israel was going by on the wall, a woman came crying out to him, and said, Help! my lord king. And he said, **If the Lord does not give you help**, where am I to get help for you? from the grain-floor or the grape-crusher?"* (2Ki.6:26,27 BBE emphasis mine)

Our God is an awesome God. He reigns from heaven above, with wisdom, power and love. Our God is an awesome God. Said the singer and composer, Donnie McClurkin. Indeed, our God is awesome. He not only does awesome things but He is awesomeness personified. He is a good God. He is a just God. He is a wonderful God. He is a great God. Most importantly, He is a helpful God. Our God is not only a helpful God but He is the Creator of Help! He is the One that makes help relevant. Without Him, help will be useless. A woman calling upon the King in the old kingdom of Israel for help got the shocker of her life when the king retorted that he cannot grant help without God's permission.

As the 'designer of help,' God knows how helpless and hopeless mankind will be without His assistance (Isai.41:14). The Writer of the Book of Acts vividly captured this when he remarked, *'For in him we **live**, and **move**, and **have our being**...'* (Act.17:28 emphasis mine). Without God, there can be no man. In fact, nothing (if we believe what is written in Genesis chapter 1) will be in existence. In His kindness, love, mercy and grace, He created us and continues to sustain us. For a better understanding of what is being explained, envisage a loving mother who has just put to bed. All her thoughts, waking and otherwise will be toward the new born. With time, as the baby ages, the mother's eyes will be on him, ensuring that he is safe. Up till he gets old, 'the baby' will still be under the watchful eyes of the mother; ever ready to extend the hand of assistance when needed. That is how God is with us. We are ever under His watchful eyes. Always the *"very present help' in the time of need"* (Ps.46:1).

By creating help, God exhibits His supremacy over His creation. This means that God retains the right of supremacy over every of His creation by virtue of being able to be of assistance to them. Everything in creation subsists in God. Everything relies on His power to be what they are ordained to be. Without Him, nothing will be.

Man, a creature of formidable force is specially created to have the greatest need for God. Every other creature needs God in smaller dose compared to man. The essence of man is rooted in God. Any man that tries to survive outside of God will find out the hard way how impossible that will be. God specifically created man to need Him (Hos.13:9). We need Him to be conceived, we need Him to be born, we need Him to grow, we need Him in our daily pursuits, we need Him to live and fulfill purpose, we need Him even at the point of death when we get scared of the Great Beyond; man needs God all the time!

To maintain His supremacy over all of creation, God has put in place structures of sustenance that ensure perfect operation. Everything in nature works in harmony, in agreement with one another. This is why scientifically; the whole of creation is called COSMOS (an ordered system or harmonious whole). When creation is in discordance within itself, there is the opposite of cosmos which is CHAOS. It happens in man's life too. Whenever he is in agreement with God, his life has a semblance of order but whenever he steps out of His will, chaos becomes the order of his life. This is because it is God in man that is 'helping' him to live. Man needs God to live. Without Him, we cannot live a fulfilled life.

God is the source of help. Every form of help that man enjoys emanates from Him. Any form of help outside of Him is negative and unprofitable. God created everything (man inclusive) for His pleasure (Rev.4:11). Just like every good father, He always desires for us to come to Him for help. No help is too small for Him to render neither is any too big for Him. He is the Omniscient, Omnipotent, and He uses these qualities to render necessary assistance to mankind. In fact, not seeking His help is an affront to Him.

It is like a father who, as a billionaire, expects his child to seek his help for anything vital but the child instead of going to his father decides to seek the neighbour's assistance. As the father, how would you feel? God, your Heavenly Father, can help you and He is willing to help you. Why then are you not seeking His help?

The devil might want you to think otherwise but God is the fountain, the cause and source of all help. As your Creator, He knows what is wrong in your life and how to fix it. Will the manufacturer of a car not know what the problem is with the car with little or no diagnosis? They will, because they know the components of the car having made it. The same way, God knows you more than anyone. He knows where you need help the most and that is where He focuses.

Beloved, God is the source of all help. He is the one that makes other helps work. You might be in the midst of 'helpers' and still languish. They will not help you unless God directs it. If you need help from anyone, do not go to them first, I repeat, do not go them first. Go to God. When you acknowledge God first, He will take care of the rest and instead of you pursuing them, they will be pursuing you to help you. David understood this principle; he never pursued men but rather pursued God and God in turn compelled men of valour to 'pursue' him (cf. 1Chr.12).

CONFESSIONS

- God is the Almighty, without God nothing can work, with God nothing can fail, God is a God of possibilities, God is a God of all grace.

- God helped the Israelites crossed over the Red Sea, God helped David kill Goliath, God helped Sarah conceived at old age, God helped Daniel to interpret difficult dreams, God helped Hezekiah to defeat enemy nations.
- Because God is on my side, I have no fear, because my God cannot lie, I have confidence in him, there is no regret in following God.
- God is a Rewarder, God is a Blesser, God is a Healer, God is a Redeemer, God is a Leader, God is a Teacher, God is a Helper.
- Because God knows all things, I will obey His instructions. I shall not die, I shall see what God has packaged for me.
- God is a Miracle Worker. Miracle is a wonder of help to a man, miracles are the grace of God to become what we are destined to be.
- God is a compassionate God, He can wipe all tears. He can give me a new beginning, He can give me a new name, he can restore what is lost, he can lift me up from the dunghill.
- With the help of God, my joy has come, with the help of God my dancing has been

multiplied, with the help of God I can renew my strength, with the help of God all things are possible, Hallelujah!

- God can pay my debt, God can build my career, God can provide for all my needs, God can multiply the little I have in my hands.
- I receive the breath of life, I receive the spirit of wisdom, I receive a new mind, I receive grace, I receive help. Hallelujah! Amen.

PRAYER POINTS
PSALM 46

1. Sing a song to Jesus the Author and Finisher of your faith.
2. Lord, fill my heart with Your love, so that Your love may flow through me to others.
3. God of Mercy, abide with me, make my body Your dwelling place, and give me the grace to resist any temptation to misuse my body in Jesus' name.
4. God of Mercy, baptize Your Church with true love and bind the body of Christ together with a strong cord of unity in Jesus' name.

5. It is written, "male and female created He them". My Father, cause every male and female You have created to help me and my children in Jesus' name.

6. Oh Lord my God, every creation You have attached my help to, I call them forth now in Jesus name.

7. Father, as I pray now cause the implication of my help to begin in Jesus' name.

8. My Father, my Father, give to all my helpers grace and the willingness to help me, in Jesus' name.

9. Lord, help my children to co-operate with Your plans for their life in Jesus' name.

10. My Father, place around me men that will help me fulfill my destiny in Jesus' name.

11. Every dormant gift and grace in me be stimulated into action in Jesus' name.

12. I refuse to work as a blind man in this season of divine assistance in Jesus' name.

13. All the fullness of the earth belongs to my God, and as a result, it belongs to me because I am a Joint-Heir with Christ.

14. I liquidate by fire every power occupying my territories physically or spiritually in Jesus' name.

15. Earth, O earth, O earth, yield my help unto me in Jesus' name.

16. Lord, let the riches of the gentiles and the abundance of the sea flow into my life in Jesus' name.
17. Pray in the Spirit for the minimum of 25 minutes.

HYMNS/ORIN IYIN

YORUBA TRANSLATION OF CONFESSIONS AND PRAYER POINTS
IJEWO ATI KOKO ADURA: OJO KINI DE OGOJI

OJO KINI

ASIRI IRANLOWO
IJEWO

- Mo ni eto si iranlowo nitori Olorun Oluranlowo to ga ju lo ni Baba mi. Iranlowo je ara ebun fun irapada mi. Iranlowo wa fun mi ninu Oluwa. Iranlowo n bo lodo mi loni. Iranlowo wa ti a ti ko oruko mi si lori. Emi ko ni padanu iranlowo ti a ti yan mo mi.

- Emi Olorun ni Oluranlowo mi; nitorina a ti fun mi lokun. Ororo iranlowo n be lori mi. Mo gba iranlowo ti to sowon. Mo gba iranlowo taara, mo gba iranlowo eburu, mo gba iranlowo ti ko wopo, mo gba iranlowo lati oke, mo gba iranlowo ogidi.

- Iranlowo ko won mi laye mi. mo pe fun iranlowo, mo gbadura iranlowo, mo gbagbo ninu iranlowo. Mo wa iranlowo, iranlowo si mu aranse wa fun mi, iranlowo mu ipin mi wa fun mi, iranlowo mu itusile wa fun mi.

- Orun iranlowo si sile fun mi. n ko le wa ninu igbekun. A ko le fi aye su mi, iranlowo gbe ayo wa fun okan mi, iranlowo mu atunse pipe wa si aye mi.

- Oluwa ni Oluranlowo mi. Nitorina mo gba iranlowo to se gbarale, mo gba iranlowo ti ki i ye. Mo gba iranlowo kaakiri agbaye.
- A na owo iranlowo si mi; nitorina n ko le ni ijakule. N ko le se alaini. N ko le di eni ti ko ri ona lo, n ko le wa lojukan naa, n ko le d'eni apati.
- Eniti n ran mi lowo wa nitosi. Emi ko da wa. Iranlowo wa ni arowoto mi, iranlowo wa nitosi mi. Ko si idaduro mo. Ko is iduro laisi ona abayo mo. Ko si ireti ofo mo, ko si ile gbigbe mo.
- Olorun wa loju ise nitori mi. Ohun gbogbo n sise po fun rere ninu aye mi. ko lee re oluranlowo mi. Oluranlowo mi ko lee sonu, oluranlowo mi ko lee ku nitori Olorun Alagbara ni o ran si mi; nitori naa mo ni ireti aye to dara.
- Iranlowo si awon ilekun to soro fun mi. Iranlowo mu fo gbogbo idena kuro lona mi, iranlowo ni ese ti mo fi duro lati je gaba, iranlowo ni agara ti o mu gbogbo idiwo kuro.
- Iranlowo ni eun ti nfoun fun mi, iranlowo a je ki gbogbo kosese di sise. Haleluya! Ati ran mi lowo.

KOKO ADURA

ORIN DAFIDI 121

1. Oluwa modupe fun ipinu atoke wa Re fun ipade Ojo Aanu ti odun yi.
2. Modupe lowo Re fun awon oun ti O ni ni ipamo ti o ju oye wa lo.
3. Modupe lowo Olorun fun otito ati iranlowo ateyin wa Re ti a ti ri gba (ko orin kan si Oba awon oba).
4. Oluwa, we mimo kuro ninu gbogbo aisododo ki O si dari gbogbo ese mi ji mi.
5. Pariwo, Olorun aanu ni igba mokanlelogun, ki o si so wipe, fun mi ni ibapade ti yio mu mi lo si ipele ti o kan.
6. Mo ko lati dawa, se eto iranlowo ti o to fun mi (Gen.2:18).
7. Nibi ti iranlowo ko si, wa iranlowo fun mi (Gen.2:20).
8. Je ki ile ki o ran emi ati awon omo mi lowo.
9. Olorun, lati inu gbogbo ahamo idajo, dide fun iranlowo mi ki O si ra mi pada ni oruko Jesu (O.D.44:26).
10. Iranlowo lowolowo, wa mi ri lesekese (O.D.46:1).
11. Baba mi, Baba mi, ji iranlowo to nsun ni tori temi (Mk.4:37-39).
12. Olorun, yi gbogbo ero buburu ota ti o lodi simi sir ere ni oruko Jesu (Gen.50:20).
13. Olorun, ran mi lowo lati bori ounkoun ti mo nse lowolowo ti o le je ki O wa elomiran

ropo mi ni ijoba Re ni oruko Jesu (ISam.15:28).

14. Baba mi, Baba mi, kun mi pelu imolara ipadabo Re leekeji ni gbogbo igba (Efe. 5:14-16).

15. Olorun aanu, se aanu Re fun gbogbo ebi mi ti emi ko fi oju ri. Boju wo won ki O si wo gbogbo aisan won san (Lk 19:10).

16. Baba mi, Baba mi, dari gbogbo aisedede ana mi ji mi ki O si fun mi ni anfaani miran lati le gbe aiye mi fun O (Joh.8:11).

17. Baba mi, Baba mi, fi opin si gbogbo laala aileso ninu aiye mi   (Gen. 27:20-30).

18. So mi po mo awon eniyan ti o ni oun ti mo nwa ati awon ti onilo oun ti mo ni (Gen. 41:14-46).

OJO KINI ASOTELE

1. Akoni kan yio bu jade lati inu ohun gbogi kan lati di akoni.

2. Isoro nla kan yio gba yiyanju ni ona ara.

3. A o gba ore-ofe lati mo igbese awon ota.

OJO KEJI

JESU IRANLOWO TO DI ENIYAN

IJEWO

- Mo je alajogun igbala. Mo n sogo ninu ibasepo mi pelu Olorun. A ti gbami saarin awon ayanfe, a ti so mi domo ninu ogun ajoni Israeli. Mo je eso Abrahamu. Omo Olorun ni mo je.

- Nitorina ko si idalebi fun mi nitori mo wa ninu Jesu Kristi. A ti da mi lare nitori a ti se mi logo lati ibere.

- Jesu ti duro fun mi. O san igbese ese ti ko je. O gbe ijiya ti n ko le gbe, o san adiyele ni kikun, o se asetan ohun gbogbo, o segun nitori mi.

- Ni bayi mo ti di atunbi. Mo ti wa laaye si isododo. Iku ko lagbara lori mi, Jesu ti se pasipaaro fun mi. Tele mo je alailagbara, nisinsinyi mo ti di alagbara. Tele a ti da mi lebi, bayi mo ti gba idalare. Tele a ti fi mi sinu ibinu, ni bayi mo ti di omoloju Oluwa.

- Ofin ti Emi Iye ti so mi dominira kuro ninu ofin ese ati iku, eran ara mi alaare ko le se amuse ofin ti Olorun, iye Jesu ninu mi ti fun mi ni isegun lori eran ara.

- Emi lee se ohun gbogbo nipase Jesu ti n fi agbara fun mi. Jesu n gbenu mi. Mo ni ireti ogo. Orun ko ti mo mi. Emi mo Jesu tii se ilekun si orun.

- Jesu ni imole aye; nitori naa okunkun ko lee joba lori mi, nitori mo je ti Jesu, okunkun ko le joba lori mi.
- Jesu ni ounje iye; nitori naa ebi ko lee pa mi. Jesu ni omi iye, mo ni itelorun. Jesu ni ajinde ati iye, nitorina emi ko lee ku, Jesu ni ona, nitori naa emi ko lee sonu. Mo layo pe mo je ti Jesu.
- Iranlowo w ani arowoto mi loorekoore nitori Jesu ni iranlowo mi. Jesu ran mi lowo lati mo Baba, Jesu ran mi lowo lati mo emi mimo, Jesu ran mi lowo lati se aseyori ise iranse mi, Jesu ran mi lowo lati se awari ayanmo mi lati orun, Jesu ran mi lowo lati segun ese ati ifekufe.
- Jesu ni Oluranlowo to see gbara le fun mi, Jesu ni Oluranlowo mi ti ki i ye, Jesu ni Oluranlowo to wa nitosi, Jesu ni Oluranlowo ti kii re. Jesu ni Oluranlowo to daju. Haleluya!

KOKO ADURA
ORIN DAFIDI 22
1. Jesu, modupe wipe Oun bami rin, bi mo tin dagba soke ninu ibasepo mi pelu Re.
2. Jesu O se, wipe o tobi ju gbogbo omiran ninu aiye mi (O.D. 20:7).

317

3. OLUWA, se iribomi ifami ororoyan irorun fun mi ni oruko Jesu.
4. Baba mi, Baba mi, ni akoko ewu igba ikeyin yi, gbe mi pamo si abe ojiji Re.
5. Emi Mimo, si oju mi si awon oun ikoiko ti ijoba orun (1Kor. 2:9,10).
6. Oluwa, ran mi lowo lati le to si ere omo-odo rere ni oruko Jesu (Ifi.22:12).
7. Jesu, fa mi sun mo O ju ti atehin wa lo (Gal.4:6).
8. Olorun, fagile gbogbo adehun pelu iku ninu aiye mi (Joh.8:1-8).
9. Olorun, fi bi mo se le ri iranlowo gba ati bi mo se le fa oluranlowo (Mk.10:46-52).
10. Awon ala okunkun ti a yan lati le oluranlowo kuro lodo mi, dawo duro ni oruko Jesu.
11.Jesu, rin si aiye mi ki O si ran mi lowo (Mt.14:25).
12. Olorun, saanu fun mi ki O si yanju oro mi (Mt.15:32).
13. Olorun, Iwo Omo Dafidi, s'aanu fun mi, ki O si ran mi lowo (Mt.20:20).
14. Ounkoun ti a gbe ise fun lati so mi di ije iku aitojo, Jesu, Olugbeikumi, gbe mi (IIKor.15:54).
15. Olorun, dide ki O fi ariwo odi mule lodi si awon aninilara ni oruko Jesu (Mt.28:1-3).

16. Awon oluranlowo ti o ti salo, tun pada farahan lati mu ayanmo mi tesiwaju ni oruko Jesu (Joh.11:11).
17. Oluwa, ran mi lowo lati le fi idi ipile ti o dan moran mule fun awon ebi mi (IITim.6:9).
18. Olorun, ru igbagbo mi soke ki O si ran mi lowo lati gbeke le O ninu oun gbogbo ti mo n se (Heb.11:6).

OJO KETA

EMI MIMO - IRANLOWO LATOKE
IJEWO

- Mo gba iranlowo latoke. Mo gba itosona latoke. Mo gba aranse to ga ju agbara aye. Mo gba ibasepo Emi Mimo.
- Iranlowo eniyan ko to. Mo ni anfaani si ogbon latoke. Eniti ko ba ni ogbon, ki o beere lati odo Olorun ti n fi fun ni lopolopo ti ki i si baniwi. Orun si sile fun mi, mo ri aranse latoke gba.
- Mo je atunbi ninu Kristi, a ti ri mi bomi ninu Emi Mimo; emi yoo jere laye mi. Awon eniyan yoo si ri ere je lati ara mi. Orun yoo jere lara mi, Emi Mimo ni atona mi.
- Ohun ti o soro fun eniyan, o seese fun Olorun. Nko ni jakule. A fi asiri orun han mi. Mo ni ona si ogbon lati odo Olorun, agbara wa fun mi, Oro imo si wa fun mi.

- Emi je eni imole. N ko lee rin ninu okunkun. Jesu ni imole aye. Mo ko emi itanje. Mo ko emi arekereke, mo ko emi igba ikeyin, mo ko okunkun.
- Ti emi ko ba mo ohun ti mo fe se, mo mo eni ti mo gbodo to lo. Emi Mimo ko lee ko mi. Emi Mimo yoo fun mi ni imisi. Emi mimo yoo fi ona otito han mi, emi ko le sina.
- Ona kan wa ti o dara loju eniyan, sugbon opin re, ona iku ni. Emi Mimo yoo tan imole si ipase mi. Emi ki yoo kose. Emi ko ni din ni iye. Emi yoo ma lesi ni.
- Itiju ni ere awon asiwere. Emi ni ogbon arugbo ojo. Emi ko le jakukle bi awon alailogbon. Olorun ni oluko mi. Olorun ni Oluranlowo mi. Emi ko ni di eni ti ko wulo.
- Iranlowo wa fun mi ninu Olorun. Ireti wa fun mi. Ona wa fun mi. Nko le sonu.
- Iku ki i se ipin mi. Mo je ti Olorun alaaye. Mo je alabukun fun. Haleluyah!

KOKO ADURA
ROMU 8
1. Baba, modupe fun agabra Re lati gba mi, ni oruko Jesu.
2. Modupe wipe O mo riri mi.

3. Olorun, ran mi lowo lati le gbekele ipese Re fun gbogbo isoro mi (O.D.18:32).

4. OLORUN, ran mi lowo lati le da si ise ton se daradara ninu aiye mi (Luk.2:19).

5. Olorun, dari ese mi ji, ki O si ran mi lowo lati rin bi tire (O.D.119:133).

6. IMISI EMI MIMO, fun mi ni afoju sun si oun gbogbo (IIKor .2:10).

7. Igboya Emi Mimo lati le wo gbogbo agbegbe ki nsi jogun won fun Olorun, gbe mi wo.

8. Agbara EmiMimo lati le bai se esu je, gbe mi wo ni oruko Jesu.

9. Emi ogbon, gbe mi wo lati je eni ti o wulo (Eks.28:3).

10. Pariwo, Emi Mimo ni igba mokalelogun, fi mi han oluranlowo mi ni oruko Jesu.

11. Gbogbo emi asise ti yi o da asotele duro ninu aiye mi, gbina sonu ni oruko Jesu.

12. Ifami ororo yan ogbon, eleyi ti o nfa oluranlowo, gbemi wo ni oruko Jesu.

13. Emi Mimo, gbe oun ti yi o je kin je itewogba niwaju oluranlowo wo mi.

14. Iwo emi ayeleri eleyi tin tele mi kiri, akoko re ti to, fi mi sile, ki o si s'ofo danu ni oruko Jesu.

15. Emi Mimo, kun mi fun emi ayo ni oruko Jesu.

16. Iwo pepe adura mi, gba ina titun.

17. Olorun aanu, fi ara Re han mi.

18. Majele ese ninu omi ara ati eje mi, Eje Jesu fo danu.

OJO KERIN

AWON ANGELI TI NJISE
IJEWO

- Mo ni eto si iranlowo awon angeli. Angeli je iranse mi. Angeli ni ise lati se fun mi. Awon angeli yoo mu wa si imuse ipinnu Olorun lori mi.
- Angeli a maa jise fun mi lati odo Olorun. Angeli yoo kun mi lowo loju ogun. Angeli a maa jise fun mi, awon angeli yi mi ka nigbagbogbo.
- Awon angleli a maa so ohun ini mi. Awon a maa yi ohun ini mi ka kiri. Awon angeli a maa gbo oro si mi lenu. Awon angeli a maa pese ohun ija fun mi. Awon angeli a maa gbe mi lowo won.
- Nko le fi ese mi gbun okuta. Nko le je alabapin ninu ijamba. A ko lee ji mi gbe. Nko lee ku iku aitojo.
- Awon angeli mi ko sun. Awon angeli mi ko saare; awon angeli mi ko gbabode, awon angeli mi dara. Awon angeli mi n so mi.
- Awon angeli mi yoo mu iroyin ayo wa fun mi. ki awon angeli mi so mi po mo awon

anfaani nla. Ki awon angeli mi mu gbogbo idena kuro lona mi.

- Awon angeli mi ko sonu. Awon angeli mi ko fi mi sile. Awon angeli mi ko se imele. Awon angeli mi ki i se alailagbara. Awon angeli mi ki seka.

- Awon angeli mi yoo se atona mi si ibi iranwo. Awon angeli mi yoo mu mi lo si ibi aanu. Awon angeli mi yoo to mi lo sibi iloro. Awon angeli mi yoo jeki awon eniyan yonu si mi.

- Mo gba iranlowo angeli. Mo gba awon angeli ti n sise fun mi. Mo n je anfaani iyonu latoke. Mo n je anfaani idasi latoke. Mo gba iranlowo latoke. Mo gba aranse latoke. Mo gba oore ofe.

- N ko lee sonu. A ko lee pa mi. N ko le sina. Oju ko lee ti mi. Anfaani yoo maa wa fun mi. Ona abayo yoo maa wa fun mi. Emi lee se ohun pupo nipase iranse awon angeli. Emi yoo gba gbogbo anfaani irapada mi ni kikun. Haleluyah!

KOKO ADURA
ORIN DAFIDI 68

1. OLORUN, modupe lowo Re tori wipe O lora lati binu. O si po ni aanu (O.D.145:8).

2. Ko orin nla si Olorun aanu pelu ORIN DAFIDI 89:1

3. Baba mi, Baba mi, fun mi ni emi iranse ti Jesu, Ki nba le ma se si awon elomiran gegebi O ti se.

4. Baba mi, Baba mi, ko owo mi ni ogun jija ati ika mi lati le ja kiki ogun ti O fe ki nja.

5. Oluwa, si oju mi si ibi ti mo ti padanu Re, ki O si ran mi lowo lati le pada si odo Re.

6. Oluwa, fun mi ni ore-ofe lati le tele O ninu emi ati otito.

7. Angeli Olorun, so mi po mo ibi ayanmo mi.

8. Pariwo, Olorun aanu ni igba mokanlelogun, ran angeli isopo pada saaju mi ki O si so mi po mo eni to yan fun mi (Gen.24:7).

9. Angeli iranlowo, yo simi ninu ala mi (Gen.31:11).

10. Angeli itusile, yo simi (Eks.32).

11. Angeli isipaya, farahan mi (Oniwasu 1:9).

12. Angeli iroyin ayo, farahan mi (Luk.2:10).

13. Angeli afunni lokun, yo simi ki o si sise iranse fun mi.

14. Oju to nfa iranlowo je ipin mi l'oni.

15. Gbogbo agbekale okunkun lati le pin mi lemi, tuka pelu in ani oruko Jesu.

16. Gbogbo oluranlowo ti mo yan to di okunkun ni oru lati doju ti mi, s'ofo danu ni oruko Jesu.

17. Gbogbo ohun okunkun to nse ayidayida oluranlowo ayanmo mi dake ni oruko Jesu.

18. Ko orin iyin kan si Olorun ki o sig be ga fun idahun adura re.

OJO KARUN

ORISUN IRANWO: AWON WOLI

IJEWO

- Awon woli je agbenuso Olorun, woli mi a soro alaafia sinu aye mi. woli mi a soro iye sinu aye mi, woli mi a soro ayo sinu aye mi, woli mi a soro aannu sinu aye mi. Nigbati woli mi ba gbadura fun mi, Olorun yoo gbo.

- Awon woli je eyin oju Olorun, awon woli a maa ri koja ohun afojuri, woli a maa ri nigbati ibi ba n bo, woli a maa ri nigbati ire ba n bo, woli a maa mo ohun to ye ni sise ni gbogbo igba. Woli mi yoo so ohun to ye ki n se.

- Woli mo okan Olorun, woli a maa fun ni ni itosona latorun, woli a maa mu ni de Ile Ileri, woli tooto ki i si ni lona, woli mi yoo mu mi de Ile Ileri.

- Emi ko ni soro odi si woli mi, emi ko ni fi owo yepere mu woli mi, n o maa yee woli mi si, emi yoo jere ebun woli, emi yoo gba iranlowo latodo woli mi.

- Orisun iranlowo mi ko ni gbe. A ko ni di orisun Iranlowo mi. Ota ko ni mo asiri mi.
- Woli mi yoo so ohun to ye ki n se fun mi, woli mi yoo to mi sona pelu Emi Olorun, woli mi yoo si ilekun ti a ti ti.
- Iranlowo ko ni jinna si mi. Iranlowo ko ni di awa ti ninu aye mi. Nko ni gba itiju ati egan.
- Iranlowo yoo fo ajaga idaduro ninu aye mi. Iranlowo yoo fo ajaga isinru ninu aye mi.
- Iranlowo yoo wa mi ri lati orun. Iranlowo yoo wa mi ri lati ile okeere. Iranlowo yoo je iriri mi lojoojumo.
- Nko ni jinna si iranlowo. Nko ni sina. Nko ni deni awati nibi ti ibukun mi wa. Awon omo mi yoo ri iranlowo. N ko ni padanu ohun rere lati odo Olorun. A o gbe ori mi soke. N ko ni je erunrun. Woli mi yoo duro fun mi. Emi yoo ri iranlowo.

KOKO ADURA
2OBA 3:1-21

1. Baba modupe fun iranse Re ti O mu itusile wa fun gbogbo awon aye ti o wa ninu ibode.
2. Iwo emi igberaga ati asise, mo de o ni oruko Jesu.
3. Ohun okunkun ninu ipile mi, dake ni oruko Jesu.

4. Nibo ni woli mi wa, farahan nipase aanu ni oruko Jesu (Hos.12:13).
5. So wipe ina Emi Mimo ni eemejila, yi emi ati awon omo mi ka.
6. Gbogbo panapana, akoko yin ti pari.
7. Olorun awon baba wa, si iwe iranti fun mi ni oruko Jesu (Est.6:1-3).
8. Iranlowo 'Olorun ni kan ni ogbodo je' wa mi ri nipa aanu (Mk.5:1-20).
9. Oluwa, so kekere mi di nla nipase aanu Re ni oruko Jesu. (Joh. 6:1-14).
10. Oluranlowo mi ti a ti yan ni orile-ede korilede, wa mi ri kiakia (1Kor.2:1).
11. Olorun, se mi ni eni ti o to si iranlowo ojiji (O.D.40:13).
12. OLORUN, ran mi l'owo lati le gbekele O wipe o wa pelu mi paapa julo ni akoko iji aye (Isai.43:2).
13. Ayanmo mi alarambara ti a so mo pepe okunkun, mo tu o sile nipase itoni woli (Mk.11:1-7).
14. Ifami ororoyan fun isokan san si ise iranse w ani oruko Jesu (O.D.33).
15. Bi mo ti se bere si ni gba adura ninu emi, mo gbe ina Emi Mimo titun lati le je gaba ni agbegbe mi.
16. Olorun aanu, yi itan mi pada (Mk.10:36-42).
17. Ariwo ijaya lati oke, died ki o si lepa awon to nlepa mi ni oruko Jesu (2Ki.6:24; 7:6).

18. Yin pelu orin kan (O.D.149).

OJO KEFA

ORISUN IRANWO: IRANLOWO TI KO WOPO IJEWO

- Orun mi si sile. A gbo ohun mi, awon anfaani mi di piposi. Iranlowo mi ti de. Emi ko se daduro emi kosi ni dawa.

- Itiju ki i se ipin mi. Egan ki i se ipin mi. Nko ni di eni ijakule. Nko ni padanu ibukun mi. Iranlowo ti de fun mi.

- A bukun fun mi koja egun. Mo je eni to ni buruji ju ki a fi aye su lo. Aluyo ni temi. Ko si ipadanu mo fun mi.

- Owuro mi ti de. Oru ti lo. Ayo mi ti po si. Ayo Olorun ni agbara mi.

- Oore ofe po si fun mi. Alaafia po si fun mi, ojurere po si fun mi. Emi ki i se eni akoti. Emi ki i se eni ofo.

- Olorun ti ran iranlowo si mi. Ohun to je temi ko ni di ti elomiran. Olorun mi lee se ohun gbogbo. Mo ga soke ju idaduro lo. Iranlowo ti de fun mi. O dara fun okan mi.

- Mo gba iranlowo. Mo gba iranlowo ti ko wopo. Mo gba iranlowo to sowon. Mo gba iranlowo ti a ko lee yipada. Mo gba iranlowo to se pataki.
- Emi ko dawa. Olorun wa pelu mi. Nko lee ku soju ogun. Ota ko lee bori mi. Eni ti n gbenu mi ga pupo, iranlowo mi ti de. Oluranlowo mi wa nitosi. A ko lee fi aye su mi.
- Ebun yoo maa wa fun mi nigbagbogbo. Oluwa ni Oluso Aguntan mi, emi ko ni se alaini iranlowo. Bi awon omo kinihun tile n se alailounje, Olorun yoo ba gbogbo aini mi pade. Emi n sin Olorun to po ni ohun gbogbo.
- Aye ko ni yi koja mi. Aye ko ni koro fun mi beni aye ko ni le mo mi. Emi yoo de ibi Ile Ileri mi. Emi yoo tun agbara mi se ninu Oluwa. A ko ni fi ohun to dara du mi. Haleluyah!

KOKO ADURA
ORIN DAFIDI 84

1. Ko orin kan si Oba awon oba ati Olorun awon olorun.

2. E je ki a yin oruko Olorun, tori nipas ease Re a da wa (O.D.148:5).
3. Iranlowo Olorun, farahan mi ni ibi ti n ko lero.
4. Emi Mimo, mom o wipe emi ko ni agbara ni ti ara mi lati dojuko adanwo, mo nilo Re, ran mi lowo.
5. Ran mi lowo Oluwa lati le tele idari Re (Isai.42:16).
6. Onise iranlowo ti ko wopo, wa mi ri, ati awon omo mi ni oruko Jesu.
7. Awon asiri iranderan lati odo Olorun, fi han mi Olorun.
8. Afefe ibi to nfe lodi simi, yi pada ni oruko Jesu.
9. Eje Jesu, pa ipin mi ati ayanmo mi mo ni oruko Jesu.
10. Olorun, se mi ni oun elo ti o to lati mo asiri iranlowo mi ti ko wo po.
11. Iwo agbara ile ana ti o ndi awon iranlowo mi ti ko wopo mu, tuka pelu ina.
12. Gbogbo agbara to nso aiye mi di ibudo ogun, e sofo danu ni oruko Jesu.
13. Gbogbo idena si ifami ororoyan titun, jade kuro ni aiye mi ni oruko Jesu.
14. Olorun, ran mi lowo lati le fi owo so wopo pelu ipinu Re fun aiye mi.
15. Olorun, si oju oluranlowo mi ti ko wopo si mi ni oruko Jesu.

16. Baba mi, Baba mi, so mi po mo orison iranlowo ti ko wopo.
17. Gbogbo idena emi ati oluranlowomi ti ko wopo, tuka ni oruko Jesu.
18. Gbadura ninu emi fun iseju mewa.

OJO KEJE

ORISUN IRANLOWO: AANU OLORUN

IJEWO

- Abajade oore ofe ni emi i se. Mo je oludije fun aanu. Mo je ipari ise iyonu. Mo je apere fun didara Olorun. Ayanfe Olorun ni mi. Mo je ohun elo ola.

- Oore ofe ti gbe itiju mi ninu aye mi. Iyi ti gbe itiju mi ninu aye mi. Ogo ti bo aye mi. aanu tib o asise mi mole. Aanu ti fi ewa is laala mi. O dara fun mi.

- Aanu ko jinna si mi, mo ni ajogunba rere. Mo ni majemu aanu to wa laaye. Olorun ko le paro. Olorun ko lee paro. Olorun ti soro, emi si gbagbo. Oro mi ti yanju.

- Bo se le wu ko ri, ona abayo yoo maa wa fun mi. Olorun mo ohun ti yoo se. Dafidi gba ikolo re, Esteri se gbogbo ogun re, kinihun ko je nkankan niwaju Samsoni, Mose segun Egypti.

- Ibikibi ti mo ba wa ninu aiye, aanu Olorun yoo sawari mi. Ijakkule ki i se ipin mi. N ko ni subu.
- Afonifoji ojiji iku ki i se ibudo ikeyin mi. Emi yoo jajaye. Nko ni ku. Olorun yoo saanu fun mi. Olorun yoo fi iranlowo ranse. Itan mi yoo yipada si rere.
- Emi ko ni gbe igbe aye ikabamo. Nko ni kedun lori ohunkohun. Ohun to n dun mi ninu ko ni pa ayo mi re. Olorun ko ni gba mi laaye lati gbe igbese buburu. Nko ni subu sinu koto.
- Aanu yoo soro fun mi. Aanu yoo pa idajo lenu mo. Aanu yoo pa awon alatako lenu mo, aanu yoo pa gbogbo idalebi lenu mo. Aanu yoo ma lepa mi, yio si ba mi.
- Aanu yoo yi omi ikoro mi si didun, aanu yoo maa so alaafia sinu aye mi. Rudurudu ki i se ipin mi, ijamba ki i se ipin mi.
- Mo gba kokoro iranlowo. Mo si awon ilekun iranlowo. Haleluyah!

KOKO ADURA
ORIN DAFIDI 30

1. OLORUN, modupe l'owo Re tori wipe O je alaanu ati oloore ofe.
2. Baba mi, modupe tori wipe aanu Re yi o mu mi yege ninu ogun aiye.
3. Gbogbo emi ti o je kin je alabapin ninu iwa aisotito, baje ni oruko Jesu.
4. Olorun, dari gbogbo aisododo mi ji mi ni oruko Jesu.
5. Gbogbo ihale esu ni ayika ebi mi, dawo duro lesekese ni oruko Jesu.
6. Aanu Olorun, wo ogbe mi san, ki O si wo gbogbo irora mi san ti mo ti gba nipase aijafara mi.
7. Isera eni ti mo nilo lati duro niwaju Re Olorun, fi fun mi ni oruko Jesu.
8. Olorun aanu, died ki O si ja ogun iani iranlowo yi fun mi.
9. Gbogbo eyin alase oru, akoko yin ti to, e so fo danu ni oruko Jesu.
10. Ipolongo ti yi o pe mi, jade w ani oruko Jesu.
11. Olorun, to awon omo mi ki O si ko won ni ona ti o ye ki won lo (O.D.32:8).
12. Mo yo oruko mi kuro ninu iwe akosile awon ti o ti jakule ni oruko Jesu.
13. Olorun aanu, fun mi ni iranlowo mi ibi ti ko wo po ni oruko Jesu.

14. Olorun aanu, fun mi ni iranlowo ni akoko ti mo wopo ni oruko Jesu.
15. Olorun aanu, fun mi ni iranlowo lati odo awon ti ko wopo ni oruko Jesu.
16. Baba mi, Baba mi, ran mi lowo kin le pari daradara.
17. Iyanu 'Olorun nikan ni o le je' gba laaye ki o sele ninu aiye mi ni oruko Jesu.
18. Modupe l'owo Re Olorun fun adura gbigbe ni oruko Jesu.

OJO KEJO

EREDI ATI ANFAANI IRANLOWO
IJEWO

- Nko lee da se. Mo nilo iranlowo Olorun. Olorun yoo ran mi lowo. Olorun ko ni pe.
- Mo ko iranlowo ibi. Mo ko iranlowo lati odo Satani. Mo ko iranlowo elebo, mo ko ayinike, mo ko iranra eni lowo. Mo yan iranlowo lati orun.
- Iranlowo yoo mu irin ajo mi ya. Iranlowo yoo mu ajaga mi fuye. Iranlowo yoo so aseyori mi di pupo, iranlowo yoo so ohun ti o le di riro.
- Mo gba iranlowo lakoko. Mo gba iranlowo ti ko wopo. Mo gba iranlowo to se deede, Mo

gba iranlowo to n tu ni lara. Maa gba iranlowo lai se 'yonu. Mo gba irnalowo laisi igbimo. Mo gba iranlowo laisi abamo.

- Iranlowo ko jinna si mi. Iranlowo ko sonu ninu aye mi. Ise mi gba iranlowo lakoko. Igbega mi wa nipase iranlowo.

- Iranlowo mi ti odo Oluwa wa. Ilekun iranlowo si fun mi. Odi iranlowo si fun mi. Emi ki i se eni ti aye n kaanu. Emi je eni ti aye fe dabi re. Won o fun mi ni iranlowo. Aranse yoo wa fun mi. Won so daradara nipa mi. Ati fowo soro mi.

- Mo gba ade iranlowo. Mo gba ami orororo iranlowo. Mo gba ase iranlowo. Mo gba ofin iranlowo. Iranlowo ko sowon ninu aye mi. Iranlowo wa nitosi mi.

- Ede iranlowo yoo maa wa lenu mi nigba gbogbo. Mo gba iranlowo lati irandiran. Mo gba iranlowo kaakiri agbaye, mo gba iranlowo jakejado orile-ede.

- Mo gba iranlowo itosi, mo gba iranlowo latoke wa, mo gba iranlowo lati ona jinjin, mo gba iranlowo latokeere, mo gba iranlowo lorekoore, mo gba iranlowo lati odo alejo.

- Mo gba iranlowo ninu ara, mo gba iranlowo ninu emi, mo gba iranlowo eto isuna, mo gba iranlowo lopo yanturu, mo gba iranlowo lati lo si ibi to ga ju ibi ti mo wa bayi lo, mo gba iranlowo lati di eni giga.

KOKO ADURA
ORIN DAFIDI 46

1. OLUWA, modupe tori wipe Iwo nikan ni o ye lati gba iyin mi ni oruko Jesu.
2. Baba mo yin oruko Re tori wipe akoko iranlowo mi ti bere lati oni ni oruko Jesu.
3. Omiran asise, fo jade kuro ni aiye mi ni oruko Jesu.
4. Ifami ororoyan asegun, gbemi wo ni oruko Jesu.
5. Iranlowo ti mi o fiwe pe, farahan laiye mi lesekese ni oruko Jesu.
6. Okan ti o nse idajo awon igbese ati eniyan ni tooto, gbe mi wo.
7. Iranlowo ti o gbe itiju mi, gbe mi wo ni oruko Jesu.
8. Iranlowo ti ogbe ibi ati iporuru okan mi, gbe mi wo lesekese ni oruko Jesu.
9. Olorun aanu, so mi po mo agbegbe aanu mi.
10. Iwo ojulowo aiye mi, ki londuro se ninu igbekun, jade pelu ina.
11. Iranlowo ajeji, to mi wa lojiji pelu aanu.
12. Olorun, ran mi lowo lati leje alagbara ati lati le duro de O (O.D.27:14).

13. Iranlowo ti yio je ki nrin jina, gbe mi wo lesekese ni oruko Jesu.
14. Emi adura ati isipe, ba si ori aiye mi ni oruko Jesu.
15. Emi Mimo, gbe igbe aiye adura mi wo.
16. Iwo odo iranlowo, san si inu aiye mi ni oruko Jesu.
17. Iranlowo ti mi o leto si, ba le mi ni oruko Jesu.
18. Gbadura ninu emi fun iseju mewa.

OJO KESAN
IPELE IRANLOWO: ORO OLORUN

IJEWO

- Mo ri imubosipo ninu Oro Olorun. Mo ni ireti ninu Oro Olorun. Mo ri iranlowo ninu Oro Olorun. Mo ri iloro ninu Oro Olorun. Mo ri itusile ninu Oro Olorun.

- Nigba ti mo ba ti gbo, 'bayi ni Oluwa wi', ireti mi yoo soji. Mo mo pe isele iyanu maa sele. Mo mo pe didasi lati orun yoo waye, nigbakugba ti mo ti gbo 'ma se beru', mo wipe oro mi ti pari.

- Itiju ki i se ipin mi. Egan ki i se ipin mi. Oluwa n be pelu mi. Alaafia pipe wa fun awon to ba pa oro Olorun mo, ohunkohun ko le da won laamu.

- Oro re je fitila si ese mi. Oro re je imole si ona mi, pelu oro re, emi ko le sonu. Oro eniyan lee kunna, Oro Olorun ko lee kunna. Mo ni ireti ninu Oro Re.
- Oro Olorun lagbara. Oro Olorun ni Ibukun, Oro Olorun logo. Oro Olorun ni atona.
- Oro Olorun a maa la oju afoju. Oro Olorun wuwo, Oro Olorun ni igboya mi, oro Olorun ni aala mi.
- Gegebi ejo Mose se gbe ejo Farao mi, oro Olorun ninu aye mi gbe oro ota mi. Oro Dafidi bori oro Goliati, awon ota mi ko lagbara to Olorun mi.
- Oro Olorun ki i jani kule. Agbara Oro Olorun ki i ti. Oro Olorun ko ni bo sile lofo, Oro Olorun gbe mi duro.
- Oro Olorun yoo so bi aye mi yoo se ri. Oro Olorun fun igbagbo mi ni imisi, Oro Olorun so oke mi dile, Oro Olorun mu iyi wa.
- Emi yoo bu ola fun Oro Olorun. Emi yoo se amulo Oro Olorun. Emi yoo gba Oro Olorun gbo. Emi yoo se ajoyo ninu Oro Olorun. Emi yoo fun Oro Olorun ni aaye to to ninu aye mi. Oro Olorun duro titi lae. Haleluyah!

KOKO ADURA
ORIN DAFIDI 119

1. Baba modupe tori wipe oro Re yii o sise iyanu ninu aye mi loni.
2. Ran mi lowo Oluwa, kin ba le fi igboya simi le idaniloju wipe O wa pelu mi ni gbogbo igba.
3. Baba mi, Baba mi, fun mi ni ore-ofe anfani elekeji, ni oruko Jesu.
4. Ran mi lowo kin ba le dabi Ire si ni oruko Jesu.
5. Jesu, kun aye mi fun agbara Emi re ni oruko Jesu.
6. Oluwa, ran mi lowo lati le bori iberu kii le maa ba elomiran soro nipa Re l'oruko Jesu.
7. Oluwa, je ki oro Re di pupo si ninu mi, ki eran ara mi si waale ni oruko Jesu.
8. Gbogbo onise itiju tin sise lodi simi, e yaro ni oruko Jesu.
9. Agbara aseyori ni ekunrere gbe mi wo ni oruko Jesu.
10. Mo fo gbogbo egun ijakule lori aye mi ni oruko Jesu.
11. Oluwa se mi ni eni ton se afihan eri ni oruko Re ni oruko Jesu.
12. Olorun, mu oro Re ya Kankan lati le se iyanu ni gbogbo agbegbe aye mi ni oruko Jesu.
13. Agbara ton fa iranlowo mi seyin, e s'ofo danu ni oruko Jesu.
14. Olorun fo ahun mi pelu ina Re.

15. Gbogbo eni ti o waa ni isakoso iranlowo mi, laarin ojo merinlelogun, e ma jowo re fun mi, ni oruko Jesu.

16. Ohun alatako, e panu mo ni ayika mi l'oruko Jesu.

17. Mo gba ore-ofe lati se ise ti o lere fun igbe dide mi ni oruko Jesu.

18. Gbadura ninu Emi fun isegun marundinlogun.

OJO KEWA

IPELE IRANLOWO: IRANLOWO AFINIMENI
IJEWO

- A ko le faye su mi. A ti fi mi mo orisun iranlowo, nko le di eni ti ko rona lo. A ti fi mi mo orisun iranlowo, a ko le ru mi loju. A ti mu mi mo orisun iranlowo.

- Iranlowo wa fun mi. Mo gba iranlowo lati ibi giga, mo gba iranlowo lati ibi ti a ko wopo. Mo gba iranlowo lati odo angeli, mo gba iranlowo eniyan, owo ti n ranni lowo ni a na si mi.

- Emi ko si atimole, emi ko si ninu ahamo, emi ko si ninu igbekun, iranlowo wa fun mi ninu Olorun, Olorun ti si orun fun mi, oluranlowo mi wa nitosi mi, oluranlowo ti wa mi ri.

- Ilekun iranlowo ti si fun mi, mo rin wonu ipele iranlowo tuntun, ferese iranlowo di sisi fun mi, gbogbo awon to fe ran mi lowo yoo ri mi, iranlowo loniruuru ona yoo maa wa fun mi.
- Mo gba iranlowo to bo si deede, mo gba iranlowo latodo Olorun, Mo gba iranlowo arowoto, mo gba iranlowo ni kikun, mo gba iranlowo itura.
- Olorun yoo lana fun mi nibiti ko ti si ona, emi ko sonu, a ran mi lowo, emi ki i se eni ti ko ri anfaani gba, a ran mi lowo.
- Eru mi fuye nitori oluranlowo mi ti ran mi lowo, a ti mu awon idiwo mi kuro, oluranlowo mi ti ran mi lowo, a ti gbe oke mi kuro nitori oluranlowo mi ti ran mi lowo.
- Iranlowo ni iyonu ti n mu aye derun, aye mi ko ni nira. Iranlowo ni atileyin ti n mu irin ya, aye mi ko ni fa seyin; emi yoo si tesiwaju ninu aye, emi yoo ri ojurere gba lopolopo.
- Itiju ni fun awon ti n pegan mi. Itiju ni fun awon to ro mi pin. Itiju ni fun awon ti won ti ilekun kan mo mi nitori pe Olorun yoo si ilekun pupo fun mi. Mo ni anfaani lopolopo. Halleluyah!
- O dara fun okan mi. Ori ni mo je. Emi ki i se iru. Emi ti Olorun Alaaye. Mo ti ri iranlowo!

KOKO ADURA
ORIN DAFIDI 89

1. Ko orin kan si Olorun ti ko se bi leere.
2. Olorun ran mi lowo lati le da iwalaye ati ifowokan Re mo laarin awon oun ti onn deru bami.
3. Olorun, mu ki eto akosile ayanmo mi sare, ni oruko Jesu.
4. Olorun yi gbogbo egan aye mi pada ni oruko Jesu.
5. Olorun, se itoni igbese mi ki o si to gbogbo igbese mi ti mo gbe ni oruko Jesu.
6. Je ki ogo Re bo gbogbo awon omo mi mole ni oruko Jesu.
7. Gbogbo omo esu ti o joko si aga awon omo mi, yikuro ni oruko Jesu.
8. Baba mi, Baba mi, se iribomi ojurere ti kowopo fun mi ni oruko Jesu.
9. Olorun, je ki gbogbo eto mi ni ibi ise mi wa mi ri ni oruko Jesu.
10. Olorun, so ogbon gbogbo awon alatako mi di ope ni oruko Jesu.
11. Igbega mi latoke, wa mi ri pelu aanu ni oruko Jesu.
12. Mo gba ore-ofe lati gba oju rere niwaju oga mi ni oruko Jesu.
13. Baba mi, Baba mi, fi ipinu Re latoke wa han mi ni oruko Jesu.
14. Iranlowo Oluwa ti o gbe ikosile mi, ba le mi ni oruko Jesu.

15. Mo ja gbogbo emi eru ninu mi ni oruko Jesu.

16. Oluwa, mu mi wa si ojurere nla pelu gbogbo awon ti yo pinu lori oro mi ni oruko Jesu.

17. Olorun, si oju mi lati le mo bi mo se maa sise lori ailera ti oun sise lodi si ayanmo mi.

18. Gba adura fun iseju mewa.

OJO KOKANLA

IPELE IRANLOWO: IRANLOWO IGBADEGBA
IJEWO

- Olorun mi ko ni odiwon, emi ko ni wo lule. Olorun mi to fun mi, emi ko lee se alaini, Olorun opo yanturu ni Olorun mi, nitorinaa owon ki i se ipin mi. Olorun mi lee se ohun gbogbo, emi ko lee padanu ohun to dara.

- Emi je oludije fun iranlowo, mo wa fun iranlowo, emi yoo maa ri eni ti yoo ran mi lowo, mo ti ri eso iranlowo, emi ko lee se alaini ohun ti o dara. Akoko ikore mi ti to, mo ti setan fun Ibukun.

- A ko ni fi mi sawati nibiti o ye ki n wa. N ko ni sonu nibi ti mo ti wulo. A ko ni bo mi mole nibiti o ye ki won ti ri mi, orun mi si.

- Kosi ohun ti o lee da eri mi duro. Emi je ori, emi ki i se onigbese, n ko ni poora, n ko ni padanu ipo mi. Emi ko ni ku.

- Ajoyo mi yoo maa posi. Aseyori mi yoo po, orin ope mi yoo lo soke pupo, kosi ohun ti yoo tu ohun ti mo ti kojo ka. Mo wa labe ojiji Olodumare.

- Mo wa larowoto iranlowo. Mo wa nitosi oluranlowo mi. Oju oluranlowo mi ko ni fo. Oluranlowo mi ko ni ku iku ojiji.

- A ran mi lowo lowuro, a o ran mi lowo losan, a ran mi lowo lale, a o ran mi lowo lojoojumo.

- Olorun yoo pa awon alatako mi lenu mo. Oluranlowo mi ko ni ba awon ota mi pade, ko ni si alatako fun ebun iranlowo mi. Oni je ojo oore ofe.

- Ohun to soro fun eniyan je irorun fun Olorun, agbara Olorun lee sawari ohun ti o ti sonu, mo je anfaani agbara iranlowo, mo je anfaani iranlowo to wa nitosi. Nko ni jakule. Haleluyah!

- Iranlowo yio fohun fun mi. iranlowo yio si ilekun titun fun mi. iranlowo yio mu mi lo si ipo to kan. Iranlowo yio bo asise mi mole. Asise ki yio bai se mi je. Iranlowo yio fun mi ni anfaani titun. Haleluya!

344

KOKO ADURA
ORIN DAFIDI 118:1

1. Baba, modupe tori wipe Iwo ni Olorun ati wipe aanu Re wa titi lae   (O.D.118:1)
2. Ko orin kan lati yin Gbongbo Idile Jesse.
3. Olorun, joba ninu okan mi, ki elomiran le ri O ninu mi.
4. Ran mi lowo lati le gba adura pelu otito fun awon ti ko'ti mo O.
5. Oluwa, gba mi l'owo ijegbaba eran ara.
6. Aki yio pa oruko mi re kuro ninu iwe iye ni oruko Jesu.
7. Gbogbo ofa asini l'okan kuro ni ibi adura, pada sori eni ti o ta o ni oruko Jesu.
8. Olorun, je ki gbogbo agbegbe aye mi ti o nilo akiyesi, di agbegbe eri mi ni oruko Jesu (O.D.2:1-5).
9. Olorun, fagile gbogbo adehun pelu iku ni aye mi, ni oruko Jesu.
10. Gbe oun soke lati ja fun mi, ni gbogbo ibi ti a tin se ipinu lori oro mi ni oruko Jesu. (Ise.5:33-40).
11. Baba mi, Baba mi, yi aye mi ka pelu oluranlowo ayanmo (Luk.8:1-3).
12. Olorun, kun mi pelu oun ti yio je kin di itewogba niwaju oluranlowo mi   (I Sam 16:18).

13. Gbogbo agbara ti onn lo aworan mi lati gbogun ti awon oluranlowo mi, sofo danu ni oruko Jesu.

14. Gbogbo atako lodi si oluranlowo mi, tuka ni oruko Jesu.

15. Mo ko iranlowo abo ni oruko Jesu.

16. Gbogbo ibi ti ase lodi simi ni ojo isomo l'oruko mi eleyi ti onn yo itesiwajumi lenu, e wa si opin ni oruko Jesu.

17. Gbogbo alatako si iranlowo deede mi, tuka ni oruko Jesu.

18. Gbadura ninu Emi fun Iseju maarundinlogun.

OJO KEJILA
IPELE IRANLOWO: IRANLOWO IBI

IJEWO

- Dafidi pa Yuraya tori pe o fe ran ara re lowo, Sara gba Abramu niyanju lati ran Olorun lowo, eyi si ko sinu idaamu, Rebeka ran Jakobu lowo lati tan Isaki lati ja Isau lole. Iranlowo ibi ki i se iranlowo. Iranlowo ibi yio mu idalebi wa. Iranlowo ibi yio mu iparun wa. Iranlowo ibi ko ni ojo ola.

- Mo ko iranlowo Satani. Mo ko iranlowo emi esu, mo ko iranlowo ti ko ti odo Olorun wa, mo ko aba ibi, mo ko iranlowo ti n mu

346

idaamu wa, kosi ohun ti yoo ba ise mi je, kosi ohun ti yoo ba ipe mi je.

- Emi yoo duro niwaju Oluwa, Oun yoo si ran mi lowo. Egbe ni fun awon to lo si Egypiti fun iranlowo nitoriti esin ko ni le sare, emi ko ni wa iranlowo nibiti ko ye, emi yoo duro de Oluwa.

- Saulu lo si odo aje Endo, o pada pelu idalebi, Woli kekere to gba iranlowo Wolii agba di eni ti kinihun faya. Egun ni iranlowo ti ko ba ti wa lati odo Olorun.

- Emi ko iranlowo odi, Olorun ni agbara ti o to lati ran mi lowo. Ohun ti Olorun ko ba ti ni se fun mi, nise ni ko duro. 'RARA' Olorun te mi lorun ju 'BEENI' Satani lo. Emi ko lee padanu anfaani mi.

- Iranlowo mi ti odo Olorun wa, eniti o da orun oun aye. Olorun mi ki i pe. Bi o tile je wipe Lasaru ku fun ojo merin, nigba ti Jesu de, okiki Lasaru kan kaakiri gbogbo ilu.

- Kosi itiju ninu pipe ki ire to de. Olorun n ko mi ni suuru ati ifarada ni. O dara fokan mi. Mo ko iranlowo odi.

- Nko ni padanu anfaani mi fun idasi lati orun. Adamu ati Efa kabamo igbese won nikeyin. Iranlowo Satani ti won gba fi won sile lofo. Won padanu ohun ti won ko le ri pada.

- Iranlowo Olorun wa fun mi. Emi yoo duro de akoko mi. Gegebi Jobu, emi yoo dide pada.

KOKO ADURA
ISAIAH 31

1. Ko bi orin iyin meje si Olorun.
2. Baba, Ese ti E fi owo kan oju mi lati ri ipele tuntun ti E tun nmumi lo.
3. Gbogbo adawole ti mo ti pa ti saaju akoko yi, bere ise pelu aanu, ni oruko Jesu.
4. Olorun, modupe fun agbara lati doju ko ojo ola laisi iberu.
5. Mo gba ore-ofe lati rin ninu ogbon pelu gbogbo eniyan.
6. Gbogbo idekun ti o farajo iranlowo ni ayika awon omo mi, eje Jesu gbe mi, ni oruko Jesu (Isa.18:21).
7. Gbogbo ibasepo odi ti o so mi po pelu iranlowo okunkun, mo ja ara mi kuro pelu agbara ajinde ni oruko Jesu.
8. Iwo emi ope ati eti didi emi, so agabara re nu lori aye mi ni oruko Jesu.
9. Mo gba iranlowo lati oke ati isopo ti yio ran aye mi lowo, fun rere ni oruko Jesu.
10. Mo ja ara mi gba kuro ni gbogbo orisun iranlowo odi ni oruko Jesu.

11. Gbogbo agbara ton ba mi ja lori ini mi, e parun ni oruko Jesu.

12. Olorun, ko owo mi ni ogun jija, ati ika mi ni ija, kin ba le gba ini mi pada.

13. Gbogbo agadagodo agbara okunkun ti o ti so mi mole si oju kan, fo pelu ina ni oruko Jesu.

14. Gbogbo onfa ajoji eleyi ti on fa mi lo si ibi iranlowo odi ati oluranlowo odi, e di asan pelu eje Jesu.

15. Mo pase fun aye ati oun gbogbo ti o wa ninu re, ki o fi owo so owo po pelu mi ni oruko Jesu.

16. Je ki gbogbo enu bode okunkun ti o ti ti mi jade kuro ninu ipin mi si lesekese ni oruko jesu.

17. Agbara lati bori ninu ogun ayanmo gbe mi wo ni oruko Jesu.

OJO KETALA

IPELE IRANLOWO: IRANLOWO NI KIAKIA/IRANLOWO WAKATI KOKANLA

IJEWO

- Iranlowo wa fun mi, orun iranlowo si sile fun mi. Mo ni iranlowo pataki. Awon ohun ti mo se alaini ko le gbe mi mi, oluranlowo mi wa nitosi mi.

- Emi ko ni idaduro, a ko fi ohun ti mo nilo du mi, a ko si di mi lowo. Emi ko sina. won ko le faye su mi, emi ki yio le e le.

- Ororo iranlowo n san si mi lori. Gbogbo oke ko seese ni a ti bori, gbogbo awon ota ilosiwaju ti gba ere itiju, oro temi ko lo buru ju. Mo gba iranlowo ni kia kia. Mo gba iranlowo ologeere.

- Dafidi gba iranlowo ni kia kia, ko ku soju ogun bi o tile je pe o ti re, o ku die ki Solomoni padanu ori ite re amo Woli Natani ran lowo, Mordecai o ba ti ku, amo Esteri ran lowo. Iranlowo je ipin mi.

- Iranlowo ko jinna si mi. Eniti n ran mi lowo wa nitosi. Awon ohun gbogbo to je temi n wa sodo mi boti ye. Mo ni ajogunba rere.

- Mo gba iranlowo nipa eto isuna ni kiakia, Mo gba imoran ni kiakia, Mo gba iranlowo ni kiakia niti ero okan. Oluranlowo mi, nibo lo wa? Wa mi ri loni!

- Gbogbo owo ti a ko ri to n mu iranlowo mi kiakia dani, oya jona danu!

- Oluwa ti pe oruko mi, iranlowo ko ni jinna si mi. Mo je oludije fun iranlowo. Mo wa ni arowoto fun iranlowo.

- Emi ko ni padanu iranlowo kiakia mi. Mo ko lati maa kedun. Mo ko lati padanu anfaani mi. Nko lee padanu ohun ti o se pataki fun mi.

- Iranlowo yoo bo asise me. Iranlowo yoo bu ewa kun aye mi. Olorun yoo so kekere ti mo ni di pupo. Olorun yoo lana fun mi. Ko si idi fun mi lati se ofo. Iranlowo wa fun mi. Orun iranlowo si sile fun mi. Haleluya!

KOKO ADURA
ORIN DAFIDI 94

1. Oluwa, mo dupe wipe E ka mi ye lati je olugbe agbara Re wo.
2. Olorun, mo dupe tori wipe ipinu Re lati oke ju ala mi lo.
3. Ojurere lati oke, fi afikun ninu oun gbogbo ti mo ba se, gbe mi wo lesekese ni oruko Jesu.
4. Afojusun ti ko wopo ati idari deede ti Emi MImo, gbe wo mi ni oruko Jesu.
5. Asiri okunkun ni ibi ise, tu fun mi pelu aanu ojo ni oruko Jesu.
6. Olorun Ojo Aanu, ma je ki ota ki o pa awon omo mi, ki won ma baa le pami lenu mo, ni oruko Jesu.
7. Iwo adigunjale ti oju ala, ina Emi Mimo fi so fo ni oruko Jesu.
8. Oun gbogbo ti o wa ninu mi ti oun ti mi si asise, eje Jesu ti won jade.
9. Pe Olorun aanu ni igba mesan, ki osi so wipe ran angeli wakati kokanla si mi, ni oruko Jesu.

10. Iwo enu ibode ati odi Jericho, subu lule fun mi, lati le wo'nu waakati kokanla iranlowo mi, ni oruko Jesu.

11. Iwo ese mi gbo oun Olorun, ooni dari mi lo si inu iparun ni oruko Jesu.

12. Olorun o, ijo re kuro ninu orun Emi ni oruko Jesu.

13. Ile, Iwo ile, yon da asokun re fun mi ni oruko Jesu.

14. Ase fun iranlowo kiakia, wo inu aye mi ni oruko Jesu.

15. Olorun, je kin tayo ni oruko Jesu.

16. Gbogbo ami ikosile ti a ko si iwaju ori mi, di fifo danu ni oruko Jesu.

17. Gbadura ninu Emi fun iseju mewa.

OJO KERINLA
IPELE IRANLOWO: IRANLOWO TI KO SISE

IJEWO

- Mo ko awon olutunininu iponju, mo ko aanu ti ko denu, Mo ko atileyin ti ko fese mule. Mo ko ileri etan. Mo ko ibasepo etan.

- Mo gba iranlowo latoke. Mo gba iranlowo lati oke okun, mo gba iranlowo ninu orile-ede, mo gba iranlowo kaakiri agbaye, mo gba iranlowo ti emi, mo gba iranlowo ti ara. Iranlowo wa fun mi. Halleyah!

- Ohun to soro fun eniyan, o seese fun Olorun. Oro temi ko lo buru ju. Ireti si wa fun mi, Olorun dara si mi. Olorun ti pese awon ohun ti mo ni lo fun mi.

- Iwo lee ri iranlowo Olorun nigba gbogbo. Olorun ti si awon ile iranlowo, emi yoo gbadura fun iranlowo, Emi yoo wa iranlowo. N ko ni ni ijakule.

- Ororo iranlowo n san si ori mi. Emi yoo furugbin eso iranlowo. Emi yoo kore iranlowo.

- Ko si nkan to nse ayanmo mi, ko si nkan to nse orile-ede mi, oluranlowo mi ko sonu, ori mi o gbe, mo ko iranlowo ti ko wulo.

- Olorun wa nibi gbogbo nitori naa iranlowo wa nibi gbogbo. Emi ko ni se alaini iranlowo, nigbakugba ti mo ba beere iranlowo, emi yoo ri iranlowo gba, ki n to beere, ilekun yoo si.

- Ikorira le tilekun, iranlowo yoo si i. Ilara lee tilekun, iranlowo yoo si. Isoroeni leyin nibi le tilekun, iranlowo yoo si. Emi ko ni se alaini iranlowo.

- Mo je asepe ise iranlowo, mo wa ninu ipinnu Olorun fun iranwo, emi ki yio w ani gbendeke, emi ko ni so ohun to wulo nu.

- Itijju ki i se ipin mi. Egan ki i se ipin mi. Emi ko le poora. A ko le gbe mi mi. Ijakule ki i se ipin mi. Nko ni fi tipatipa gbe ile aye. Itiju ba eyin ota mi. Emi je omoloju Olorun. Haleluyah!

KOKO ADURA
ORIN DAFIDI 107

1. Olorun modupe wipe E gbami laye lati je alabapin ninu ise Re laye.
2. Oluwa, fun mi ni igboya lati je alabapin ninu ise re laye.
3. Olorun ran mi lowo lati le gbekele otito oro re nigba ti o le fun mi lati mo riri iwalaaye Re.
4. Baba mi, fun mi ni okun ti Emi lati le tako ese atimaba ibasepo mi pelu re ati awon elomiran ni oruko Jesu.
5. Isele konireti, aini iranlowo, ko eru re kuro ninu aye mi ni oruko Jesu.
6. Ofa ijakule ti a ta lodi simi pada sori eni ti o ta o ni oruko Jesu.
7. Iwo emi mi, ki lonse ninu tubu ota, jade pelu ina.
8. Eleyameya ti o le mu kin padanu oluranlowo, wa si opin lesekese ni oruko Jesu.

9. Ofa ijakule ti a ta lodi si aye mi pada sori eni ti o ta o ni oruko Jesu.

10. Abanilorukoje ton sise iba mije niwaju oluranlowo mi, pade ijakule lono meji loruko Jesu.

11. Olorun je ki ayo ropo ekun ti ayan fun mi ni oruko Jesu.

12. Iwo emi akitiyan alailere ti a yan lodi si ori mi e so fo daanu ni oruko Jesu.

13. Olorolowo ti ojina, aye mi wani ipese sile fun o wa mi ri ni oruko Jesu.

14. Angeli Olorun, pase fun oluranlowo mi, ki o sare wa si odo mi lesekese ni oruko Jesu.

15. Iranlowo ayederu lati odo awon ti ko to, tuka pelu in ani oruko Jesu.

16. Abogbo iranlowo ti yi o yori si ekun, epare ni oruko Jesu.

OJO KEEDOGUN
RIRAN OLORUN LOWO
IJEWO

- Emi ko ni ba ilana ise mi je. Nko ni ba ipe mi je. Nko ni ba anfaani ti mo ni lati gba iranlowo latoke je. Abramu gbiyanju lati ran Olorun lowo, ko gba idalare fun igbese yi.

- Emi yoo duro de Oluwa; nipa bee yoo so agbara mi dotun. Emi yoo gba ohun to dara ju ti Olorun ti pese sile fun mi. A o fun mi ni igboya. Nko ni so ireti nu. Mo ko iranlowo ajoji.

- Ologbun ni Oluwa. Jagunjagun ni Oluwa. Oluwa ni Alagbara Julo. Olorun ni o gbon julu, kosi opin si agbara Re. Mo sinmi le Oluwa.

- Emi ko ni sare koja Olorun. N ko ni padanu akoko mi. Awon omo mi yoo wa lakoko ti Olorun ti yan. Igbeyawo yoo wa lakoko ti Olorun ti yan. Iwe igbega yoo de.

- Akoko Olorun ni o dara ju. Kosi abamo ninu aye mi. Nko ni ni ibanuje nigba ti mo ba n duro. Nipase diduro de Oluwa, aye mi yoo dara si.

- Irin ajo mi ko ni pari lojiji. N o sare ije mi pelu suuru. N ko ni gba ona eburu. N ko ni wa atileyin ibi. N ko ni wa aranse buburu, n ko ni gba iranwo ti ko mo. Ohun ti Olorun yoo se fun mi yoo dara pupo.

- Awon to gbiyanju lati ran Olorun lowo ni ibanuje won posi. Akoko ti a fi duro ki i se akoko ti a fi sofo. Akoko iduro je akoko imurasile.

- Olorun gbon ju mi lo. Emi yoo re ara mi sile niwaju Olorun; Oun yoo si ran mi lowo.

- Awon miran a maa ran Olorun won lowo; Olorun won ko lagbara. Olorun won nilo won, won n gbe Olorun won, won n ja fun

Olorun won. Olorun won ko wulo, Olorn won ko mona ko si lee se nkankan.

- Olorun mi wa laaye. O ran mi lowo. Olorun mi lagbara. O n gbe mi. Olorun mi wulo. Olorun mi lee se ohun pupo, Olorun mi wulo, Olorun mi gbon. Olorun ko le paro. Olorun ki i pe. Olorun yoo mu mi posi nigba gbogbo. Haleluyah!

KOKO ADURA
ORIN DAFIDI 115

1. Oluwa, modupe lowo Re fun alafia Re ti ko se fi enu so ti o fifun mi.
2. Korin titun kan si Olorun oga oggo julo.
3. Gba ase lori ifarahan iwa ipa, oogun oloro, iyale ati awon ifarahan okunkun ni ayika re ni oruko Jesu.
4. Mo ko beni emi o fe gbogbo ijewo odi lori gbogbo awon omo mi l'oruko Jesu.
5. Emi Mimo pin awon omo mi niya pelu awon afi akoko eni sofo l'oruko Jesu.
6. Lowo gbogbo eru ojo ola, mo tu awon omo mi sile pelu eje Jesu.
7. Emi Mimo, ran mi lowo kii maba pari ere ije ti mo bere ninu emi sinu ara.
8. Gbogbo iranse idojuti ti o nsise lodi si awon omo mi, e yaro l'oruko Jesu.

9. Mo yonda ayanmo awon omo mi Oluwa, gba ise se ni oruko Jesu.

10.Gbogbo pakute ti a de sile fun mi ni ibi ise mi, mu eni ina ti o de o sile ni oruko Jesu.

11.Emi Mimo mu asotele aye mi ya kankan pelu ina ni oruko Jesu.

12.Ororo isipe, aye wa ni ipese fun o gbe mi wo nisinsinyi l'oruko Jesu.

13.Ina Emi Mimi mu asotlele aye mi mo ni oruko Jesu.

14.Mo gba gbogbo Ibukun mi eleyi ti a pamo sinu ile iso okunkun pada ni oruko Jesu.

15. Mo dariji gbogbo eni ti o se mi ni ona kan tabi omiran ni oruko Jesu.

16. Mo gba ore-ofe lati fi gbongbo ati ese mule ninu Kristi ni oruko Jesu.

17. Oluwa, fun minioakn omo leyin ni oruko Jesu.

18. Gbadura ninu emi fun iseju marundinlogun.

OJO KERINDINLOGUN

IRANLOWO TI A KO FOJURI: IRANLOWO LATOKE

IJEWO

- A ti bi mi ninu emi. Ati ipa eso aidibaje bi mi. A bi mi ninu Oro Olorun. A bi mi ninu Emi Ayeraye.
- Agbara ko lee padanu okun. Agbara Olorun n sise ninu aye mi. A daabo bo mi pelu agbara Olorun. Mo niye pupo si Olorun.
- Mo je ohun oso to niye pupo lowo Olorun. Mo je eni ti a kaye ninu eto Olorun. Mo ninu okan Olorun, a ti ko mi si ateleowo Olorun. Ohunkohun ko lee mi mi. A bi mi ninu ogo.
- Eniyan to se pataki pupo ni mi. A ti fi pamo sinu Kristi Jesu. Emi ko ku, mo wa laaye ninu Olorun. Igbe aye Olorun sise lara mi. Mo ga ju idibaje lo. Haleluyah!
- Ohun otun yoo sele si mi, ohun atijo ti koja lo. Mo mo eni ti mo je, mo je omoloju Olorun. Mo je aya (Jesu) to lewa. Mo je omo ogun Oluwa. Mo je ara Re.
- Iranlowo ko jinna si mi. Iranlowo lona kan tabi omiran yoo wa fun mi. N ko lee sina. N ko lee sonu.
- Olorun lee lana nibi ti ko sona. Olorun lee so egungun to ti doku di alaaye. Ko tii tan fun mi.
- Ireti wa fun igi ti a ge nigba ti gbongbo re ba si wa ninu ile. Ti o ba ti fara kan omi, yoo tun so pada. Mo ni ireti to wa laaye. Mo wa laaye.

- Aja to wa laaye dara ju kinihun to ti ku. Awon ota mi ko lee bori mi. Mo ni ajogunba daradara.
- Ohun to n sise fun mi tobi ju ohun to n sise lodi si mi. Mo ni anfaani ninu Olorun, mo wa ni ipele to ga. Haleluyah!

KOKO ADURA
ORIN DAFIDI 121

1. Modupe lowo Re pe o ka mi ye lati je olugbe agbara re lati oke.
2. Modupe Olorun, fun anfani ati agbara lati di omo Olorun.
3. Modupe lowo re fun ise iwosan ti O ran si mi.
4. Mo gba ore-ofe lati je atokun alafia ninu ara Kristi.
5. Oluwa, ko mi bi a tise ngadura si Emi Mimo.
6. Olorun, to isise mi si odo eni ti o nilo ireti ti oti odo emi nikan wa.
7. Oluwa, ran mi lowo lati kuro ninu ise ti ewe bo sinu ijinle ti emi.
8. Oluwa, si oju mi si awon Ohun ti o jinle ni ayika mi loruko Jesu.

9. Mo gba ore-ofe lati ni isinmi lori ohun gbogbo gegebi ti eiye idi l'oruko Jesu.
10. Gbogbo ibasepo ti ko ni ran mi lowo lati mu ayanmo se wa sopin l'oruko Jesu.
11. Baba mi, Baba mi jeki iwalaye Re to mi ni gbogbo odun yi.
12. Iranlowo lati oke be emi ati awon omo mi wo ni oruko Jesu.
13. Iwo emi abalaye ti o joko lori aluyo mi tuka pelu ina.
14. Oluwa, yi gbogbo egun afowofa mi pada si ibukun ni oruko Jesu.
15. Esu ki yio ko iwe ti o gbeyin lori awon omo mi l'oruko Jesu.
16. Mo gba iranlowo lati oke fun aseyori gbogbo ise ti Olorun yan fun mi lati dawole ni oruko Jesu.
17. Jowo, gbadura ninu Emi fun ogun iseju.

OJO KETADINLOGUN

IRANLOWO OKUNKUN
IJEWO

- Mo ko iranlowo emi okunkun, mo ko iranlowo ajeji. Mo ko iranlowo to je ikekun. Awon to ran Absalomu lo ko ba a.

- Olorun mi to lati ran mi lowo. Olorun mi kunjuwon. Olorun mi wa nitosi. Olorun mi ti seleri lati ranmi lowo.

- N ko lee se Olorun nigba ti mo ba wa ninu aini. Ti O ba tile so pe beeko, o temi lorun. BEEKO Olorun dara ju BEENI esu lo. Emi yoo duro de Olorun. Mo ko iranlowo Satani.

- Saulu lo ba abokusoro fun iranlowo, o pada pelu ibanuje ati iporuuru okan. Ni igbeyin o padanu ite ati aye re.

- Ohunkohun ti Olorun ba fun eniyan o dara. Ibukun Olorun ki i mu laalaa wa. Ibukun Olorun a maa mu alaafia wa.

- Egbe ni fun awon to gbekele eniyan. Ohun ti o dara ju ti eniyan se, ti eniyan naa ni. Emi yoo di nla.

- Olorun ti pese ohun to dara julo fun mi. Olorun ti pari oro mi ki a to fi ipinle aye sole.

- Emi yoo ri igbala Oluwa. Emi yoo ri ire Oluwa ni ile alaaye.

- Olorun ko ni je ki oju olododo ri ibaje. Ireti wa fun mi. Iranlowo wa fun mi.

- Olorun lee la ona nibi ti ko sona. Ohun to le fun eniyan se seese fun Oluwa. Emi yoo duro de Oluwa. Ibukun ni fun awon to duro nitori won ko ni ri ijakule. Haleluyah!

KOKO ADURA
ORIN DAFIDI 116

1. Ko orin iyin kan.
2. Oluwa, dariji mi fun aini suru de o.
3. Oluwa, dariji mi fun aisin o gege bi mo ti deje.
4. Ohun gbogbo ti o wa ninu mi, eleyi ti o ntimi lati ma se asise, poora ni oruko Jesu.
5. Gbogbo ebun Emi Mimi ti o ti farasin ninu mi, soji nisisiyi l'oruko Jesu.
6. Gbogbo iranlowo okunkun eleyi tii o ja mi lole ogo, mo pinya pelu re nipase aanu.
7. Lowo gbogbo ogun ti o ni agbara ofin lori mi, gbami o Olorun aanu.
8. Asiri odale ti o nse bi ore ni ayika awon omo mi, tu ni oruko Jesu.
9. Pariwo, Olorun aanu ni igba mokanlelogun ki o si wipe: gbami lowo iranlowo okunkun ni oruko Jesu.
10. Adura ti ayanmo mi nilo, Oluwa fi han mi nipase aanu.
11. Majemu aanu, fe gbogbo kurukuru itiju danu lori aye mi.
12. Akoko buburu ki yio bori akoko rere ninu ye mi l'oruko Jesu.
13. Lati inu pakute iranlowo buburu, Olorun aanu tu mi sile l'oruko Jesu.

14. Mo pase fun ojulowo eto Olorun ki o fi idi mule ninu aye awon omo mi l'oruko Jesu.

15. Ipile mi, gba iwosan fun eri Olorun ni oruko Jesu.

16. Fun iseju marundinlogun gbadura ninu Emi.

OJO KEJIDINLOGUN
KIKIGBE FUN IRANLOWO
IJEWO

- Olorun mi ki i se Olorun ti o diti. Yoo gbo igbe mi fun iranlowo. Oju Oluwa n rin kaakiri agbaye ti o si n fi ara re han gegebi alagbara si awon ti okan won se deede pelu Re. Nko ni kigbe lasan.

- Iranlowo mi wa latodo Oluwa; eniti o da orun ohun aye. Nigba ti ekun mi ba de orun, orun mi yoo si.

- Kosi itiju lati kigbe fun iranlowo. Nigba ti Peteru kigbe fun iranlowo, Jesu gba a la kuro ninu riri omi. Nigba ti Samoni kigbe fun iranlowo, irun ori re wu pada, nigba ti Elisha kigbe fun iranlowo, o gba ewu ileke, nigba ti mo ba kigbe, emi yoo gba ini mi.

- Kikigbe je ona lati gbadura, kikigbe je ami irele, kikigbe je ona ifaraeniji, kikigbe je ona iwopale.

- Olorun a ma fun awon onirele okan ni ere. Olorun a maa lo ohun elo ti awo pale.

364

Olorun a maa feti si alaini. Nigba ti emi ba kigbe, Oluwa n gbo.

- Akoko mi ko ti i tan. Oro mi ki i se eyi to buru ju. Orun ko ti mo mi. Olorun ko binu si mi. Igbagbo mi yoo sise fun mi.
- A gbo igbe Bartimeu oju re si la. A gbo igbe obinrin Sirofenikia, omobinrin re si gba iwosan. Olorun ko lee ko ekun atokanwa. Olorun ko lee ko ekun gidi. Ekun mi si Oluwa je ami omo tooto. Haleluyah!
- Itiju kosi ninu kikigbe fun iranlowo. O je amin igbagbo, Olorun a si maa bowo fun gbigbabo. Igbe ninu igbagbo je igbe ti n mi orun.
- Olorun feran omode, ijoba Olorun si wa fun awon to ni okan bi omode. Awon omode a maa sunkun fun iranlowo nigba gbogbo. Olorun ki i gbeti kuro ninu ekun awon tire.
- Okan lara oriki Olorun ni **OLURANLOWO NLA ISRAELI**. Olorun je Baba, oun si ni baba mi. Nigba ti mo ba kigbe, Baba mi to tobi ju yoo dahun.

KOKO ADURA
ORIN DAFIDI 60
1. Yin Oluwa pelu orin kan.
2. Oluwa o, fo ahan mi pelu ina.

3. Oluwa o, so mi di eni tin fi ami han ni oruko Jesu.

4. Gbogbo agbara ti n sun aluyo siwaju, sofo pelu ina ni oruko Jesu.

5. Oluwa o, jeki ibeere mi pade ojurere lodo olore mi.

6. Pariwo Olorun aanu ni igba mokanlelogun, so mi po mo awon ti o ni oun ti mo nilo ati awon ti o nilo ohun ti mo ni, ni oruko Jesu.

7. Oluranlowo akako wa mi ri pelu aanu.

8. Sekeseke igbekun ti a kojo lodi si awon omo mi fo pelu ina.

9. Orun mi ti o si fun iranlowo, farahan pelu aanu.

10. Olorun o, je ki ibugbe awon ota mi di ahoro ni oruko Jesu.

11. Oluwa, ran mi lowo lati ma mu ogbon jade kuro ninu ohun gbogbo ti mo ba la koja laye.

12. Mo gba ore-ofe lati fi gbile ninu Kristi.

13. Oluwa, fun mi ni okan omo lehin.

14. Aye bi ti Josefu, a mu lati inu tubu lo si aafin iranlowo ti yio mu mi lati inu tubu lo si aafin gbe mi wo ni oruko Jesu.

15. Gbogbo eto ibi ota lodi si ijo Olorun sofo danu ni oruko Jesu.

16. Fun iseju ogun si isinyi, gbadura ninu Emi.

OJO KOKANDINLOGUN

IDIWO SI IRANWO: ESE

IJEWO

- Ododo a maa gbe orile-ede leke, sugbon ese ni egan orile-ede.
- Nko ni gba ese laaye lati ba ise owo mi je. Emi ko ni tele ogunlogo lati se ibi. Emi ko ni duro ni awujo awon elegan.
- Emi yoo sunkun niwaju Oluwa fun aluyo mi. Emi yoo to ipase Olorun fun isegun mi. Olorun ti se ileri lati ma ko mi sile.
- Emi ko ni se awawi nipa ese mi. Nko ni wa idalare fun aisedeede mi, Emi ko ni bo ese mi. Nko ni tan ara mi je.
- Emi yoo jewo ese mi. Emi yoo ko ese mi sile. Emi yoo gba idariji. A so mi dotun. A o we mi ninu Omi Mimo Oro Olorun.
- Aso mi yoo funfun. Ororo ko ni gbe lori mi. Ese a ma mu ifoju emi wa. Emi ko ni da ese.
- Ese lo mu eniyan padanu ogo Olorun, ese amaa mu iwa mimo di alailesese, ese amaa mu itiju ati ihoho wa, emi ki yoo dese.

- Emi yoo to ipase Kristi. Emi yoo tele apere awon asiwaju to ni emi Olorun. Emi yoo je ologbon.
- Ese ko ni boju orun mi. Ese ko ni mu abuku baa so ala mi. Ese ko ni ba aye mi je.
- Emi ki i se elese. Emi ki i se alaisedeede. Emi ki i se elegan. Emi ki i se ajeji si Olorun. Ese ko ni yi idanimo mi pada. Mo ko abawon ese lara aso.

KOKO ADURA
ORIN DAFIDI 147

1. Yin Olorun aanu pelu orin kan.
2. Mo gba ore-ofe lati wa ninu ife Oluwa patapata.
3. Mo n gbadura lojojumo, fun ore-ofe lati ma sise ninu iwa mimo niwaju Oluwa.
4. Oluwa, we mi mo kuro ninu gbogbo aisododo.
5. Ore-ofe lati mo gbogbo eto awon ota, gbe mi wo ni oruko Jesu.
6. Gbogbo irugbin orun apaadi ninu aye mi, fa tu ti gbongbo ti gbongbo ni oruko Jesu.
7. Gbogbo igbese odi ti mo ti gbe eleyi ti o ja mi lole iranlowo lati oke, Olorun aanu dami pade.
8. Emi Mimo ran mi lowo lati ri asise mi ati lati yipada ni oruko Jesu.

9. Ohun ti o tako iranlowo, mo pa o lenu mo lori aye mi.

10. Gbogbo ipejopo ti nja awon omo mi lole ini won, pinya l'oruko Jesu.

11. Baba, dariji mi fun gbigbeke le oye mi dipo ki wo O fun iranlowo.

12. Ifami ororo yan fun isegun gbe mi wo ni oruko Jesu.

13. Oun ti ko latun se, ma se faye gba lati wo inu ayanmo mi, l'oruko Jesu.

14. Olorun aanu, ma fi aye gba ota lati pa awon omo mi ki won le pami lenu mo.

15. Oun rere gbogbo ti agbara okunkun ti ji lo ninu aye mi, majemu aanu, da pada l'oruko Jesu.

16. Gbadura ninu Emi Mimo.

OJO OGUN

IDIWO SI IRANLOWO: AWON IWA ODI

IJEWO

- Nko ni ba anfaani ologo mi je. Nko ni ba aaye mi je. Nko ni padanu ibukun Olorun.

- Iwa mi ko ni da ati goke mi duro. Emi yoo ko bi a se n soro, emi yoo ko bi a se n huwa, emi yoo ko bi a se n ko ara eni nijanu, emi yoo ko iwa irele ati iwa rere.

- Jesu fi omobinrin kan we aja, sibe o re ara re sile, o si ri ibukun gba. Rahabu gba idile re la kuro ninu isubu Jeriko nitori o wuwa daadaa.

- Omo obirin to fun Elisha lounje ji pada nitori o se ijewo daradara, emi ko ni je ki ohun to n sele mu mi siwa wu.

- Emi ki yoo ku. Yiye ni emi yoo ye. Emi yoo ri rere Olorun ni ile alaaye.

- Kanga mi ko ni gbe, orisun iranlowo mi ko ni di, emi yoo ri ibale okan. Emi yoo ri isinmi fun okan mi. Awon to fe ran mi lowo ko ni yi okan won pada. O dara fokan mi. Haleluyah!

- Emi yoo pari ere ije mi. Kosi ohun ti yoo da mi duro. Awon alatako mi ko ni ri ohunkohun lodi si mi.

- Esu ko ni tan mi je. Emi ko ni le oluranlowo mi danu. Nko ni lo enu mi lati fa isubu ara mi.

- Iranlowo ko ni jinna si mi. Iran odi ko ni wa si imuse lori ebi mi. Awon angeli mi ko ni fi mi sile.

- Emi Mimo ko ni fi mi sile. Emi yoo tele itosona lati orun. Emi yoo gba eko latodo asiwaju. Emi yoo se ara mi ni pipe.

KOKO ADURA
ORIN DAFIDI 42

1. Yin olorun olotito.
2. Iwo emi ailoye ati iditi, so agabara re nu ninu aye mi l'oruko Jesu.
3. Mo dide mo tan tori wipe imole mi tide.
4. Baba mi, Baba mi, gbemi kuro lowo emi aimokan ati ailese botito.
5. Mo ronupiwada kuro ninu gbogbo ijafara, ati ayi malese on ti Olorun nreti ninu aye mi.
6. Gbogbo ofa okunkun ti o ti wo ara mi ni pase oju ala, sofo danu ni Oruko Jesu.
7. Iwo agbegba mi, so owo po pelu mi ni oruko Jesu.
8. Gbogbo agbara ti on yo ayika mi lenu, e sofo danu ni oruko Jesu.
9. Pelu ina ati ipa mo gbe ipin mi ni oruko Jesu.
10. Gbogbo agbekale ota mi lati pami saju akoko mi, e tuka pelu ina
11. Iyanu mi, kii lonse ninu iyewu okunkun, fo jade pelu ina ni oruko Jesu.
12. Gbogbo agbakale ota mi lati pa mi saaju akoko mi, etuka pelu ina.

13. Gbogbo agbegbe aye mi ti mo tin ri ijakule, teriba pelu ina ni oruko Jesu.
14. Gbogbo ana ti aye mi gba jo ifami-ororo danu, e di pa ni oruko Jesu.
15. Olorun, se iribomi mi pelu ifami-ororo irorun l'oruko Jesu.
16. Egba adura ninu Emi fun ogun iseju.

OJO KOKANLELOGUN

IDIWO SI IRANLOWO: AIMOKAN ATI IKUNA LATI BERE

IJEWO

- Ailesoro lo n siwaju oriburuku; emi o ni panumo, n kigbe fun iranlowo; n o gba Ibukun.
- Iranlowo mi ko ni ri idaduro, a ko ni fi iranlowo mi du mi, a ko ni si iranlowo mi gbe fun eleomiran, n ko ni wa lojukan; mo ko ijakule.
- Olorun yoo fun mi ni oso dipo eeru, Olorun yoo rojo ibukun sori mi, n o ni aaye ti ko nipekun, aluyo mi yoo seese.

- N o bere imo, n o beere fun atileyin, n o rin ninu ijegbaba, emi yoo ba awon ologbon rin, emi yoo bori.
- Ijakule ki i se ipin mi, anfaani ko ni fo mi ru, ogo mi ko ni di itiju; n ko ni sise lasan, emi yoo jere, n ko ni padanu.
- Olorun yoo lana fun mi, Olorun mi je ogbontarigi onise iyanu, Olorun onise ara ni mo n sin, oore ofe lopo yanturu wa fun mi.
- Kosi ohun to lee dami duro. iranlowo wa fun mi; ipin mi ni aseyori; n ko ni subu, emi yoo ba eni to to pade.
- Orun si si je ipin mi; isegun je ipin mi, Agbelebu je ipele otun fun mi, nko lee sina, iranlowo wa fun mi.
- Olorun mi je onise iyanu, awon oke ko lee duro niwaju Re, nipa agbara Olorun awon oke yoo di petele, a ti bukun mi, mo ni anfaani pupo, iranlowo wa fun mi.
- Jeremiah gba iranlowo, ko ku sinu aja ile. Peteru gba iranlowo lasiko, ko ku sinu tubu. Sadraki, Mesaaki ati Abedinigo gba iranlowo lasiko, won ko ku sinu ina ileeru. Emi yoo gba iranlowo lasiko. Haleluya!

KOKO ADURA
ORIN DAFIDI 38

1. Oluwa, modupe lowo Re nitori wipe mo le ko aini mi wa s'odo Re. ko orin kan si abani gberu.
2. Agba, Baba, ranmi lowo lati yi kuro ninu ese ti o wa ninu aiye mi, ki n si bere ni otun pelu re loni.
3. Ranmi lowo lati gbekele otito oro Re, nigbati o ba nira lati mo iriri iwalaye re.
4. Gbogbo owo eru ti o lodi simi, di opin l'oruko Jesu.
5. Gbogbo alagbara okunrin ti a yan lati ma topinpin awon omo mi, e yaro l'oruko Jesu.
6. Oluwa, fi mi se itesiwaju agbara Re lati tu awon eniyan sile ati lati so won di ominira lowo agbara okunkun.
7. Iwo omiran aimokan, ki lo n duro se ninu aiye mi, fo jade pelu ina.
8. Iwo agbara ijakule ni bebe iranlowo nla, fo pelu ina.
9. Baba, fun mi ni iranlowo lati ibi Mimo wa ni oruko Jesu.
10. Oluwa, si oju awon oluranlowo mi lati ri mi l'oruko Jesu.
11. Iwo arolu ala ti o ma so mi di alailagbara ninu emi gba ofa ina l'oruko Jesu.
12. Oluwa, fun owo mi lokun lati ja ati awon ika owo mi fun ogun jija.
13. Obiri ina yi awon omo mi ka l'oruko Jesu.

14. Ofa ailegbadura fo jade kuro ninu aya mi l'oruko Jesu.
15. Mo toro idariji fun aikii tete dahun si awon ami pataki ti Emi Re fi han mi l'oruko Jesu.
16. Emi ogbon gbe gbogbo ipa aimokan eeyi ti o ndi ayanmo mi lowo ni oruko Jesu.
17. Gbadura ninu Emi fun isegu marundinlogbon.

OJO KEJILELOGUN
GBIGBOGUN TI AWON EMI TI N TAKO IRANLOWO

IJEWO

- Iranlowo ko jinna si mi, ipile mi ko lee da mi duro, gbolohun odi ko lee dami duro, emi ko ni padanu ohun to dara.
- Olorun yoo fun mi ni oso fun eeru, awon ti n fi ayanmo sofo ko lee fi ayanmo temi sofo, odo Olorun nikan ni ajaye wa.
- Nibi ti ko ba ti si iranlowo, Olorun yoo ran iranlowo, ohun ti eniyan ko mo, Olorun mo o, mo wa larowoto iranlowo latoke.
- Mo ri ojo tuntun; mo ri anfaani tuntun, oore ofe n sise fun mi, Olorun mj je agbenuso ti o se gbarale, Olorun mi yoo lana, mo ni ipin daradara.

- Kosi idiwo lona mi, kosi itiju fun mi, kosi adanu ohun to dara fun mi, oro mi ti di aseyori, kosi ohun buburu to sele si mi.

- Oluranlowo mi ko ni ku, oluranlowo mi ko ni saisan, oluranlowo mi ko ni sina, oluranlowo mi ko ni yi okan re pada, emi yoo ri ohun ti i se temi gba.

- Mo po niye, Mo je eni ti a kaye, mo je eni ti a o lee diyele, mo je eni ti a kasi, Olorun ti fi ami ororo yan mi, Olorun ti fi ona han mi, mo je alabukun fun.

- Eyin emi ti n tako iranlowo, e jade! A ko lee fi eto mi du mi, a ko lee dami duro, ona tuntun wa fun mi, anfaani wa fun mi.

- Emi yoo ko orin isegun, n ko ni je iru, n ko ni di eniyan lasan, emi yoo ri didara Olorun.

- Akoko mi re, iranlowo mi ti de, akoko ti to fun mi lati tan imole. Halleluyah!

KOKO ADURA
ORIN DAFIDI 22

1. Oluwa o, modupe lowo Re fun igbala okan mi, ko orin kan si Olugbala re.
2. Oluwa, mu mi gbon ju ota mi lo.
3. Ninu apapo igbekun nibi ti ayanmo mi se mo, jade pelu ina l'oruko Jesu.

4. Ariwo ijiya lati oke, dide ki o si le awon alenipa mi l'oruko Jesu.

5. Ororo isokan ma san sinu ijo ara Kristi l'oruko Jesu.

6. Pepe adura ise-iranse mi gba ina titun l'oruko Jesu.

7. Ofa asise jade kuro ninu aye mi ati aye awon omo mi l'oruko Jesu.

8. Olorun o, ranmilowo kuro lowo iyemeji l'oruko Jesu.

9. Ororo imo-emi yato bale mi l'oruko Jesus.

10. Emi ma ri awon omo-omo mi, beni emi ma wa laye lati ri akoko ogo won.

11. Gbogbo ami ti o wa laarin wa, eleyi ti nsise fun ota ki asiri re ki o tu, ki o si gba ere itiju l'oruko Jesu.

12. Oluwa, ko mi bi a tin gba agbayori adura.

13. Ojo aanu ro le mi lori fun isegun ti ko wo po.

14. Ida awon ota mi, ki yi opa awon omo mi ni olurko Jesu.

15. Oluwa, be ise-iranse wa wo pelu ise ami ati iyanu, ni oluko Jesu.

16. Gbogbo awon alaisan tin be ni ile iwosan, gba iwosan l'oruko Jesu

17. Gbadura ninu Emi fun iseju marundinlogbon.

OJO KETALELOGUN
AMUSEYA IRANLOWO: AAWE ATI ADURA

IJEWO

- Nko ni gbadura lasan, adura mi yoo de orun, adura mi yoo so oke dile, adura mi yoo mu ibukun wa.

- Nko ni si adura gba, n ko ni gbadura si Olorun ti ki i gboran, emi mo pe oludande mi n be laaye. Nigbakugba ti mo ba kigbe, oun yoo da mi lohun.

- Adura je ibukun lati gbe owo Olorun dide, emi yoo gbadura ati aawe, emi yoo gbe igbese igbagbo, a o se Olorun logo.

- Emi yoo gbadura nigba to rorun, nigba ti ko rorun, emi yoo gbadura titi ti yoo fi rorun, adura mi ki i se lasan, Olorun yoo kiyesi adura mi.

- Adura ati aawe mi yoo mu iranlowo wa fun mi, Olorun yoo fi ere si aawe mi, Olorun yoo fowo si aawe mi, gegebi Koniliu, Olorun yoo fere si aawe ati adura mi.

- Aawe ati adura n sise, aawe ati adura n se ayipada, adura ati aawe a maa mu iyato wa, nko ni sole.

- Orun a maa dahun si aawe ati adura, isodotun okun a maa waye nigba ti mo gba gbaawe, emi yoo gbaawe lati mu ara mi

378

kuro ninu isoro, emi yoo si oke nidi pelu adura mi.

- Josua da oorun ati osupa duro, Elijah pe ina sokale, Mose pin okun niya, Debora segun iko ogun.
- Adura je ifiwepe fun idasi Olorun. Emi yoo gbadura, emi yoo gbaawe, emi yoo pe ogun orun sise, nkan yoo yi pada fun mi. Haleluyah!

KOKO ADURA
ORIN DAFIDI 30

1. Mo mo riri Oluwa ti o n fun wa ni isegun ni gbogbo igba – ko orin titun kan si Jesu.
2. Iwo ofa ko si oluranlowo ninu ayanmo mi ba ina jade (Joh.5:7).
3. Ojo aanu ro le mi lori fun iranlowo ti o soro gbagbo.
4. Emi-Mimo di awon oluranlowo ayanmo mi lowo lati san, kan nipa fun won lati ran mi lowo.
5. Igbese ti o ye kin gbe lati bori ogun 'maranlowo' Emi-Mimo, fi han mi l'oruko Jesu.
6. Angeli ifihan, be ala mi wo.
7. Gbobo asise awon obi mi ti o nfarahan nini aye mi, eje Jesu gbe won mi.

8. Ina titun ti Emi-Mimo sokale sori pepe adura mi fun ipele ogo ti o kan ni oruko Jesu.
9. Ina titun be ayika mi wo l'oruko Jesu.
10. Gbogbo afefe buburu ti nfe awon anfani mi danu, dakeje ni oruko Jesu.
11. Gbogbo ila buburu ti mo jogun ninu iran mi, sofo danu, l'oruko Jesu.
12. Gbogbo oba ti n joba ni agbegbe mi, mo ro o loye pelu ina l'oruko Jesu.
13. Ofa apani die-die ninu eje mi ti o nduro d'ojo ayo mi lati farahan, jade pelu agbara.
14. Emi ki yio sun orun iku l'oruko Jesu.
15. Ojo aanu ro le mi lori fun iwosan.
16. Oluwa, so ekun me di erin.
17. Gbadura nimu Emi fun ogun iseju.

OJO KERINLELOGUN

AMUSEYA IRANLOWO: ORE, IRUBO ATI IFURUGBIN

IJEWO

- Iranlowo mi towo Olorun Alagbara wa, Olorun ni orisun iranlowo to se gbarale julo; iranlowo lati odo Olorun ki i mu ibanuje wa, inu mi dun lati duro niwaju Oluwa. Iranlowo lati odo Olorun ki i jani kule.

- Ofin ifurugbin yoo gbe mi. Emi yoo furugbin lopolopo. Oju kokoro ko ni bori mi, Olorun yoo fi ona iye han mi.

- Orun mi ko ti. Aye mi ko si lowo awon ota mi, Olorun lee ba gbogbo aini mi pade. N ko le tan sile. Olorun mi wa laaye.

- N o ran awon miran lowo. Emi yoo fi ara mi sile fun iranwo awon miran. Emi yoo furugbin iwa rere, emi o fi owo funni, emi yoo je iranlowo ti elomiran nilo, emi yoo je idahun si elomiran.

- Ohun ti aye mi n fe wa fun mi, ohun ti n ko ni wa lopo yanturu nibikan, emi o maa ba awon to nilo mi pade. Ohunkohun ti eniyan ba furugbin, oun naa ni yoo kore. Emi o kore ohun rere.

- Oluranlowo yoo dide, yoo si wa mi ri. Aini ki i se ipin mi. Iran aye mi ko ni se awati ipese. Irin ajo mi ko ni se awati itosona. Ise mi ko ni ni ifaseyin. Oluwa yoo pese.

- Mo gba oso fun eeru, mo yan iye dipo iku, Mo gba ibukun dipo egun, ebi mi je alabukun, ise owo mi je alabukun, emi yoo ri rere Oluwa.

- Ibudo mi ko farasin, oluranlowo mi yoo wa mi ri, emi ki i se eni awati laarin ero. Oluranlowo mi yoo wa mi ri.

- Mo di riri, mo wa, mo wa ni arowoto, a da mi mo, a se awari mi, a bukun mi, ibukun ni mi.
- Iranlowo ko jinna si mi. ifurugbin ati irubo mi yoo sise fun mi. Olorun ko le paro. Mo ni itelorun pelu didara Olorun.

KOKO ADURA
ORIN DAFIDI 63

1. Ko orin si Oga Ogo.
2. Oluwa, ran mi lowo lati ma tele apeere re ninu ise l'oruko Jesu.
3. Oluwa, wo mi pale ki o si tun mi mo.
4. Oluwa, jeki ipade yii je ibere oun titun ninu aye emi ati idile mi l'oruko Jesu.
5. Iwo emi ikosile, di itewogba l'oruko Jesu.
6. Gbogbo ofa ifasehin ti isuwona ti a ta lodi simi pada ni oruko Jesu.
7. Ohun ti yio so mi di eni nla fun awokose, bale mi loni l'oruko Jesu.
8. Awon ero ti yio fa awon oluranlowo mo ra sinu aye mi, gbe mi wo ni oruko Jesu.
9. Gbogbo ofa "iwo ki yio se rere" ti a ta lodi simi, pada l'oruko Jesu.
10. Gbogbo oun ibi ti o npase odi, pa enu mo l'oruko Jesu.

11. Gbogbo iji ti a nyan lati gbe mi mi, dake je l'oruko Jesu.
12. Gbogbo oun ibi tin se ayidayida ayanmo orile-ede yi, pa enu mo l'oruko Jesu.
13. Baba mi, Baba mi, ru awon ebo mi soke lati fo'un fun mi nibi ti o to.
14. Gbogbo oba ajoji ti a fi sori ite lati ogbun apadi, lori ite adugbo mi, mo ro o loye pelu ina ni oruko Jesu.
15. Ohun idalare, gbe ohun idalebu mi lori awon omo mi.
16. Ore Solomoni so po mo Ibukun irande-iran, Olorun aanu, jeki ore mi so mi po mo awon oluranlowo ayanmo mi.
17. Gbadura ninu Emi fun isejji marundinlogbon.

OJO KEEDOGBON

AMUSEYA IRANLOWO: SISE IRANLOWO IJEWO

- Emi ko le tan sile; awon eniyan a dide fun mi, Olorun a ran iranlowo si mi. Nibikibi ti mo ba ti n wa iranlowo, emi a ri iranlowo.

- Ore mi yoo maa fohun fun mi, ore mi yoo maa gbohun soke fun mi, ore irubo mi yoo fohun fun mi.
- Eso iranlowo mi ko ni dake, aye mi ko ni di gbigba nigbakugba ti mo ba nilo re.
- Olorun a ran mi lowo; Olorun a ti mi leyin. Olorun yoo mu agbegbe mi gbooro, iranlowo latoke wa fun mi.
- Ota mi maa yo mi, aseyori oore ofe ni emi n se. Aanu yoo fohun mi. Iranlowo wa fun mi ninu Olorun.
- E dake jee, eyin elegan, Itiju ki i se ipin mi, emi yoo dide pada. Emi yoo wa loke, nko ni wa nisale. Olorun yoo fun mi lokun.
- Iranlowo yoo gbe mi soke. Iranlowo yoo mu mi duro soke. Iranlowo yoo lana fun mi. Emi yoo je alabukun fun.
- Nko ni kigbe lasan, n ko ni foju sona lasan. N ko ni so'reti nu. Igbagbo mi ninu Oluwa yoo sise iyanu.
- Nibi ti awon miran ti kuna, emi yoo ni aseyori. Eso iranlowo ti mo ti furugbin yoo sise fun mi. Nigbkugba ti mo ti nilo iranlowo, emi o ri iranlowo gba. Olorun mi je onidajo ododo, Olorun mi je olododo, Olorun mi dara.
- Mo gba abayo si isoro mi, a ko ni fi mi sile. Nko ni so anfaani mi nu. Olorun ti ba mi fi

ohun re ti o dara ju pamo. N ko ni padanu. Haleluyah!

KOKO ADURA
ORIN DAFIDI 27

1. Ko orin titun kan si Olorun Oga Ogo julo.
2. Oluwa, ranmilowo lati gbarati daradara ki nle pari daradara, l'oruko Jesu.
3. Oluwa, si iju mi lati ri bi O se fe kin sin O l'oruko Jesu.
4. Baba iyanu, ri mi sinu aanu, ore-ofe ati oju-rere Re, ni oruko Jesu.
5. Ororo lati di ayanfe lori awon elomiran, gbe mi wo l'oruko Jesu.
6. Gbogbo ahon ibi ti o nsoro lodi si awon omo mi, le mo orisun enu re l'oruko Jesu.
7. Ayanmo mi, dide ki o si jade kuro ninu koto esin ni oruko Jesu
8. Ipa onfa Oluwa, emi ki yio padanu eni ti o ti yan fun mi l'oruko Jesu
9. Oluwa, Olorun Oludari, lo awon adari ti o wa ni ijoba apapo, ipinle ati agbegbe lati gba orile'de yii kuro lowo inira l'oruko Jesu.
10. Gbogbo emi ti nje ki dabi eni ti ko se gbarale fun elomiran, wo inu igbekun ki o si jade l'oruko Jesu.
11. Oluwa o, yo ojukokoro ti emi kuro loji mi l'oruko Jesu.

12. Oluwa o, tu asiri ti o wa n'idi isoro mi lemi lowo, ni oruko Jesu.
13. Oluwa o, ko mi ni oun ijinle ati ikoko.
14. Oluwa, fun mi ni agbara fun ekunrere aseyori ninu ise akanse mi ti o kan l'oruko Jesu.
15. Oluwa, mo odi yi awon omo mi ka pelu agbara re.
16. Emi-Mimo, si oju mi, ki O si ran mi lowo lati se ipinnu ti o to ni oruko Jesu.
17. Gbogbo agbara ti n fi iranlowo mi sofo, fo tutu, l'oruko Jesu.
18. Gbadura fun okere ju iseju marundinlogbon.

OJO KERINDINLOGBON

AMUSEYA IRANLOWO: IMORE

IJEWO

- Emi je eniti o moore. Oluwa dara si mi; Ibukun Olorun ti so mi di oloro; ki i si mu laalaa wa.
- Olorun ti bukun mi. Olorun ti so mi di ibukun, ibukun Oluwa ti fun mi ni oso dipo eeru; ogo n be fun mi.
- Oluwa ti fi ororo si mi lori. Oluwa ti so ofo mi di ayo, Oluwa ti fo opa idabu irin.

- Oluwa ti la mi loju. Oluwa ti gba ejo mi ro, a si ti da mi lare. A ti se mi logo, mo wa laaye.
- Oluwa ti dari ji mi; Oluwa ti san 'gbese mi, Oluwa ti gba ogun mi ja, Oluwa ti mu ile mi gbooro.
- Oluwa ti fi kun mi ni gbogbo ona, Oluwa ti tu mi ninu. Oluwa ti le awon ota mi kuro.
- Emi ko ni itiju, n ko si ni abamo, Oluwa ti se ohun nla; Oluwa ti si orun mi.
- Oluwa ti mu ogun mi wa sopin, Oluwa ti so oko mi di ile, oluwa ti kun ogbun mi.
- Oluwa ti mu gbogbo ona mi gun, Oluwa ti gbe mi ga ju awon ota mi lo, Emi ko ni abamo.
- Oluwa ti fun mi lokun, Oluwa ti so mi di ninla. Oluwa ti mu egan mi kuro. Ogo ni fun Oluwa ni oke orun. Mo dupe pupo pupo.

KOKO ADURA
ORIN DAFIDI 100

1. Ko orin kan si Jesu Oluranlowo wa.
2. Oluwa modupe lowo Re fun owo airi Re ti o wa lori aye mi ni oruko Jesu.
3. Baba mi, Baba mi, kun mi pelu awon nkan ti mo nilo lati je itewogba niwaju awon oluranlowo mi, l'oruko Jesu.
4. Baba, modupe lowo Re nitoti wipe o ga ju ogbon ti a lero lo.

5. Baba mi, Baba mi, mo dupe lowo Re fun awon eri ti o soro, gbagbo eleyi ti o nse ni aarin wa

6. Modupe lowo re, nitori ti o ka mi ye lati je olugbe agbara re ti oke.

7. Ohunkohun ti o wa ninu ojo ola mi ti nduro lati doju ti mi, yipada l'oruko Jesu.

8. Modupe lowo Re fun itusile nla kuro lowo agabara awon eni okunkun.

9. Awon ofa iranlowo mi, e o ni bori mi ni oruko Jesu.

10. Gbogbo iboju okunkun, ti o bo oju mi lati maa da awon oluranlowo mi mo, gbina.

11. Olorun aanu, fun mi ni iranlowo kuro ninu gbogbo idamu mi, nitori wipe asan ni iranlowo eniyan.

12. Olorun aanu, yara lati ran mi lowo (O.D.70:1).

13. Iranlowo ti yio f'opin si aini mi, wa miri nisinsinyi (O.D.72:12).

14. Olorun aanu, o ti gbe iranlowo sowo enikan ti o tobi, so mi po mo (O. D.89).

15. Ore-ofe lati gbekele o fun iranlowo mi ti o kan, mo gba ni oruko Jesu (O.D.115).

16. Ninu ipo irele ti mo wa, ran iranlowo lati gbe mi dide ni oruko Jesu.

17. Bi mose fi imore mi mo loni yi, pese mi fun iranlowo.

18. Gbadura ninu Emi fun iseju marundinlogbon.

OJO KETADINLOGBON

AMUSEYA IRANLOWO: IGBAGBO
IJEWO

- Igbagbo mi wa laaye; igbagbo mi nga si, igbagbo mi ti digba.
- Igbagbo mi tobi, igbagbo mi nso eso; mo ni ebun igbagbo; mo n sise igbagbo; mo ni igbagbo lati ojo rere; mo ni igbgbo lati yi aye mi pada.
- Mo ni igbagbo lati wa laaye. Emi ko ni ku; mo ni igbagbo fun iwosan, n ko ni saare, mo ni igbagbo lati wa loke; n ko ni subu; igbagbo mi n sise.
- Igbagbo mi yoo f'ohun, igbagbo mi yoo f'ohun soke; igbagbo yoo si oke nidi. Igbagbo mi yo pe akiyesi orun.
- Igbagbo mi yoo ji oku; igbagbo mi mu alaisan larada. Igbagbo mi yoo te Oluwa lorun; igbagbo mi yoo sise iyanu; igbagbo mi yoo mu ibukun wa. Iyanu yoo sele.
- Eniyan meji dara ju enikan lo; Olorun yoo lana fun mi, Olorun yoo ran atileyin si mi, emi yoo ri rere Oluwa ni ile alaaye.

- Emi yoo gbadura ninu igbagbo, maa gbaawe ninu igbagbo; maa furugbin ninu igbagbo, emi yoo duro lori igbagbo mi.
- Igbagbo mi ko ni ja mi kule; igbagbo mi yoo je kokoro, igbagbo yoo bori idojuko mi, iranlowo ni igbagbo.
- Ireti wa fun mi nitori mo ni igbagbo. Olorun ko lee paro!
- Igbagbo mi yoo fo ajaga airi iranlowo lori mi. A o ran mi lowo.

KOKO ADURA
ORIN DAFIDI 119

1. Dupe lowo Olorun ti o bukun re pelu iranlowo ti o ko to si, tabi o ko ye fun.
2. Ko orin titun kan si Olorun aanu.
3. Mo da eje Jesu bo awon oluranlowo mi.
4. Ipo ti mo ma de lati ran awon elomiran lowo, farahan l'oruko Jesu.
5. Emi-Mimo, ran awon elomiran lowo nipase mi. Ki O ba le di ayinlogo l'oruko Jesu (Lefi.19:18).

6. Oluwa, pa ese mi mo kuro ninu isina, ni oruko Jesu.

7. Ran mi lowo lati sinmi le o pelu igboya ninu idaniloju pe o ma nwa ni aye re ni gbogbo igba (O.D.12:14).

8. Ran mi lowo lati ma dabi re si lojojumo bi mo ti kuro ninu eni atijo mi.

9. Fi han mi lati ran awon ota mi lowo lati sun mo o (Luk.6:27).

10. Ran mi lowo lati yipada si o nigbati mi o lagbara mo lati ri iranlowo ninu re (2Oba.19:5).

11. Oluwa, modupe fun awon onigbagbo ti o ran mi lowo lati ri iranlowo ninu re (2Oba.19:5).

12. Baba mi, Baba mi, nipase igbagbo mo ji gbogbo awon oluranlowo ti ko sise ati eleyi ti o nsun ti a yan fun aye mi ati ayanmo mi dide.

13. Gege bi a ti ko, awon ti won tipase igbagbo segun ile oba ti won sise ododo, ti won gba ileri. Fun idi eyi, nipase igbagbo, mo gba iranlowo ti o ye fun awon omo mi (Heb.11:33-35).

14. A ko wipe, "sa gbogbo." Fun idi eyi mo gbagbo pe iranlowo nwa mi bo ni akoko yi (Luk.8:50).

15. Baba mi, Baba mi, a ko ninu oro re wipe, "olododo ni yoo ye nipa igbagbo." Nipa igbagbo mi, mo pase wipe emi ni o kan lati ni iriri iranlowo (Heb.10:38).
16. Iranlowo mi ti owo Oluwa wa, nipa igbagbo mo gba iranlowo (O.D.121:2).
17. Gbadura ninu Emi fun iseju marundinlogon.

OJO KEJIDINLOGBON

AMUSEYA IRANLOWO: WIWA NIBI TI OLORUN FE KA WA
IJEWO

- Emi ko ni wa nibi ti ko ye ki n wa. N ko ni tele opo ero. Nko ni sina. Emi yoo je ori, emi ki i se iru.
- Oore ofe yoo sise fun mi; oore ofe Olorun yoo f'ohun fun mi; aanu je ipin mi. A ran mi lowo.
- N ko ni se asise. N ko ni gbe nibi ti ko ye. Okoowo mi ko ni si nibi ti ko ye, okoowo mi ko ni doju dele, A o si awon ilekun fun mi, Aanu je ipin mi. A ran mi lowo.

- Iranlowo yoo wa mi ri nibi ti mo ba wa; iranlowo ko ni fo mi ru; oluranlowo mi ko ni yi okan pada. Iranlowo je anfaani mi.
- Nko ni dorikodo, n ko lee sina, a ko lee fi mi sile seyin, emi yoo maa je eni ti a kasi, iranlowo yoo wa mi ri.
- Iranlowo yoo pa awon ti n gan mi lenu mo, Mase yoo nitori mi iwo ota mi. Emi yoo dide pada. Emi yoo ye. Nko ni ku. Olorun yoo gbo igbe mi.
- Mose ri iranwo gba ninu aginju. Ismaili ri iranwo gba ninu asale. Dafidi ri iranwo gba nigba ti o n sa fun Saulu.
- Iranlowo yoo wa mi ri. Nko jinna si iranlowo; emi ko ni duro de ojurere ota, oro awon ti n tako mi ko ni di ase fun mi.
- Ogo Oluwa ni ibori mi, nibikibi ti mo ba wa, iranlowo wa nibe. Nitori Oluwa wa pelu mi, iranlowo wa fun mi.
- Awon to mo mi yoo ran mi lowo, ajeji yoo ran mi lowo, okunrin yoo ran mi lowo, obinrin yoo ran mi lowo. Mo gba aso iranlowo. Mo gba ifami ororo yan iranlowo. Haleluyah!

KOKO ADURA
ORIN DAFIDI 33

1. Oluwa, modupe lowo Re fun igbala opo eniyan.
2. Ko orin titun kan si Jesu Olulana.
3. Oluwa, Olorun mi o, je ki n wa ni ibi ti o to ni akoko ti o to lati ba won eniyan ti o to pade (Mk.10:46-62).
4. A ko wipe "gbekele Oluwa pelu gbogbo okan re, mo on ni gbogbo ona re, oun yio si ma to ipa ona re. To ipa ona mi si odo awon olurnlowo ayanmo mi (Owe.3:5).
5. Baba mi, Baba mi, bo ba tile je wipe ibi ti mo wa lowo-lowo yi ko wa fun iranlowo lati oke, nipase eto ti orun, si mi nipo kuro nibe (2Sam.9:1-3).
6. Gbo oro Oluwa lati enu mi, iwo angeli ti o tayo ninu ipa, mo so ise iranlowo re ji ninu aye mi loni yi (O.D.103:20).
7. Gege bi ajumojogun igbala, eleyi ti awon angeli ti yan fun iranlowo, iwo emi ti nsise iranlowo lo sinu gbogbo tubu okunkun ti Jesus (Heb.1:14).
8. Iwo Emi Oluwa fe bi iji, sawari ki o si dari awon oluranlowo mi ti a ti yan si mi ni oruko Jesu (Joh.3:8).

9. Gbogbo asiri ti mo nilo lati mo nipa ayika mi, tu fun mi ni oruko Jesu (Lefi.18).
10. Mo gba gbogbo ile ti mo ti sonu pada ni oruko Jesu.
11. Oluwa, nipa afefe lile ti ile orun, le gbogbo awon okunkun ti o yi ayinka iranlowo mi ka ni oruko Jesu.
12. Pariwo Olorun aanu ni igba mokanlelogun, se atunto ninu aye ati ayanmo awon omo mi, ni oruko Jesu.
13. Emi Mimi to ipa ese mi loni si odo eniyan ti o nilo ireti ti o wa lati odo Jesu nikan.
14. Imole Jesu tu asiri ki o si le gbogbo okunkun ati iri awon ika ti o njoba ninu idile mi.
15. Orisun inira ninu aye mi, gbe danu nisisiyi.
16. Gbodura ninu Emi fun iseju marundinlogbon.

KOKANDINLOGBON
AMUSEYA IRANLOWO: ITOSONA LATORUN

IJEWO

- Emi ko ni sina. Awon to korira mi a dore mi. N ko ni padanu ohun daradara ti Olorun ni fun mi.

- Ipin mi ni oore ofe nla. Ebun Olorun fun mi yoo wa mi ri. Emi o mo ohun to to lati se. Emi o mo ona lati pade awon to ye ki n pade, emi o si mo ohun to ye lati so.

- Olorun n to igbese mi. Emi o ni sina. Mi o ni wo moto odi, mi o ni gbe ile odi, oju mi yoo ri ona.

- Okukun o ni bo mi. iruju ki i se ipin mi. ofa iruju pada sibi to ti n bo, aso iwuwo okan pada sibi to ti n bo, ofa iruju yoo jona di eeru.

- Ilana Olorun fun mi yoo yori si rere. Ipinnu esu fun mi yoo jakule; n ko ni bo sinu pakute ibi.

- Nibiti ko si ireti, iranlowo yoo dide fun mi. nibiti mo ba ti sonu, iranlowo a dide fun mi, nibiti mo ba ti sonu, iranlowo a wa mi ri. N ko ni pari pelu itiju.

- Ibere tuntun yoo wa fun mi. ilekun ti a si yoo wa fun mi, Anfaani tuntun yoo wa fun mi. Ogo wa fun mi. ijakule ki i se temi. Mo je alabukun fun.

- Oju oluranlowo mi ko ni fo, oluranlowo mi ko ni sina, oluranlowo mi ko ni lo is ibomiran. Emi o maa lesi.
- Ojo to dara ju lo wa niwaju mi. Ohun atijo ti koja lo, ewa yoo farahan. O ti dara fun mi.
- Maa ba eni to ye pade. Maa se ohun to ye. Olorun ni Olutosona mi. Haleluyah!

KOKO ADURA
ORIN DAFIDI 124

1. Oluwa, modupe lowo Re fun asiri itoni eleyi ti o so mi po moa won oluranlowo ayanmo.
2. Ko orin iyin.
3. Baba mi, Baba mi, nipase angeli itoni, to mi lo si ibi ti mo ti ma ri iranlowo (Eks.2:20).
4. Oluwa o, Olorun mi, to mi pelu oju re ki O si so mi po mo awon oluralowo mi (O.D.32:8).
5. Baba mi, Baba mi, fun ra are re, dari emi ati oluranlowo ninu aye ttiti ti a ma fi pade ara wa.
6. Gege bi a ti ko wipe "iye awon ti Emi Olorun ba dari ni omo Olorun, Oluwa o, dari mi ni

pa se Emi Re si odo awon oluranlowo ti a ti yan ti a si so mo ayanmo mi (Rom.8:14).

7. Baba mi, Baba mi, fun mi ni ni itoni ti wooli eleyi ti yo sii mi si iranlowo ati awon oluranlowo lati oke (Ise.13: 1-4).

8. Baba mi, baba mi, nibi ti iranlowo eniyan ti ye, jeki iranlowo Re gba ise se (Gen.21:14-19).

9. Oluwa mi, Olorun mi, iwo ti o ran Peteru lowo ti ko ri sinu omi, ran igbeyawo mi lowo lati ma ri (Mt.28:31).

10. Olorun aanu, fi mi si eni ti o ye fun iranlowo.

11. Olorunn aanu, fi mi se eni to ri iranlowo lai toro gba. Je ki iranlowo ti mi o bebe fun dide fun mi ni oruko Jesu.

12. Gbogbo iwa ti o wa ninu mi tiko fi aye gba iranlowo ninu aye mi fa tu ti gbongbo ti gbongbo ni pase agbara ajinde ni oruko Jesu.

13. Oluwa o, komi ni awon oun ijinle ati asiri

14. Oluwa o, gbogbo asiri ti o wa ninu idile ayanmo mi farahun nipase annu l'oruko Jesu.

15. Gbogbo awon asotele nla ati oke ti o nyi kiri layika ayanmo mi farahan nipase aanu l'oruko Jesu.

16. Oluwa o, se iribomi ti Emi adura fun mi l'oruko Jesu (O. D.119:164; 55:17).

17.Gbadura ninu Emi fun iseju marundinlogbon.

OJO OGBON
IRANLOWO LATI EGIPITI
IJEWO

- Mo ko iranlowo ajoji, mo ko iranlowo latodo awon ota. Olorun mi lee tan isoro mi. Emi o duro niwaju Oluwa, Olorun mi kajuuwon.
- Emi o ni pehinda, mi o ni padanu imole mi; ota mi o ni raaye se mi bo se fe. Aaye mi o ni sofo, awon ohun iyanu a maa sele si mi.
- Mo ko iranlowo lati ibi ajoji, mo ko iranlowo lati ibi ti Olorun ko fowo si. Kosi ibasepo laarin okunkun ati imole.
- Iji okunkun ko ni bori mi; anfaani mi ko ni koja mi, iranlowo mi yoo ti odo Oluwa wa. Mo ko ibanikedun eni ibi.
- Akoko to fun mi lati tan imole, akoko mi ti to lati dide, mi o ni peju, mi o ni padanu igba temi, a ko ni fi elomiran dipo mi.
- Ibukun mi ko ni degun. A o ni yi aseyori mi pada. Orun ko ni ti mo mi.
- Apada si buburu ko ni de ba mi, ohun to n sise ninu aye mi ko ni duro; erin mi ko ni dekun.

- Ohun to n dun ninu aye mi o ni kan, ogo mi ko ni pada seyin, maa gbadun ojo aye mi.
- Aisan ko ni ge aye mi kuru, mi o ni ko si panpe, ogun ateyinja ki i se ipin mi, adanu ki i se ipin mi.
- Kosi ohun to se mi; kosi ohun to se ayanmo mi, mi o ni kabamo laye mi, inu Olorun dun si mi. Haleluyah!

KOKO ADURA

AISAYA 31

1. Jesu, modupe lowo Re fun irubo Re (Heb.2:18).
2. Ko orin titun si Jesu fun eto irapada eleyi ti O pese sile fun wa.
3. Oluwa, ran mi lowo lati se atunto gbogbo eto mi ni isise ntele kii n bale mo riri aini awon elomiran gege bi ti temi (Fil.2:3-4).
4. Oluwa, ran mi lowo kii le te oju mi mo o, nigbati awon eniyan ba mu inu bi mi ni Oruko Jesu.
5. Oluwa, je kin ri aye bi o ti ri, ki o si ran mi lowo lati darapo mo ise igbala ti orun.
6. Gbogbo iranlowo alupayida ti ejibiti ni owo ni, mo so danu patapata, Emi Mimo gba ise se lowo mi.

7. Oluwa fun mi ni okan, eleyi tin ma se idajo ohun gbogbo ati eniyan gbogbo ni pipe l'oruko Jesu.

8. Oluwa, dariji mi fun ipinu ti o to lati pada lo si ijibiti ki o si gbami lowo abajade re. (Gen.12:10-20).

9. Baba, a ti ko ninu oro Re pe awon ajeji ni yio fun mi ni omu. Fun idi eyi, lati oni lo, jeki awon ajeji patapata ran mi lowo (Ise.28:1-2).

10. Oluwa, Olorun mi o, ran mi lowo lati ri iranlowo gba lati owo awon eniyan Orile-ede ti oniruru awo ati ede ni oruko Jesu (Mika 4:1-2).

11. Baba, gege bi a ti ko wipe oro awon kenferi yio wa sodo mi, fun idi eyi jeki iranlowo awon kenferi wa mi ri (Isai.61:6).

12. Emi isipe, ba le mi ni oruko Jesu.

13. Gbogbo agbakale ninu emi lodi si awon omo, fo pelu ina.

14. Mo gba oruko mi jade kuro ninu akosile ijakule ati aini aseyori loruko Jesu.

15. Gegebi o lo Farao lati san Josefu lesan fun ibi ti awon arakunrin re se fun, wa lo iru eyi lori ile aye fun mi l'oruko Jesu.

16. Ohun gbogbo ti mo padanu sinu ebi ikosile, mo gba won pada ni oruko Jesu.

17. Gbadura ninu Emi fun iseju marundinlogbon.

OJO KOKANLELOGBON

IGBEYIN AIBEERE FUN IRANLOWO
IJEWO

- Mi o ni ku sinu didake. Mi o ni padanu ayesi mi. Mi o ni di ohun elo ipati. N o kigbe fun iranlowo. Mi o ni ku iku yepere.
- Mi o ni jeki igberaga ba anfaani ti mo ni fun iranlowo je; mi o ni foju tembelu anfaani fun iranlowo. Mi o ni foju te eni to maa ran mi lowo; mi o ni koja lara eni t'Olorun ran si mi lati ran mi lowo.
- Eto mi ni iranlowo. Maa beere fun iranlowo. Maa kan ilekun iranlowo; maa kigbe fun iranlowo. Olorun a ran iranlowo si mi. Mi o ni ku sinu didake.
- Mo ko ijiya ti ko nidi, mo ko lati duro sinu ijiya; mo ko ko ijiya ati inira igba pipe. Olorun ti yanju isoro mi.
- Emi o beere fun iranlowo; iku Jesu ki i se lasan ninu aye mi. Iku ati ajinde Jesu ti ra iranlowo fun mi.
- Oluwa ni Oluso Aguntan mi. Mo mo pe o fe mi. Mo mo pe o lero rere lokan si mi, ohunkohun ti mo nilo, Oun ti pese. Mi o ni

padanu ipese mi. Olorun a to mi sona sibi ti maa ti ri iranlowo. Aamin.

- Ohun to soro fun sese fun Olorun; iranlowo mi seese, ko ti i tan fun mi. Oro mi a ja sope. Haleluyah!

- Emi ko ni ku. Emi yio ye. Maa ri rere Oluwa. Maa korin asegun. Maa layo nipari.

- Iranlowo yoo wa mi ri. Iboju ti ko je kaye ri mi yoo jona deeru. Mo di riri fun awon to fe ran mi lowo. Oluranlowo mi ko jinna. Ibi ti mo wa ni ibudo iranlowo. Haleluyah!

- Mo yan iteriba. Mo yan ifokansin; mo yan ifarasin; mo yan iranlowo; mo yan atileyin; mo yan anfaani. Mo yan iranlowo. Amin.

KOKO ADURA
ORIN DAFIDI

1. Ko orin kan si Eleda re.
2. Baba mi, Baba mi, ran mi l'owo lati le san idiyele fun ipe giga Olorun ninu Kristi Jesu.
3. Oluwa, wo gbogbo ile to ti daru ninu ebi mi ati Ijo Olorun san.
4. Baba mi, Baba mi, bukun igbagbo mi ki O si ran mi l'owo lati le gbe ara le O ninu oun gbogbo ti mo ban se ni oruko Jesu.
5. Emi o ni boha ninu agbajopo iranlowo ni oruko Jesu.

6. Oun gbogbo ati ounkoun ti oti ku ninu aiye mi nipase aibere fun iranlowo, e ji pada ni oruko Jesu.

7. Gbogbo irugbin okunkun ninu aiye mi, efatu ni oruko Jesu.

8. Afefe iyipada si ibi giga, ya awon omo mi soto fun rere ni oruko Jesu.

9. Gbogbo agbara ki agbara ti a yan lati mo ogiri idabu si arin emi ati awon oluranlowo mi, epade ijakule ni oruko Jesu.

10. Jesu Oluwa, ro awon omo mi pelu oun ti won nilo lati di itewogba lodo oluranlowo ni oruko Jesu.

11. Emi igberaga, fi aiye mi sile.

12. Emi okunkun, fi aiye mi sile nisinsinyi ni oruko Jesu.

13. Agbara iwosan ati imupadabosipo, gbe aiye mi wo ni oruko Jesu.

14. Ofa iku, emi ki se ti e, pada ni oruko Jesu.

15. Oluwa o, da awon oluranlowo mi lohun ki won le ranti mi ki won si ran mi lowo ni oruko Jesu.

16. Agbara iku ti odi won omo mi ni igbekun, tu won sile pelu ina.

17. Gbadura ninu Emi fun ogun iseju.

OJO KEJILELOGBON

IGBEYIN AIBEERE FUN IRANLOWO: BIBO SINU IDANWO

IJEWO

- Mo ko idanwo. Emi ki i se alailagbara niwaju idanwo. Agbara Olorun wa fun mi. Emi o segun ifekufe mi.
- Pelu Olorun, ohun gbogbo ni sise. A ti ri mi bomi ninu Emi Mimo. Maa bori ogun aiye. Ma segun ise ti ara.
- Mo ni eso Olorun ninu mi; nitori naa, emi ko gbodo dese, a ti pa ara ati ise re lara mi. Mo ti di atunbi, mo ti di eda tuntun.
- Mi o ni ru ofin Olorun; mi o ni rin sinu panpe ota, mi o ni se aikobiara si ailera mi, emi yoo fi ara mi fun ibawi Emi Mimo, ailera mi ko ni ba ayanmo mi je.
- Emi yoo so eso emi; mo dagba kuro ninu aitayo, emi yoo dagba ninu emi, maa je apere rere fun awon miran.
- Idanwo ko ni di mi loju iran mi, idanwo ko ni ba anfaani mi je, idanwo o ni ti ilekun ogo mo mi.
- Jagunjagun Oluwa ni mo je, mo n rin ninu oore ofe Oluwa, oju ko lee ti mi.

- Mo lagbara, mo loro, a fi agbara fun mi, mo ni okun Olorun. Mo ni ami ororo Olorun. Mo lee se ohun gbogbo. Aamin.
- Olorun ko ni faaye gba idanwo to ju agbara mi lo; Olorun yoo fona han lati bori gbogbo idanwo mi.
- Ofa idanwo, pada sibi ti o ti n bo; irawo ni mi, emi yoo tanmole, mo je eso isododo, oju mi ko ni ri idibaje. Oluwa wa pelu mi. Haleluyah!

KOKO ADURA

ORIN DAFIDI 28

1. BABA, modupe lowo Re nitori O dara si emi ati ebi mi.
2. Ko orin titun si Jesu.
3. Baba mi, Baba mi, ran mi lowo lati ri ara mi ninu bi O ti fe mi to ni Oruko Jesu.
4. Oluwa, ran mi lowo lati le tera mo ise ti O fun mi lati se, ko ni se pelu oun ti yio na mi ni oruko Jesu.
5. Mo gba ore-ofe lti bo lowo idanwo igbera-eni yewo ni oruko Jesu.
6. Mo jewo mo si pase pe awon omo mi yio gba enubode awon ota won ni oruko Jesu.

7. Oluwa, mo yin O fun ona ti O nla fun mi nigba to le ni oruko Jesu.
8. Oluwa o, gba mi lowo agbara okunkun.
9. Ore-ofe ti fi aye gba iranlowo, gbe mi wo ni oruko Jesu.
10. Ikekun idanwo, tu mi sile pelu ina.
11. Gbogbo imo iparun awon ota ti won nse lodi si awon omo mi, tuka pelu ina.
12. Gbogbo akore lala okunkun, e s'ofo ni oruko Jesu.
13. Gbogbo agbara ti ndari awon oso mi si bomiran, akoko yin to, e s'ofo ni oruko Jesu.
14. Iwo ejo idanwo ti nsise ninu ipile mi, ja gbangba pelu ina ki o si ku ni oruko Jesu.
15. Oluwa, fun mi ni okun lati bori idanwo ni oruko Jesu.
16. Emi Mimo, tunse ki O si yi okan mi pada sir ere ni oruko Jesu.
17. Gbadura ninu Emi fun iseju meedogbon.

OJO KETALELOGBON

IGBEYIN AIBEERE FUN IRANLOWO: PIPADANU OHUN INI ENI

IJEWO

- Mi o ni padanu ohun to se iyebiye si mi. Emi yoo jere, N o ni padanu iwulo mi. Olorun yoo fi aanu Re han mi.

- Ota o ni bori mi, maa gba gbogbo iranlowo to ye ki n gba, mi o ni ni ifaseyin.

- Mo ko iya olojo pipe. Mo ko iponju ti ko leere. Mo ko iya ainidi. Mo gba imule.

- Awon ohun ini mi wa labe ipamo Olorun, awon ohun oso mi wa nibi ti ole ko ti lee de, mo n gbadun ipamo Olorun. Mo wa labe iye Olorun Alagbara julo.

- Ohun ti ko sise laye mi ko tun bere si maa sise bayi; emi o ri ebun Olorun to dara ju, ko si ohun ija kan ti a se lodi si mi ti yoo gberi. Mo wa labebe ojiji Olorun.

- Igberaga ko ni ja mi lole, mo ko labi gberaga, mo yan lati je onirele, kosi atako ti yoo lee bori mi, iranlowo mi daju.

- Bibeli mi je iwe iranlowo; woli mi je asoju iranlowo, awon ore mi yoo ran mi lowo, awon ebi mi yoo ran mi lowo. Haleluyah!

- Mo ti furugbin eso iranlowo, emi yoo kore iranlowo. Anfaani yoo wa fun mi. Oluranmilowo mi wa larowoto.

- Ohun ti mi o lee se ko ni dami duro; ailera mi ko ni da mi duro. Mo n tesiwaju, mo n lo sibi giga, mo wa ninu iwe iranti, a ko gbagbe mi. Haleluyah!

- Mo gba ami ororo lati lesi; mi o ni pedin. Mi o ni padanu oluranlowo mi. Mo di ailemu fun awon to fe ja mi lole.

KOKO ADURA
AISAYA 41

1. Ko orin kan si Oba awon oba.
2. Bab, fun mi ni ore-ofe lati le ma rin ninu ila Re ninu aiye ki nsi ma rin nipa itona Re ninu oun gbogbo ti mob a nse ni oruko Jesu.
3. Oluwa, ran awon omo mi lowo lati ma kopa ninu oun ti yio fa egun sinu aiye won ni oruko Jesu.
4. Ififunni je ise ati emi. Baba mi, Baba mi, fun mi ni emi ififunni ni oruko Jesu.
5. Oluwa, fun mi ni ore-ofe lati le moa won oun ti nsise lodi si ati ma wa pelu Re ati ore-ofe lati bori won ni oruko Jesu.
6. Ile-ejo okunkun ti o mura lati ma fi aiye gba iranwo atoke fun mi, tuka pelu in ani oruko Jesu.
7. Agbara ki agbara ti o ba fe jami lole ogun ibi mi, e s'ofo ni oruko Jesu.
8. Gbogbo ite okunkun ti a gbekale nitori awon omo mi, e tuka pelu in ani oruko Jesu.
9. Gbogbo idabu si aseyori eko awon omo mi, tuka pelu in ani oruko Jesu.
10. Gbogbo idabu si ipe mi, tu ka nipa Eje Jesu.

11. Gbogbo agbara ti nduro de akoko aijafara mi lati dojuko mi, e wo pale ni oruko Jesu.

12. Agbara ki agbara tin lo ayida yida okunkun lati si mi nipo kuro nibi Ibukun mi, e s'ofo ni oruko Jesu.

13. Iwo emi aso ni ni agbegbe mi ti a yan lati gbogun tie bi mi, e s'ofo danu ni oruko Jesu.

14. Emi Mimo, tu asiri ota agbegbe mi ni oruko Jesu.

15. Gbogbo iranlowo mi to ti si lo, mo gba yin pada nipa aanu ni oruko Jesu.

16. Gbogbo kokoro mujemuje ninu ago ara mi tin fa aisan, jade pelu in ani oruko Jesu.

17. Gbadura ninu Emi fun ogbon iseju.

OJO KERINLELOGBON

IGBEYIN AIBEERE FUN IRANLOWO: IDADURO SOJUKAN

IJEWO

- Aye mi yoo maa tesiwaju. Emi o maa tesiwaju ati iwaju ni; mi o ni si labe ajaga ibi; emi o maa lo lati okun de okun.

- Awon ti yoo fa mi soke yoo yosi mi, emi naa yoo di mimo si awon oluranlowo mi, ipo ti mo wa yoo dara si.

410

- Idurosojukan ki i se ipin mi. Emi o wa iranlowo latodo awon to lee ran mi lowo. Emi o wa nibi to ye ni akoko to ye.
- Olorun gbo igbe Jonah lati inu eja. Olorun gbo Dafidi lati inu iho. Iranlowo ko sowon ninu aye mi.
- Okoowo mi maa tesiwaju; ise mi yoo tesiwaju, ebi mi yoo tesiwaju; ise iranse mi yoo tesiwaju.
- Mo wa labe orun to si, mo ko lati wa loju kan, mo yan iye, mo ko iku, mo yan iyara, mo ko idurosojukan.
- Ohun daradara yoo sele si mi, maa layo ninu okan mi; maa korin asegun; emi o jo ijo asegun.
- Awon to wa pelu mi ju awon to n tako mi lo. Eni to ga julo n gbe inu mi. Awon oke isoro mi di awati; mo wa loke; mo wa laaye.
- Ohun gbogbo ti mo ba dawo le yoo yori si rere, Nibiti awon yoku ti kuna, emi yoo se aseyori. Olorun fi asiri re han awon woli, awon ota mi o ni raaye se mi bi won se fe. Haleluya!
- Idunnu ati ayo ko ni jinna si mi, ile mi je ile Oluwa. Angeli iranlowo yoo yi mi ka, emi o ri rere Oluwa ni ile alaaye.

KOKO ADURA

ORIN DAFIDI 44

1. Ko orin ijosin si Olorun aanu.
2. Oluwa, ran mi lowo lati le ma koyin si ifarahan okunkun ati ti awon omo ise re ni oruko Jesu.
3. Jesu, ran mi lowo lati le ma jere okan fun O lojojumo.
4. Oluwa, ran gbogbo awon ti won ti fi aiye won fun O lati le ma so eso ironupiwada ati eso Emi.
5. Oluwa, ko okan mi lati le ma gbe gbogbo eru mi Le o ninu igbagbo kin ma sise ma ronu.
6. Oluwa, dari gbogbo asise mi ana ji mi. Fun mi ni anfaani miran lati le ma gbe aiye mi fun O.
7. Okunrin emi mi, ki lo nse ninu ago awon ota? Jade nipa agbara ajinde ni oruko Jesu.
8. Gbogbo agbara tin fi oju mi ba oluranlowo ja, tu mi sile nipa ina.
9. Iwo emi iparadiradi, tu mi sile ki o si fo jade pelu in ani oruko Jesu.
10. Gbogbo okunrin alagbara okunkun irenderan ti nlodi si igbega mi, ku nipa ina ni oruko Jesu.
11. Sekeseke aifojuri ti ode mi mo le, ja pelu in ani oruko Jesu.

12. Jeki awon ota alenimadehin mi lo si irn ajo are mabo ni oruko Jesu.
13. Emi Mimo, tu asiri awon ota agbegbe mi ni oruko Jesu.
14. Pepe odi to di iranlowo ebi mi mu, tuk pelu in ani oruko Jesu.
15. Pariwo, Eje Jesu nigba mokanlelogun, gbe mi jade ninu ewon iranderan ni oruko Jesu.
16. Pariwo, Ina Emi Mimo ni igba mokanlelogun, gbogbo edidi awon aje ninu adugbo mi, e gbina ki e si ku ni oruko Jesu.
17. Gbadura ninu Emi fun ogbon iseju.

OJO KARUNDINLOGOJI

ITUSILE KURO NINU AIRIRANLOWO
IJEWO

- Mi o ni padanu aye mi, maa ja ajasegun ninu ogun aye, Awon ero okan mi a wa si imuse; iran aye mi yoo se rere.
- Erin lo maa keyin oro mi, a o pa awon elegan mi lenu mo, Olorun ki yoo je ki iran odi se ninu aye mi.
- Itiju ati egan ki i se ipin mi, awon oke koseese yoo di petele, awon ona mi ti ko gun ti di gigun.

- Olorun ti soro si ayanmo mi. Olorun ti bukun mi koja egun. Olorun ti so okun mi dotun.
- Emi ki i se eni adojuko fun awon to fe ba temi je, Olorun ti da mi lare, gbogbo opuro ni a a o tu lasiri, gbogbo ohun ija ikoko ki yoo sise lodi si mi. Aabo wa fun mi.
- Owon ki i se ipin mi; didawa ki i se ipin mi, ainiranlowo ki i se ipin mi. Mo ko aso itiju.
- Ala buburu ko ni se mo mi lara, a o ni ki mi ku ofo, mi ni kabamo laye mi. Mo gba iranlowo.
- Mo je alabukunfun; mo ni itelorun; a ti da mi lare, mo gba iwosan. Mo wa laaye, mo ni itesiwaju, mo ri iranlowo gba.
- Emi ko ni lo seyin; emi ki i se onigbese, emi ki i se alaisan, emi ki i se elewon, emi ki i se otosi, mi ki i se eni idalebi.
- Eto ibi mi ninu Jesu duro deede, a ti ka mi mo awon ayanfe; a o tun awon asise mi se, Olorun mi kujuuwon. Olorun mi yoo so ikoro mi di didun. Haleluyah!

KOKO ADURA

ORIN DAFIDI 94

1. Ko orin kan si Jesu.

2. Baba, fun gbogbo awon tokotaya ti now Re fun eso inu ninu ijo mi, pawon le rin loni ni oruko Jesu.

3. Baba mi, Baba mi, gba mi ki O sit u mi sile lowo gbogbo agbara ti ko je ki nri iranlowo ti mo ni lo l'aiye gba.

4. Ofa airiranwo ti a ta sinu aiye mi, pada si odo eni ta o ni oruko Jesu.

5. Bi O se lo Peteru ati Johannu lati se ise ami ati iyanu, lo emi ati awon omo mi lati le ma se ogidi ise iyanu ninu iran w ani oruko Jesu.

6. Olorun gbogbo eran ara, yanju gbogbo isoro mi ki O si fun mi ni ago ara titun ni oruko Jesu.

7. Oluwa, fun mi ni okan omo odo irufe ti Jesu kin le ma sin awon miran gege bi O ti se ni oruko Jesu.

8. Oluwa Baba mi o, je ki aiye mi wa fun iranlowo ti ko wopo ni oruko Jesu.

9. Gbogbo iwa odi to nle iranlowo sa fun mi, opin de ba yin ni oruko Jesu.

10. Nipa ifami ororo yan Jesu lori mi, emi ati oluranlowo mi yio ma ko si ara w ani oruko Jesu.

11. Oluwa o, je ki nma je igbadun awon anfanni to yato papa julo ni awon ibi to yato ni oruko Jesu.

12. Emi Mimo, ru awon afi adurajagun soke lati le ma fi adura jagun fun mi ni oruko Jesu.

13. Gbogbo oju okunkun to nso awon omo mi fun iparun, e fo danu ni oruko Jesu.
14. Gbogbo kurukuru okunkun to di awon oluranlowo mi mu, e fi ona sile ni oruko Jesu.
15. Kokoro aseyori, s'awari mi nipa aanu ni oruko Jesu.
16. Pariwo Olorun Aanu nigba mokanlelogun, ki o si wipe, tu emi ati awon omo mi sile kuro ninu ahamo airiranlowo ni oruko Jesu.
17. Gbadura ninu Emi fun iseju meedogbon.

OJO KERINDINLOGOJI

GBIGBADUN IRANLOWO OLORUN: DAFIDI

IJEWO

- Olorun mi ki i se opuro. Oun a maa se ohun ti O ba ti so. O ti se ileri lati ran mi lowo. Nitrori naa emi yoo ri iranlowo.
- Emi o jeri si didara Olorun. Kosi agbara to lee fi ohun to je temi du mi, mo ga ju gbogbo agbara ati ijoba okunkun.
- Dafidi gbadun iranlowo Olorun; Solomoni gbadun iranlowo Olorun. Nitorina won se ohun ribiribi.

- Nipa iranlowo Olorun, mo lee fo odi koja, nibp iranlowo Olorun, mo lee koja laarin iko ogun, nipa iranlowo Olorun, mo lee la Okun Pupa koja.
- Iranlowo Olorun je eto ibi mi, iranlowo Olorun je anfaani mi, iranlowo Olorun je ajemonu ojoojumo mi.
- Mo je okan lara awon oso iyebiye Oluwa, kosi eniti o lee benu ate lu mi, nigba ti isoro ba de, emi yoo pe fun iranlowo.
- Oluranlowo mi ko sonu. Oju oluranlowo mi ko fo, oluranlowo mi ki i se alailagbara; ohun iloro oluranlowo mi ko le tan laelae.
- Olorun opo yanturu ni mo n sin. Mo wa nibi ti iranlowo Re lee de. Mo wa nitosi fun iranlowo. Oluranlowo mi ko ni yi okan re pada.
- Oruko tuntun ni ipin mi, ipele otun je ipin mi, agbara tuntun je ipin mi; oluranlowo mi ko ni yi okan pada.
- Oruko titun ni ipin mi, ipele titun ni ipin mi, agbara titun ni ipin mi, nipa iranlowo Olorun, aiye mi tidara.
- A ran ise iranse mi lowo, ebi mi ri iranlowo, awon omo mi ri iranlowo, ogo wa fun mi, iyi wa fun mi. Mo ri iranlowo ni gbogbo igba. Haleluyah!

KOKO ADURA
ORIN DAFIDI 146

1. Ko orin kan lati josin fun Olorun Alagbara julo.
2. Oluwa, modupe lowo Re fun eni ti mo je ninu Kristi gegebi ati kowe re ni 1Pet.2:9.
3. Oluwa, ko mi ni ona Re, ki O si ma to mi nipa ona ogbon ni oruko Jesu.
4. Olorun Aanu, ma se fi aaye gba mi lati mu abuku/itiju ba oruko Re nipa ise mi ni oruko Jesu.
5. Oluwa, fun mi ni eti ti ngbo ohun Emi Re ati okan ti ntele ilana Re ni oruko Jesu.
6. Oluwa, ko owo mi bi a ti njagun ati ika mi bi a tin ja awon ogun ti O fe kin ja ni oruko Jesu (O.D.114:11).
7. Oluwa, kan nipa fun awon oluranlowo ojojumo mi lati sopo mo mi ni oruko Jesu (1Chr.12:2).
8. Baba mi, Baba mi, ko gbogbo awon ti ajo ni dupo dije ki emi le se itewogba ni oruko Jesu.
9. Ifami ororoyan lati gba ipin ti Olorun yan fun mi, ba le mi ni oruko Jesu.
10. Ifami ororo yan lati gba awom eri, ba le mi ni oruko Jesu.
11. Gbogbo iku ajeji ninu ebi mi, so ipa re nu l'ori mi ni oruko Jesu.
12. Mo ko lati diti, yadi, ati foju emi.
13. Esu ko ni ko abala iwe to pari ninu aiye mi.
14. Oluwa, ran mi lowo ki nmase so ojo ibewo mi nu ni oruko Jesu.
15. Oluwa, fi awon apa ibi ti mo tin se aare ti emi han mi.
16. Oluwa, gbe awon oluranlowo akoko dide fun mi ki awon ota mi to bori mi (Sam.21:16,17).
17. Gbadura ninu Emi fun iseju meedogbon.

OJO KETADINLOGOJI

GBIGBADUN IRANLOWO OLORUN: ASA, JEOSHAFATI

IJEWO

- Ko si ohun ija ti a o se simi ti yoo gberi; gbogbo awon ti o korajo nitori mi ni a o tuka. Olorun mi je Alagbara julo.
- Asa bori awon egbeegberun omo ogun. Jeosafati segun orile-ede meta po, nitori Oluwa wa leyin aseyori won.
- Ti Olorun ba wa leyin re, aabo wa fun o. Mo ni igboya, mo duro deede, mo ni idaniloju, mo ni itelorun.
- Olorun mi lee se ohun gbogbo; Olorun mi le se ayipada ohun to soro, Olorun mi lee ji oku dide, Olorun mi le yi ipo mi ti ko dara pada si daadaa. Olorun daadaa ni Olorun mi.
- Olorun mi lee jeki ohun gbogbo sise po fun rere mi, n ko beru rara ohun ti ota lee se.
- Ipin mi ni lati jeri, ipin mi ni aseyori lopolopo, ipin mi ni isegun lori ijakule.
- Emi yio gbadun iranlowo Olorun, emi yoo ri oore ofe, emi o ni padanu ohu didara julo lati odo Olorun.
- Ohun ti ko to Olorun mi ko ni sogo lori mi; awon ti ko to mi o ni gba ipo mi.

- Mo ni ajogunba rere, iranlowo je ajogunba mi, iranlowo lati orun je ogun ibi mi, mo ri iranlowo gba.
- Nko ni wa lori ile gbigbe, emi yoo wa lori oke, ewa Olorun yoo bori eeru mi. Haleluyah!

KOKO ADURA

ORIN DAFIDI 108

1. Ko orin kan si Jesu.
2. Baba, ran awon omo mi lowo lati ma kopa ninu oun ti yio fa egun si ori awon aiye won.
3. Oluwa, fi aye gba mi lati se atunse ninu ona mi kin le ni eri okan to mo niwaju Re ati eniyan ni oruko Jesu.
4. Baba, modupe lowo Re fun oun gbogbo ti O ti se fun mi, papa julo fun awon ogun ti o ti ja fun mi ti mi o tile mo ni oruko Jesu.
5. Oluwa, fi agabra Re han lati tu mi sile kuro ninu idekide ti mon la koja ni oni ni oruko Jesu.
6. Oluwa, ya awon omo mi soto fun ibapade to yato ni oruko Jesu.
7. Oluwa, ran mi lowo lati le fo ara mi mo kin le wulo fun ise Re ni oruko Jesu.
8. Oluwa, ran mi lowo lati le fe O bi o se to ati bi o se ye ninu otito ni oruko Jesu.
9. Iwo ni Alagbara, se ise agbara Re ninu ebi mi ni oruko Jesu.
10. Olorun mi, iwo wipe, "asan ni iranlowo eniyan", nitori iranlowo otito odo Re ni tinwa, je kin le gbadun iranlowo Re.

11. Ati ko ninu Oro Re wipe awon eniyan na yio je ore atinuwa ni ojo ijade-ogun Re. Baba, fi agabra Re han ninu aiye mi ki o si je ki awon eniyan yara lati ran mi lowo ni orukoe Jesu (O.D.110:3).
12. Mo gba idabobo Oluwa lori gbogbo irufe ewu ni ilana Jehoshafati ni oruko Jesu (1Ki.22:32,33).
13. Niwongba ti Emi to ji Jesu dide ninu oku ngbe inu mi, Oluwa, ji ki O si gba ago ara mi ni oruko Jesu.
14. Iwo emi ailera, jade kuro ni ago ara mi ni oruko Jesu.
15. Mo tu ara mi kuro lara ibasepo to lodi eyi tin mu oko aiye mi ri ni oruko Jesu.
16. Niwongba ti mon san idamewa mi dede, mo ko lati ma fi owo mi s'ofo ni ile iwosan ni oruko Jesu.
17. Gbadura ninu Emi fun iseju meedogbon.

OJO KEJIDINLOGOJI

GBIGBADUN IRANLOWO OLORUN: ESTERI, RUTU
IJEWO

- Mo wa labe majemu iranlowo; iranlowo je ogun ibi mi, iranlowo ko jinna si mi. Iranlowo mayederun fun mi.
- Mo n gbadun anfaani iranlowo; mo gba ebun iranlowo, mo darapo mo iranlowo ti a ko lee fi du mi, iranlowo je ipin mi.

- Emi ni oludije ti a o ran lowo, a ti fowo si iranlowo mi, mo wa nitosi fun iranlowo, mo ro mo iranlowo.
- Orisun iranlowo mi ko ni gbe, orisun iranlowo si sile fun mi. Mo gba kokoro si iranlowo.
- Emi o ri iranlowo nibiti o ti soro. Gegebi Esteri, emi o ri iranlowo labe akoso botiwun kori; Olorun mi yoo fi iranlowo asiko ranse, Olorun yoo ran mi lowo lati bori isoro.
- Ohun ti ota ro si mi, ko ni se nipa oore ofe Olorun. Emi yoo bori.
- Emi yoo maa dara si ni, mo n lo soke si ni, mo je ori, mo wa loke, mo n lo so is ipele giga. Mo ri iranlwoo gba.
- Gegebi Rutuu, emi o gba oore ofe fun iranlowo, ko ti i tan fun mi. Imole wa leyin okunkun mi.
- A gbo igbe mi fun iranlowo. Igbe mi fun iranlowo yoo gba idahun ni kiakia, nibiti mo wa, iranlowo yoo wa mi ri, ilekun iranlowo si sile fun mi.
- Nibiti enikeni ko ba ti ri iranlowo, emi o ri iranlowo gba. Emi o ri iranlowo lodo awon ti ki i se iranlowo fun elomiran. Amin!

KOKO ADURA

ORIN DAFIDI 70

1. Ko orin kan si Jesu.
2. Oluwa o, ma je ki eran ara, aiye yi ati esu jami lole anfaani ti o wa ninu irapada Kristi. Jeki awon eniyan mo wipe omo Re ni mo je.
3. Oluwa, fun mi ni ore-ofe lati le ma fi Okan Re han ninu irele l'ojojumo.
4. Gegebi Omo Eniyan ko ti ni ibi ti yio gbe ori Re le ki emi le ni ile l'ori, temi da? Oluwa, nipa aanu, mo gba.
5. Oluwa, fun mi ni ore-ofe lati to aiye mi ni ibamu pelu Oro Re ni oruko Jesu.
6. Oluwa, je ki Emi Iwa Mimo bere si ni fi ara han ninu mi ni oruko Jesu.
7. Oluwa Olorun mi, gegebi eni ti Iwo ti yan ti O sim o bi Esteri, nigbakugba ti mob a nilo iranlowo Re, je ki iranlowo dise fun mi ni oruko Jesu.
8. Ati ko wipe oun gbogbo ti Re mi. nitori na, Baba mi, lati oni ati titi, je ki iranlowo igbadegba je temi lati jegbadun ni oruko Jesu.
9. Ati ko wipe, "Emi yio ran yin lo kore ni ibi ti e ko sise si." Oluwa o, mu mi jegbadun iranlowo ni ibi ti mi o se lala si ni oruko Jesu (Joh.4:38)
10. Baba mi ti nbe l'orun, Olorun gbogbo eran ara, gbe soke ki O si fi idi aiye mi mule ninu ore-ofe iranlowo akoko n oruko Jesu.
11. Oluwa, tu ore-ofe ti yio mu mi sopo mo iranlowo latoke ni oruko Jesu.
12. Oluwa, ni ilana ti Rutu, so mi po moa won ise ti yio se mi l'anfaani ni oruko Jesu (Ru.2:2).
13. Baba mi, Baba mi, ni ilana ti Esteri, je ki ojurere yamisoto ki O si fun mi ni ite temi ni oruko Jesu (Est.2:15-1).

14. Gbogbo aba iranlowo je to yimika, e lo ki e fi ara yin s'ofo ni oruko Jesu.
15. Gegebi ogo orun o se gbe pamo, be gege, ogo mi o ni se gbe pamo ni oruko Jesu.
16. Gbogbo iwe ojo okunkun ti a gbe kale lodi si awon omo mi, ejona di eru ni oruko Jesu.
17. Gbadura ninu Emi fun iseju ogun.

OJO KOKANDINLOGOJI

GBIGBADUN IRANLOWO OLORUN: DANIEL, NEHEMIAH

IJEWO

- Mo segun gbogbo alatako, mo segun gbogbo awon to korira iserere mi, enikeni ti o ba korira mi, ko ni si nibe nigba ti mo ba pe fun iranlowo.
- Olorun yoo tilekun mo awon ti n tako iranlowo mi, ki won to da iranlowo mi duro, emi o ti koja lo.
- Kosi ohunkohun ti yoo da iranlowo mi duro. Kosi ohunkohun to maa da oluranlowo mi duro. Oluranlowo mi ko ni yokan pada.
- Iwe mi yoo ri iyonu, leta mi yoo ri iyonu; ibeere mi fun iranlowo yoo gba ase; iranlowo yo sise fun mi. Amin.
- Emi o bowo fun ofin iranlowo. Maa tele ilana pipe iranlowo. Nibiti iranlowo ba ti

farasin, maa ri iranlowo. Iranlowo je ogun ibi mi, nitori naa iranlowo ko jinna si mi.

- Awon angeli iranlowo yoo be mi wo loni, ojise iranlowo yoo jise fun mi, iranlowo je ipin mi, iranlowo je ajogunba mi.
- A ko lee fi eto mi du mi, emi o le tan sile, a o le da mi pada, a ti se iranlowo lojo fun mi.
- A ti fi owo si mi lati gba iranlowo; a ti gbe mi dide lati gba iranlowo, ise mi yoo gba ayesi.
- Iranlowo yoo po pupo fun mi. iranlowo yoo to fun mi, iranlowo a sumo mi pekipeki. Haleluya!
- Ekun ki i se ipin mi, ohun to n dun laye mi ko ni dikoro, iranlowo wa fun mi. Haleluyah!

KOKO ADURA
ORIN DAFIDI

1. Yin Olorun ninu Emi ati ninu oye.
2. Baba mi, Baba mi, fun mi ni ore-ofe lati ma bu ola fun O ninu oun gbogbo ti mon se ni gbogbo ojo aiye mi.
3. Oluwa mi, fun mi ni ore-ofe lati le ma ko nipa igbe aiye Jesu ki O si ranmi lowo lati le ma gbe igbese gegebi bi Jesu ti se ni oruko Jesu.
4. Oluwa, gbe awon Kristeni to je adari ni gbogbo agbaiye ro ki won ma ba subu ni oruko Jesu.
5. Oluwa, si oju mi si ijamba apadi aiyeraye.
6. Baba mi, Baba mi, se oun gbogbo to nilo lati se lati le mu mi duro lailabuku niwaju ite Re ni oruko Jesu.

7. Baba mi, Baba mi, Baba aanu, lati oni titi de opin, je ki aiye mi je ipago igbaradi awon oluranlowo ni oruko Jesu.

8. Oluwa o, Olorun mi, fi ipa mu awon eniyan lati dide fun iranlowo mi ni oruko Jesu.

9. Danieli ni joju ninu ijoba awon oba, je ki njoju nipa iranlowo Re nigbogbo ojo aiye mi ni oruko Jesu.

10. Oluwa, fun mi ni eru-okan fun awon eniyan Re ati fun ile Re gegebi Nehemiah.

11. Gbogbo ile-iso okunkun ti o duro larine mi ati awon oluranlowo ayanmo mi, e wo pale ni oruko Jesu (Dan.10:10-13).

12. Fun mi ni ore-ofe lati moye ise Olorun lati isinsinyi ni oruko Jesu (Dan.9:1).

13. Baba mi, Baba mi, ru awon oba aiye soke ki won le fun mi ni iranwo lori iran mi pelu gbogbo ipo ati oun ini won ni oruko Jesu.

14. Ni ilana Danieli, je ki gbogbo agabagebe awon ota mi di iparun won ni oruko Jesu (DAN.6:22-24).

15. Oluwa o, gbe aso ore-ofe ati ogo titun wo mi ni oruko Jesu.

16. Gbadura ninu Emi fun ogbon iseju.

OJO OGOJI
OLORUN: ASEDA IRANLOWO

IJEWO

- Olorun ni Alagbara julo, laisi Olorun, kosi ohun to lee sise, pelu Olorun, kosi ijakule Kankan, Olorun je Olorun siseese. Olorun je Olorun gbogbo oore ofe.

- Olorun ran awon omo Israeli lati la Okun Pupa ja, Olorun ran Dafidi lowo lati pa Goliati, Olorun ran Sarah lowo lati loyun ni ogbologbo ojo, Olorun ran Danieli lowo lati tumo ala to soro, Olorun ran Hezekiah lowo lati segun awon orile-ede to gbogun ti i.
- Nitori Olorun wa pelu mi, eru ko ba mi, nitori Olorun mi ko lee paro, mo ni igboya ninu Re. emi ko ni abamo ninu titele Olorun.
- Olorun ni Olusanesan; Olorun je Olubukun, Olorun je Olurapada; Olorun je Asiwaju; Olorun je Oluko; Olorun je Oluranlowo.
- Nitori Olorun mo ohun gbogbo, emi o mu ase Re se. Emi ko ni ku; emi o ri ebun ti Olorun ti pese fun mi.
- Olorun je Onise Iyanu. Ise iyanu je ohun ara fun iranlowo eda; ise iyanu je oore ofe Olorun fun wa lati da ohun ti Olorun fe ka da.
- Olorun je alaanu ti n nu gbogbo omije nu. O lee fun mi ni igba otun, O lee fun mi ni oruko titun, O lee mu pada bo sipo ohun to ti sonu. O le gbe mi soke lati ori akitan.
- Nipa iranlowo Olorun, ayo mi ti de, nipa iranlowo Olorun mo ni idi to po lopolop lati mujo jo, nipa iranlowo Olorun, mo lee so okun mi dotun, nipa iranlowo Olorun ohun gbogbo ni sise. Halleluyah!

- Olorun lee san igbese mi, Olorun lee ba mi gbe ise mi duro; Olorun lee pese fun gbogbo aini mi; Olorun lee so kekere ti mo ni di pupo.
- Mo gba imi aaye, mo gba emi ogbon. mo gba okan titun, mo gba oore ofe. Mo gba iranlowo. Haleluyah!

KOKO ADURA
ORIN DAFIDI 46

1. Ko orin si Jesu Olupilese ati Alasepe igbagbo Re.
2. Oluwa, kun okan mi pelu ife Re ki ife Re le ma san lati odo mi odo awon miran.
3. Olorun Aanu, wa ba mi gbe, fi ago mi se ibugbe Re, ki O si fun mi ni ore-ofe ati bori idanwo to fe mu mi si ara mi lo ni oruko Jesu.
4. Olorun Aanu, se iribomi fun Ijo Re pelu ife tooto ki O si di Ijo Kristi pelu edidi irepo ni oruko Jesu.
5. Ati ko wipe, "lako labo l'O da won". Baba mi, pase fun gbogbo okunrin ati obinrin ti O da lati ran emi ati awon omo mi lowo ni oruko Jesu.
6. Oluwa Olorun mi o, gbogbo iseda ti O so iranlowo mi mo, mo pe won jade ni oruko Jade.
7. Baba, bi mo se ngbadura nisinsinyi, je ki ipa iranlowo mi bere ni oruko Jesu.
8. Baba mi, Baba mi, fun gbogbo awon oluranlowo mi ni ore-ofe ati itara lati ran mi lowo ni oruko Jesu.
9. Oluwa, ran awon omo mi lati sopo moa won ipinnu Re fun aiye won ni oruko Jesu.
10. Baba mi, fi awon eniyan yi mika ti yio ran mi lowo lati mu ayanmo mi se ni oruko Jesu.

11. Gbogbo ebun emi ati ore-ofe to ti dobu ninu aiye mi, ji soju ise ni oruko Jesu.

12. Mo ko lati ma sise bi afoju ni akoko iranlowo latoke yi ni oruko Jesu.

13. Gbogbo ekun ile je ti Olorun, nipase eleyi, o je temi nitori mo je Ajumo-Jogun po pelu Kristi.

14. Mo fi won sofo, gbogbo agbara to nje gaba lori agbegbe mi ninu ara ati ninu emi ni oruko Jesu.

15. Ile, ile o, ile o, fi iranlowo mi fun mi ni oruko Jesu.

16. Oluwa, je ki oro awon keferi ati asunkun okun san wa sinu aiye ni oruko Jesu.

17. Gbadura ninu Emi fun iseju meedogbon okereju.

APPENDIX

SECTION SIX
APPENDIX

1

PRAYERS FOR SPIRITUAL RENEWAL (PS.11)
CONFESSION

- I am renewed by the Spirit. I am lifted by the spirit. I am Spirit filled. My Spirit man is lifted. I have overcome.
- The Blood of Jesus has purified me. I am worthy of His Presence. My inner man is empowered. I carry the grace of God. I carry the fire of God.
- My Spirit man is set on fire. The Word of God has set me on fire. I know who I am. I am a terror to the kingdom of darkness.
- Because I am renewed, I carry fresh fire, fresh anointing. I am unstoppable for enemies. When the enemies see me, they shall flee.
- My household is renewed. My family is renewed. My business is renewed. My Church is renewed. My destiny is renewed. It is well with my soul! In Jesus' name.

PRAYER POINTS
Joel 2: 28-32; Ezek.37: 1-14

1. Oh Lord, I need spiritual renewal to serve You the more.
2. My Father, my Father, renew my prayer life by fire.
3. Holy Spirit, renew my evangelism life, kindle fresh fire in me.
4. Father, let there be holiness renewal in my life.

5. Lord Jesus, rekindle the fire of the word in my life.
6. Oh Lord, let the study and meditation of Your Word be renewed in my life.
7. My inner man, receive fresh fire to fulfill God's mandate.
8. Every area of my life that needs to be renewed, oh Lord, let there be fire of renewal there.
9. Holy Spirit, have Your way in my life for my spiritual advancement.
10. Holy Spirit, refresh my life for the next level of my assignment.

2

PRAYERS AGAINST BESETTING SINS (PS.51)
CONFESSION

- I am born again. My body is born again. My Mind is born again. Besetting sins cannot have dominion over my life.
- Christ in me the hope of glory. I can do all things through Christ that strengthens me. I will live a victorious life over besetting sin. I will overcome at last.
- Jesus is the author and finisher of my faith. He knows my struggles and is ready to help me. My Redeemer lives, I will triumph over sinful life.

- I am born to rule. I will live a dominion life in this crooked world. Besetting sins will not overcome my life in Jesus' name.
- Satan, get thee behind me! Impure thoughts, get thee behind me! Immoral acts, get thee behind me. My body is the Temple of God!

PRAYER POINTS
Psalms 19: 7-14, Psalms 51; Psalms 119:9
1. Every power of besetting sins over my life, loose your power by fire.
2. Every yoke and bondage of besetting sins in my life, break by fire in Jesus' name.
3. Every power of besetting sins that held my life captive, break by fire.
4. Every areas of my life that besetting sin is affecting, Holy Spirit deliver me.
5. Satanic bondage of besetting sin over my life, catch fire in Jesus' name.
6. By the power in the Word of God, I am delivered from every besetting sins.
7. Holy Spirit, help me to overcome every form of besetting sin in my life.
8. I receive grace to live a victorious life over besetting sins in Jesus' name.
9. Through your Word oh Lord, let my soul be converted to live a holy life.

10. My Father, give me grace to be more desirous of Your Word than every other things.

3

PRAYERS FOR AWAITING MOTHERS (PS.29)
CONFESSION

- My God is my creator. I am created excellently, wonderfully and perfectly.
- I reject barrenness. I embrace fruitfulness because that is the will of God for my life.
- The Word of God is higher than any other word, therefore every negative report of my fruitfulness is cancelled by the Word of God.
- I have the life of God in me. I possess the gene of God. I will bear my own child/children in Jesus' name.
- I and the children that the Lord will give me shall be for signs and for wonders. My children shall surround my table in the name of Jesus.

PRAYER POINTS

Psalms 113; 123

1. Father, I thank You because I will not be barren in my life.

2. Every hindrances to my fruitfulness, be scattered in the name of Jesus.
3. Every covenant that is hindering my child bearing, be destroyed by the power in the Blood of Jesus.
4. Every satanic instrument used to block my womb, be removed by fire.
5. Oh ye my womb, receive power of conception in the name of Jesus.
6. Power that is resisting my conception, die by fire in Jesus' name.
7. Wherever my womb is being kept by the powers of darkness, come out by fire.
8. Every negative words and curses that has blocked my fruitfulness, be nullified in Jesus name.
9. Oh ye power of conception, come upon my life now in Jesus' name.
10. Every arrow of miscarriage programmed against my life, jump out by fire.

4

PRAYER FOR THE CHRONICALLY ILL (JER.17)
CONFESSION
- Heal me oh Lord and I shall be healed. Save me oh Lord and I shall be saved.
- Christ has been wounded for my transgressions. He has been bruised for my iniquities. The chastisement of my

peace is upon Him. By His stripes I am healed and I am delivered.

- I shall not die but live to declare the glory of the Lord. This sickness shall not be unto death in the name of Jesus.
- Thou shall keep me in perfect peace because my mind is stayed on thee. The peace of God is my portion in the name of Jesus.
- He forgives me of all my iniquities and heals all my diseases. He redeems my life from destruction, therefore I am set free. Hallelujah!

PRAYER POINTS
Isai.53; Psalms 103: 1-5

1. Thank You Lord for all the provision for my healing.
2. Father, be glorified for the power in Your Word to heal me.
3. My Father, my Father, I appreciate You for the power in the Blood of Jesus to heal and set me free.
4. Arrow of sickness in my body, you are a stranger there, jump out by fire.
5. Every attack of sickness in my body back fire in the name of Jesus.
6. Every bondage of sickness, affliction in my life, be destroy by fire.

7. Covenant of sickness in my lineage, break by the Blood of Jesus.
8. Inherited sickness in my body, Blood of Jesus, flush them out.
9. Recurring sicknesses in my life, disappear by the power in the Blood of Jesus.
10. Sickness is not my portion; I receive new body and sound health in Jesus' name.

5

PRAYER FOR BUSINESS EXPANSION (PS.68) CONFESSION

- My business will prosper. My business will increase. My coast shall be enlarged.
- My business will flourish like the cedar of Lebanon. My business will expand locally and internationally in the name of Jesus.
- My business shall be profitable. Devourers shall not have power over my business. I am a tither.
- My God will bless the work of my hand. I shall be the head and not the tail. I will be a lender and not a borrower. My work is blessed.
- Evil seed germinating in my business is uprooted by fire. My staff shall lead a godly life. My business shall express the glory of God in the name of Jesus.

PRAYER POINTS

Deut.28: 1-13; Psalms 1:1-3

1. Oh Lord, I appreciate Your grace and mercy over my business.
2. My Father, my Father, let Your hand of increment rest upon my business.
3. Father, bless and enlarge the coast of my business indeed.
4. Anointing of prosperity, rest upon my business for expansion.
5. Every environmental power attacking my business expansion, be wasted by fire in the name of Jesus.
6. Demotion powers set against my business expansion, be consumed by fire of the Holy Ghost.
7. Oh Lord, give me connecting helpers for my business.
8. Holy Spirit, endow me with wisdom to expand my business in Jesus' name.
9. Isai. 60:1,2. The glory of my business begin to shine now by the power in the name of Jesus.
10. Every demonic or satanic power buried or hanging in my business environment, Holy Ghost thunder, bury them for me.

6

PRAYER FOR THE UNSAVED (PS.38)

CONFESSION

- For the wages of sin is death; but the gift of God is eternal life through Jesus Christ our Lord. The unchurched around me will not die in sin.
- Save them oh Lord and they shall be saved. Deliver them from the power of sin and they shall be delivered.
- Because God loves them, they shall receive eternal life through Christ Jesus.
- Behold the kind of love God bestowed upon them that they should be called the son of God. They are children of God.
- Like the Prodigal Son, they shall find their way home. They are possessed by the spirit of God, they shall be born again.

PRAYER POINTS

Psalm 1: 3-6; Psalm 57

1. Oh God of Mercy, I thank You for the love You have for the sinners. You do not want them to perish.
2. By your Mercy oh Lord, encounter every sinner in my family and in my environment.
3. Father, open their spiritual eyes and ears of understanding that they may know You.
4. Every power holding them captive, be wasted by fire.

5. Holy Spirit, open the door of salvation to all unbelievers around me.
6. Father, break every power of sin over their lives in Jesus' name.
7. Lord Jesus, give them a new heart and renew their spirit man in the name of Jesus.
8. By Your mercy Father, lead them to Calvary for the salvation of their soul in Jesus' name.
9. My Father, my Father, open the spiritual eyes of the sinners that they may see beyond physical.
10. Spirit of holiness, possess as many that seek You for their salvation.

7

1. PRAYER AGAINST BUSINESS OPPOSITION (PS.12)
CONFESSION

- My business will not run aground. Loses will not swallow my business. The traps of the opposition will not kill my business.
- I will not make foolish business discussions. I will not use my hand to wreck my business. I will not be out of business.

- I will not be reduced in business. I will not lose my capital. I will not lose my investments. I will not lose my profits.
- My business will go to the next level. My business partners will not damage my business.
- My business will go from strength to strength. My business will enjoy supernatural assistance. Like Peter, my business will see abundance. The Lord will give me divine direction.

PRAYER POINTS

1. Lord, visit the foundation of my work place and expose the activities of the opposition in the name of Jesus.
2. Lord, do not allow the activities of opposition to close down the business of my work place in the name Jesus.
3. Lord, deliver my staff and colleagues from the arrow of debt and indebtedness in the name of Jesus.
4. Lord, guide my company and industry from unfriendly business atmosphere in the name of Jesus.
5. Lord, break the yoke and bondages of loss over the business of my work place in the name of Jesus.
6. Lord, give me victory over those who want to swallow and consume my business in the name of Jesus.
7. Lord, let every power that wants to take over my business be neutralized immediately in the name of Jesus.

8. Lord, your Word says You will fight against those who are fighting me, take over my battles over my business in the name of Jesus.

9. Lord, give me superior wisdom over the antagonist and opposition in my business in the name of Jesus.

10. Lord, nullify every evil prophecy against my business now in the name of Jesus.

8

PRAYER FOR THE GRADUATES SEEKING JOB (ISAI.14)

CONFESSION

- My life cannot be stranded. I shall receive uncommon help in Jesus' name.

- Mercy of God shall locate my life. Door of opportunity shall be opened for my life. The Lord shall order my steps to profitable job in Jesus' name.

- My God shall remember me for good. Divine doors shall be opened for me. I shall be highly favoured in Jesus' name.

- Good job shall locate me; I shall locate good job. God's mercy, favour and grace will speak for me.

- My certificates and other documents shall be endorsed and highly favored in Jesus' name. Every mark of rejection is hereby removed from my documents in Jesus' name.

PRAYER POINTS
Psalm 1, Deut.28:1-13
1. Father, thank You for Your daily provision for my life.
2. God of mercy, let the doors of opportunity be opened for me in Jesus' name.
3. Oh Lord, let my credentials find favour wherever I present them.
4. My Father, my Father, provide for me a good and satisfying job. The one that will give me the freedom to serve You.
5. Every power of rejection upon my life and credentials be nullified in the name of Jesus.
6. Every evil mark upon my forehead, be wipe away by the power in the Blood of Jesus.
7. Father, let every of my rejection be turned to acceptance by mercy in the name of Jesus.
8. Oh Lord, grant me my heart desire in regard to my dream job in Jesus' name.
9. Where others are experiencing let down, I shall experience favour in the name of Jesus.
10. Prepare me oh Lord, for the task ahead in my new place of work in the name of Jesus.

PRAYER FOR MARRIAGEABLE SINGLES (ISAI.58)
CONFESSION

- I shall be married. I will no longer be single unnecessarily. He that created them, created them male and female. I shall locate my spouse in the name of Jesus.

- Every mark of negativity, antagonizing my union with my God ordained spouse, be washed away by the Blood of Jesus.

- He that finds a wife, finds favour from the Lord. My husband shall find me. I shall no longer be hidden from my husband.

- Mark of acceptance, envelope me. I reject rejection. I embrace marital acceptance.

- Wrong partner, get away from me. Evil partner, get away from me. Wrong relationship, get away from me in the name of Jesus.

PRAYER POINTS

Gen.2: 18-24; Psalm 19

1. Oh Lord, I appreciate You because You will not allow me to choose the wrong partner.
2. Holy Spirit, guide me in choosing the right partner for my life.

3. My Father in heaven, give me the bone of my bone and the flesh of my flesh.

4. God of mercy, let me not enter the wrong house when choosing my partner in Jesus' name.

5. Every power of delay in marriage be broken over me by fire in Jesus' name.

6. My God, give me my day of joy and let people celebrate with me.

7. Every evil or demonic mark hindering my marriage, Blood of Jesus wipe it away.

8. Foundational powers and curses that does not allow marriage in my lineage, be broken now in Jesus' name.

9. Marital effort wasters in my generation, be wasted by the Blood of Jesus over my life.

10. Whatsoever has been done negatively in the spirit realm concerning my marriage, be cancelled by the Blood of Jesus.

10

PRAYER AGAINST THE SPIRIT OF UNTIMELY DEATH (PS.91)
CONFESSION

• My life, reject untimely death. My family, reject untimely death. My household, reject untimely death.

• Spirit of untimely death, we are not your candidate; disappear by the Fire of God.

- Hand of God, cover me and mine and protect us from evil powers looking for whom to kill.
- I and my family shall abide under the shadow of the Almighty. We choose life. We reject untimely death. We are for signs and we are for wonders.
- Forces beheading people around me, I am not your target, blow up by fire. I shall live to declare the glory of God in the name of Jesus.

PRAYER POINTS

Psalm 123

1. Thank You Lord for the settlement of my debt on the Cross of Calvary.
2. Every power of death ruling my life, loose your power now.
3. Every chain and padlock of death in my life, break by fire in Jesus' name.
4. God of mercy, deliver me from every form of untimely death in Jesus' name.
5. Every arrow of untimely generational death, leave my life, by fire.
6. Spirit of sudden death, leave my ministry in Jesus' name.
7. Every blood sucking demons, sent to suck our blood while sleeping, catch fire!

8. The grace to live my life to the fullest in the will of God, possess my by mercy.
9. Holy Spirit, cover me and mine with the Blood of Jesus.
10. Jehovah Nissi, let Your Banner of protection cover us in the name of Jesus.

11

2. PRAYER AGAINST EATING IN THE DREAM (PS.17)

CONFESSION

- My destiny will not be aborted. My glory will not be exchanged. Night caterers get lost.
- My body is the temple of the Almighty God. I will not be destroyed by demonic food.
- I am sanctified. My house is sanctified. My bed is sanctified. My dining table is sanctified. I reject demonic food.
- I will increase, I will multiply. I wll grow, I will rise. I will not be reduced. I will not be caged. I will not be tied down.
- I will not die prematurely. I will not be a figure head. I will not be wasted. Amen

PRAYER POINTS

1. Lord, paralyze every night caterer cooking food for me in my dream in the name of Jesus.
2. Lord, set ablaze every kitchen house and evil canteen feeding me in my dream in the name of Jesus.
3. Lord, protect my bed chambers from the attacks of the evil night caterers in the name of Jesus.
4. Lord, blindfold the agents of darkness sent to feed me in my dreams in the name of Jesus.
5. Lord, sanctify my house and shield it from the agents of night caterers.
6. Lord, purge my soul from the pollution and contaminations of food I have eaten in the dreams in the name of Jesus.
7. Lord, restore all my exchanged virtues and glory which happened when I was eating in my dreams in the name of Jesus.
8. Lord, restore my spiritual gifts and fruits which had been lost as a result of eating in the dreams in the name of Jesus.
9. Lord, give me immunity against poison and corruption in my dream life in the name of Jesus.
10. Every poisonous food I have ever ingested physically and spiritually, Blood of Jesus, purge it out of my system in Jesus' name.

12

3. PRAYER FOR MINISTRY GROWTH AND & FRESH FIRE (PS.27)

CONFESSION

- God is on our side. The gate of hell cannot prevail against us. The Church is marching on. Through our God we shall prevail against our foes. We shall not bow down to satanic threat.
- Our ministry will enjoy unusual signs & wonders. The Lord will enlarge our coast. The Lord is on our side. Evil laws will not stop us.
- Growth is a symbol of living. Growth is a sign of development. Growth is a symbol of increase. The Lord will increase us on every side. Our ministry will not be stagnated.
- Zion is a place of comfort. It is a place of recovering. It is the mountain of deliverance. Great deliverance will take place in our midst. Destiny will be restored. Signs and wonders will not be scarce in our midst.
- Fire is a purifier. Fire is a refiner. God will baptize us with fresh fire. Our ministry shall be noted for fire brand. Fire is a limit breaker. We shall not be limited.

PRAYER POINTS

1. Lord, I thank You for the unusual signs and wonders we have experienced so far in our ministry.
2. Fresh fire of God that sustains the ministry & every member rest upon our lives in the name of Jesus.

3. Every environmental power working against the ministry and the members be disgraced by the Blood of Jesus.
4. Every evil law enforcers within and without our ministry receive the judgment of God in Jesus' name.
5. Heaven of unusual signs & wonders that will enhance the growth of the ministry and enlarge our coast be opened in Jesus' name.
6. Every resource You have given to us in our ministry both physical and spiritual we refuse to lose any in Jesus' name.
7. Evil gate of hell that is lifted against our ministry will not prosper by the Blood of Jesus.
8. Every spy in our most midst working for our enemy, be exposed and disgraced in Jesus' name.
9. Grace of God to grow both physically and spiritually rest upon our ministry in Jesus' name.
10. You satanic voice of slander will not prosper in our ministry in Jesus name.

13
PRAYER FOR GOD'S VESSELS (PS.23)
CONFESSION

- I am chosen by God; His grace is sufficient for me. I am of the generation that serves God. I shall not wander away.

- The Potter shall mold me. Every impurity shall be removed. In the hands of the potter, I shall turn our well. I will serve my generation well.
- I shall be a vessel unto honour always. I shall not be a vessel unto dishonor. My life shall be forever consecrated unto the Lord.
- Devil, you have no place in my life. Every area of my life has been filled up with the Spirit of God.
- I am useful. I am wanted. I will not be discarded. I will not be thrown away. in the name of Jesus.

PRAYER POINTS
Isai.61

1. My Lord, thank You for choosing me to be a vessel of honour in Your hand.
2. Father, sanctify me and consecrate me for Your glory.
3. My Father let your grace be sufficient for me till the end of my life.
4. Lord Jesus, help me to fulfill the ministry You have committed into my hands.
5. Oh Lord, empower me to do exploits in my ministry.
6. Every attack of the enemy over my ministry, Father, give me victory over them.

7. Every power that is standing against my ministry, let them be wasted by fire.
8. Father, I pray let not all my labours be in vain, lest I should be a cast away.
9. Holy Spirit, continue to be my guide in every step I be take.
10. Oh Lord, let Thy will be done in my life.

14

PRAYER AGAINST THE SPIRIT OF DEBT (PS.2)
CONFESSION

- The promise of God for me is that I shall lend unto nations and not borrow. I claim this promise in the name of Jesus.
- I reject the spirit of debt. I reject the spirit of borrowing. I reject the spirit of lack.
- I embrace the spirit of abundance. I embrace the spirit of restoration. I embrace the spirit of overflow.
- Power that force people into indebtedness; loose your hold over my life. My financial life, be on fire.
- Henceforth, my financial life will turn around for good. In the name of Jesus.

PRAYER POINTS

Psalm 21

1. Oh Lord, I thank You for pulling me out of the net of debt.
2. Father, please forgive me for knowing entering into the den of debt.
3. Oh Lord, empower my business so it can flourish.
4. My Father, my Father, seal the pit of debt that the enemy has dug for me.
5. Hand of God, pull me out of the pit of debt.
6. My Father, bless the work of my hands so I can pay off all my debt.
7. I receive the grace to be a blessing to people.
8. I receive the grace to be a lender and not a borrower.
9. I receive the grace to have in abundance.
10. Father, deliver me from the spirit of stagnation.

15
PRAYER AGAINST THE SPIRIT OF BACKSLIDING (PS.51)
CONFESSION

- I refuse to backslid. I refuse to be lukewarm. I refuse to be cold. I shall be hot and fervent for my God.
- I refuse to be a Demas. I refuse to be a Judas. I refuse to be a Saul.

- Spirit of God, possess me for the journey ahead. Hand of God, lead me on this journey called life.
- Godly companions, surround me. Holy Spirit, surround me with godly companions.
- My challenges shall not overcome me. I shall always overcome all of my challenges in the name of Jesus.

PRAYER POINTS

Psalm 51

1. Oh Lord, thank You for opening my eyes to discover my spiritual downfall or setback.
2. By Your mercy oh Lord, restore unto me the joy of thy salvation.
3. Create in me a new and right spirit in the name of Jesus.
4. Renew my spiritual life oh Lord in prayer, in Word and in Holiness.
5. Give me the spirit that cries against sinful desire.
6. Every area my life that is leaking spiritually, Blood of Jesus, block them for me.
7. My Father, my Father, separate me from all the friends that are causing my spiritual backwardness by fire.
8. Let every stumbling stone be removed from my way in the name of Jesus.

9. Spirit of holiness, possess my life in the name of Jesus.
10. Holy Spirit, envelop me with the grace to forge ahead in the face of adversity.

16
PRAYER FOR OUR CHILDREN (PS.127)
CONFESSION

- My children are for signs. My children are for wonders. My children are miraculous. My children are marvelous.

- My children are not children of belial. My children are not demonic. My children shall not die untimely. They shall live to the glory of God.

- My children will serve the living God. My children will never serve the devil. All the days of the lives of my children, they shall sing the praises of God.

- My children are wise. My children are knowledgeable. My children are sensible. My children are not foolish.

- The eyes of the Lord are the guide of my children. My children will not take the wrong steps. It is well with my children in the name of Jesus.

PRAYER POINTS
Psalm 127

1. Father, thank You for all these wonderful gifts (heritage of God) given to me.
2. Blood of Jesus, speak better things over all my children in Jesus' name.
3. Father, let my children be taught of the Lord.
4. Father, let my children be established in righteousness. Let them be far from every oppression in Jesus' name.
5. Father, let all my children fulfill their destinies on the land of the living in the name of Jesus.
6. My Father in heaven, do not let me know the graveyard of my children in the name of Jesus.
7. Oh Lord, let the prospering of my children be rapid, and they shall never disappear in the midst of their glory in Jesus' name.
8. Holy Spirit, let I and the children whom the Lord has given me be for signs and wonders in the land of the living in Jesus' name.
9. As the Lord liveth, all my children shall be a light and salt in their own generation.
10. Spirit of God and the fear of God, possess all my children in the name of Jesus.
11. Any arrow targeted against my children, go back to the sender in the name of Jesus.
17

4. PRAYER FOR RECOMMENDATION (PS.90)

CONFESSION

- As David was recommended for the palace. Naaman got his miracle/healing through the recommendation of a prophet by the house maid. Jesus was recommended by God. I shall enjoy divine recommendation.
- I shall get to my palace. The throne is my destination. No forces will be strong enough to waste my chances in life.
- I shall be considered for lifting. My location will change through recommendation. My status will be enhanced through recommendation. Dignitaries shall stand for me.
- My God will raise a spokes man for me. My Aaron will not be silenced. Men will not sit until my arrival.
- The power of satanic excuses against my life is broken. Evil dew will not work against my Godgiven chance. Evil opposition will not succeed over me and my business.

PRAYER POINTS

1. Oh Lord, by mercy, connect me to the individual that will connect me to my dream in Jesus' name.

2. Every invisible power working against my opportunity, fire of God waste them in Jesus' name.
3. Anointing for divine favour, rest upon my life before the end of this Mercy Rain in Jesus' name.
4. That spokesman that You have positioned to recommend me in great places, oh Lord stir him/her up in Jesus' name.
5. Every foundational powers monitoring my God given opportunity be blindfolded in Jesus' name.
6. Every invisible power turning the heart of men against my life and business be paralyzed in Jesus' name.
7. Those You have positioned strategically to speak for me will not speak against me in Jesus' name.
8. Every evil that is arranged to put me down, oh Lord by Your great mercy use it lift me up.
9. I receive grace to be sensitive to Your plan and purpose for my life.
10. Everyone that needs what I have and those that have what I need we are connected by mercy in Jesus' name.

18

PRAYER FOR THE CHURCH OF GOD (PS.133)
CONFESSION

- Christ is the Head of the Church. The devil will never become her head. The Church of

God is an end-time Movement. Her mandate is to select, train and equip heavenly bound saints.

- The Church of God shall keep waxing stronger while the gates of hades keep waxing weaker.
- The Church of God shall be continually made holy. Every impurities and unrighteousness shall be purged out in the name of Jesus.
- The Church of God shall not be closed. It shall be opened always welcoming and converting sinners in the name of Jesus.
- The Church of God shall remain a sanctuary. A place of rest for the weary and a place of joy for the heavy in heart.

PRAYER POINTS

Psalm 83

1. Holy Father, we thank You because You are the head of the church which the gate of hell can never prevail.
2. Oh Lord, let not the gates of hell prevail over the Church of God in Jesus' name.
3. Oh Lord arise, and let all the enemies of the Church of God be scattered in Jesus' name.
4. Every evil gathering or meeting or conspiracy over the Church of God shall never stand in the name of Jesus.

5. Every weapon fashioned against the Church of God shall be paralyzed in Jesus' name.
6. Lord, reveal every satanic agenda over the Church of God and nullify it in Jesus' name.
7. Our Father in heaven, give the Church of God power to preach the Word in due season and out of season.
8. Holy Spirit, empower all the leaders of the Church to succeed in their mandate.
9. Any form of attack against the Church of God shall never stand in the name of Jesus.
10. Let every work of darkness over the Church of God be destroyed by the power in the Blood of Jesus.

19

PRAYER WHEN IN FOREIGN LAND (ISAI.54)
CONFESSION

- Joseph moved from nobody to somebody in a foreign land. Daniel became a voice in a strange land. Esther assumed a position of honour in a strange land. In this land where I am, I shall become a voice.

- Strangers will build my walls. Those I do not know will serve me. The Lord will quench my thirst in a foreign land. I will not eat the bread of affliction.
- The earth is the Lord's and the fulness thereof. I will suck the breast of kings, I will drink the milk of the nobles.
- When I appear, fear will disappear. When I speak, favour will answer. When I sit, mockers will bow.
- Evil conspiracy could not resist Daniel. Potiphar could not succeed over Joseph. God will connect me to my Goshen. I will eat and be satisfied in this foreign land.

PRAYER POINTS

1. Lord, by Your mercy I am connected to the fatness of this land and the dews of heaven upon it.
2. Oh Lord, I thank You for Your provision for my needs in this land.
3. Every power from my foundation that is waiting for my shame at home, be roasted by the Holy Ghost fire in Jesus' name.
4. Oh Lord, I prophecy that I shall not return empty in Jesus' name.
5. Unusual grace for great achievement, rest upon my life in this land in Jesus' name.

6. Oh Lord let the profit of this land begin to flow in my direction in Jesus' name.

7. The sure mercies of God for unusual protection rest upon my life in Jesus' name.

8. Every evil in operation upon this land will not swallow me and my family up in Jesus' name.

9. Daniel prospered in a strange land, Joseph also prospered by the grace of God, I must prosper in Jesus' name.

10. Grace of prosperity in a foreign land in the order of Isaac, rest upon me now in Jesus' name.

20

5. PRAYER WHEN APPLYING FOR VISA (ISAI.54)

CONFESSION

- God's purpose for my life will not be frustrated. Evil gate keepers will not succeed over my life. Forces that stopped others will not stop me. Where others are stuck, I shall make progress.

- Joseph was favoured in a strange land. Daniel and his colleagues were also favoured. I shall not be rejected. Favour will speak for me. I am unstoppable.

- I shall be preferred. Wherever I appear, they will see God in me. My Visa shall command divine approval. No power shall be able to stand before me.

- God's promise for my life will not be delayed. Evil dreams will not materialize. Every of my breakthrough in the dream shall be fulfilled.
- My long-time visions and promises shall be fuifilled. God will answer every of my life question. Money will not disappoint me. Grace will be my currency.

PRAYER POINTS

1. Oh Lord, I receive unusual grace to work in line with Your purpose for my life in Jesus' name.
2. Great doors of unusual favour open to me by mercy in Jesus' name.
3. Every agent of opposition on my way of advancement, be paralyzed in Jesus' name.
4. By mercy oh Lord, I receive a mouth and wisdom that cannot be opposed in Jesus' name.
5. Every evil monitoring agent position to frustrate me and my opportunities, be frustrated by the Blood of Jesus.
6. Oh Lord, let everything work for my favour before my interviewer.
7. Every evil mark upon my Visa causing rejection, Blood of Jesus, erase it in Jesus' name.
8. The good hand of the Lord for unusual favour, rest upon my Visa in Jesus name.
9. Every time I appear before my interviewers, let unusual favour speak for me.

10. Every mark of rejection upon my Visa, Blood of Jesus erase them in Jesus' name.

21

PRAYER FOR SPIRITUAL FREEDOM (PS.86)
CONFESSION

- Whom the Son sets free shall be free indeed. Jesus has set me free. I am free indeed.
- My spirit man is free. I am no longer in the dungeon of the enemy. Even lawful captives shall be free says the Lord; I shall be set free.
- My mind is free. I shall think clearly. My mind shall dominate negative thoughts.
- My body is free. My mind if free. My spirit man is free. I am an embodiment of freedom.
- Evil dungeon, spew me out. I am not you candidate. I am free; to do the will of my Heavenly Father.

PRAYER POINTS
Isaiah 41: 10-20, Job 11: 13-20

1. Oh Lord, I appreciate You for my spiritual freedom perfected on the Cross of Calvary.

2. If the Son sets you free, you shall be free indeed! Lord Jesus, set me free from spiritual bondage.
3. Holy Ghost fire, set my life free from every demonic prison that I am in the name of Jesus.
4. Every power that is holding me captive spiritually, loose your power over my life in Jesus' name.
5. He that lives in me is bigger than he that lives in the world. Victorious power to live above spiritual bondage, possess me now.
6. Blood of Jesus (21 times), set me free from every demonic entanglement that is holding my life captive.
7. I am created to live a life of dominion, from today my life receive dominion anointing in Jesus' name.
8. Every foundational power ruling my life, be destroyed by the power in the name of Jesus.
9. I receive power to live a victorious life above sinful life from today in Jesus' name.
10. Every power assigned to waste my spiritual life, be wasted by fire in the name of Jesus.

AFIKUN
1. ADURA FUN SISO DI TITUN NINU EMI

1

ADURA FUN SISO DI TITUN NINU EMI (ISAI.11)
IJEWO

- Emi Mimo ti so mi di otun A gbe mi ga ni pa ti Emi. Emi Mimo kun inu mi. A gbe okunrin emi mi ga. Mo ti bori.

- Eje Jesus ti we mi nu. Emi ye ni waju Re. Okunrin Emi mi gba agbara. Mo gbe Ore-ofe Olorun ru. Mo gbe Ina Olorun.

- Okunrin emi mi ti gba ina. Oro Olorun ti da ina sinu mi. mom o eni ti mo je. Mo je ijaya fun ijoba okunkun.

- Nitori a ti so mi di otun, mo gbe ina titun, ifami ororo yan titun. Emi ko se daduro fun awon ota. Ti awon ota ba ri mi, won ma be lu gbo.

- A so ile mi di titun. A so ebi mi di titun. A so okoowo mi di titun. A so Ijo mi di titun. A so ayanmo mi di titun. O ti dara fun okan mi! ni oruko Jesu.

KOKO ADURA
Joeli 2:28-32; Ezek.37:1-14

1. Oluwa o, mo fe iso di titun tie mi lati le sin O si.
2. Baba mi, Baba mi, so igbe aiye adura mi di titun nipa ina.
3. Emi Mimo, so igbe aiye ihinrere mi di titun, da ina titun sinu mi.
4. Baba, je ki igbe aiye iwa mimo mi di titun.
5. Jesu Oluwa, tun ina Oro Re da sinu aiye mi.
6. Oluwa o, je ki kika ati ijiroro Oro Re di otun ninu aiye mi.
7. Okunrin emi mi, gba ina titun lti le se ise Olorun.
8. Gbogbo agbegbe aiye mi to ni lo ati di otun, Oluwa o, je ki ina iso di titun ma jo nibe.
9. Emi Mimo, ma joba lo ninu aiye mi fun itesiwaju tie mi.
10. Emi Mimo, tun ina iye mi da fun ipele ise to kan fun mi.

2

ADURA LODI SI AWON ESE TO SORO KO SILE (O.D.51)
IJEWO

- A ti tun mi bi. A ti tun ago ara mi bi. A titun okan mi bi. Ese to so ro ko sile ko le jegaba l'ori aiye mi.

- Kristi ninu ki,ireti ogo. Emi le se oun gbogbo nipa Kristi tin fun mi l'agbara. Emi ma gbe igbe aiye to nbori ese to soro ko sile. E mi ma bo ni kehin.

- Jesu ni Olupilese ati alasepe igbagbo mi. O mo ilakaka mi O si se tan lati ran mi l'owo. Olurapada mi ye, emi yi o bori igbeaiye ese.
- Abi mi lati dari. Emi yi o gbe igbe aiye olubori ninu aiye rudurudu yi. Ese to so ko sile ki yio bori mi ni oruko Jesu.
- Satani, dehin lehin mi! ero ti ko mo, dehin lehin mi. iwa ti ko to, dehin lehin mi. ago ara mi je Tempili ti Olorun!

KOKO ADURA
O.D. 19:7-14; 51; 119:9

1. Gbogbo agbara ese to soro ko sile, so agbara re nu nipa ina.

2. gbogbo ajaga ati ide ese to soro ko sile ninu aiye mi, ja nipa ina l'oruko Jesu.

3. gbogbo agbara ese to soro ko sile to di aiye mi ni igbekun, ja nipa ina.

4. gbogbo agbegbe aiye mi ti ese to soro ko sile ti ba je, Emi Mimo, gba mi.

5. ide satani nipa ese to soro ko sile ninu aiye mi, egbina ni oruko Jesu.

6. nipa Oro Olorun, mo bo ri ese to soro ko sile ninu aiye mi.

7. Emi Mimo, ran mi lowo lati bori gbogbo irufe ese to soro ko sile ninu aiye mi.

8. Mo gba ore-ofe lati gbe igbe aiye asegun lori ese to soro ko sile ni oruko Jesu.

9. Nipa Oro Re Oluwa o, je ki a yi okan mi pada lati gbe igbe aiye mimo.

10. Baba mi, fun mi ni ore-ofe lati ma nani Oro Re ju oun gbogbo lo.

3
ADURA FUN AWON TIN WOJU OLUWA FUN OMO (O.D.29)
IJEWO

- Olorun ni eleda mi. A da mi towotowo, a da mi tiyanutiyanu ati pipe.
- Mo ko iyagan. Mo so mo ileso nitori ife Olorun fun aiye mi ni eyi.
- Oro Olorun bori gbogbo oro, nitorina gbogbo akosile odi lori ileso mi, a pa won re ni pase Oro Olorun.
- Mo ni iye Olorun ninu mi. Mo ni iseda ti Olorun. E mi ma bi awon omo temi ni oruko Jesu.
- Emi ati awon omo ti Oluwa yi o fun mi wa fun ise ami ati ise iyanu. Awon omo mi yi o rogba yi tabili mi ka ni oruko Jesu.

KOKO ADURA
O.D. 113; 123

1. Baba, modupe lowo Re nitori emi ki yio yagan ni aiye mi.
2. Gbogbo idabu ileso mi, e tuka ni oruko Jesu.

3. Gbogbo majemu ti ndi ati bimo mi lowo, e sofo nipa agbara ti o wa ninu Eje Jesu.

4. Gbogbo irinse satani tin di ile omo mi, ina mu kuro.

5. Iwo ile omo mi, gba agbara ati gbe omo ni oruko Jesu.

6. Gbogbo agbara ti nlodi si ati loyun mi, e ku nipa ina ni oruko Jesu.

7. Ibikibi ti agbe ile omo mi pamo si ninu ijoba okunkun, jade pelu ina.

8. Gbogbo oro odi, epe ti o di ile ileso mi, e so yin ti out bante ni oruko Jesu.

9. Iwo agbara ati loyun, bale mi nisinsinyi ni oruko Jesu.

10. Gbogbo ofa ki oyun ma jabo ti ata lodi si aiye mi, fo jade pelu ina.

4

ADURA FUN AWON ALAISAN OJO PIPE (JER.17)
IJEWO

• Wo mi san Oluwa emi yi o si san. Gba mi Oluwa emi yi o si di eni igbala.

• A ti sa Kristi logbe nitori irekoja mi. A ti pa lara nitori aisedede mi. Ina alaafia mi wa ni ara Re. Nipa ina Re ni amu mi lara da asi ti gba mi la.

- Emi ki yio ku bikose yiye lati ma fi ogo ogo Oluwa han. Aisan yi ko ni jasi iku ni oruko Jesu.
- Iwo yio pamimo ninu alaafia pipe nitori okan mi duro lori Re. Alaafia Olorun ni ipin mi ni oruko Jesu.
- Oti dari gbogbo ese mi ji mi osi ti wo gbogbo aisan mi san. O ti gba aiye mi kuro ni owo iparun nitorina mo ti gba itusile. Haleluya!

KOKO ADURA
ISAI.53; O.D.103:1-5

1. Oluwa modupe fun gbogbo ipese imularada mi.
2. Baba, gba gbogbo ogo lori agbara to wa ninu Oro Re lati wo mi san.
3. Baba mi, Baba mi, mo mo riri Re fun agbara to wa ninu Eje Jesu lati wo misan ati lati tu mi sile.
4. Ofa aisan ninu ago ara mi, alejo ni e nibe, fo jade pelu ina.
5. Gbogbo idojuko aisan ninu ara mi, pade si ini ti oti nbo ni oruko Jesu.
6. Gbogbo ide aisan, iponju ninu aiye mi, e sofo danu pelu ina.
7. Majemu aisan idile mi, fo nipa Eje Jesu.
8. Aisan ajogunba ninu ara mi, Eje Jesu, fo danu.

9. Asian alalobo ninu aiye mi, poora pelu agbara inu Eje Jesu.

10. Aisan ki se ipin mi. mo gba ara titun mo si wa ni alaafia ni oruko Jesu.

5

ADURA FUN IMUGBORO OKOOWO (O.D.68)
IJEWO

- Okoowo mi yio serere. Okoowo mi yio ma ga si. Agbegbe ni yio di nla.

- Okoowo mi yio ma serere bi igi Lebanoni. Okoowo mi yio gboro lati ile yi ti ti de ile ajoji ni oruko Jesu.

- Okoowo mi yi o lere. Ajenirun ki yio ni agbara lori okoowo mi. Emi a ma san idamewa mi.

- Olorun yio bunkum ise owo mi. emi yio je ori, emi ki yio je iru. Emi a ma win, emi ki yio toro. Ise mi di alabukun fun.

- Gbogbo irugbin okunkun tin gberu ninu okoowo mi, a fa yin tu pelu ina. Awon alabasise mi yio gbe igbe aiye mimo. Okoowo mi yio ma fi ogo Olorun han ni oruko Jesu.

KOKO ADURA
DEUT.28:1-13; O.D.1:1-3

1. Oluwa o, mom o riri Re fun ore-ofe ati aanu Re lori okoowo mi.

2. Baba mi, Baba mi, je ki owo Re fun igberu re lori okoowo mi.

3. Baba, bukun ki O si so agbegbe okoowo mi di nla nitoto.

4. Ifami ororo yan lati se rere, re lori okoowo mi fun isgbro.

5. Gbogbo agbara agbegbe ti ndojuko imugboro okoowo mi, ina jo yin run ni oruko jesu.

6. Agbara ijakule ti a gbe dide lodi si imugboro okoowo mi, ina Emi Mimo jo yin run.

7. Oluwa o, fun okoowo mi iranlowo.

8. Emi Mimo, fun mi ni ogbon to ma mu okoowo mi gboro ni oruko Jesu.

9. Isai.60:1,2 – Ogo Okoowo mi, bere si ni tan bayi bayi nipa agbara to wa ninu oruko Jesu.

10. Gbogbo agbara emi okunkun tabi ti satani ti a sin tabi ti a fi ko ni agbegbe okoowo mi, ara Emi Mimo, gbe won sin fun mi.

6
ADURA FUN AWON TI KO TI MO OLORUN (O.D.38)
IJEWO

- Nitori iku ni ere ese; sugbon ebun Olorun ni iye aiyeraye nipase Jesu Kristi Oluwa wa.

Awon ti ko I ti mo Olorun ni ayika mi ki yio ku sinu ese.

- Gba won Oluwa o a o si gba won la. Gba won kuro lowo agbara ese a o si gba won.
- Nitori Olorun nife won, won yio gba iye aiyeraiye nipa Kristi Jesu.
- E wo iru ife ti Olorun ni si won eyi ti o mu ki a ma pe won ni omo Olorun. Omo Olorun ni won se.
- Bi omo oninakuna ni, won yi o wa le pade. Emi Olorun wa ninu won, won yi o di atunbi.

KOKO ADURA
O.D.1:3-6; O.D.57

1. Olorun aanu o, modupe l'owo Re fun ife ti o ni si awon elese. Oo si fe ki won parun.

2. Nipa aanu Re Oluwa o, ba gbogbo awon elese ninu ebi mi ati agbegbe mi pade.

3. Baba, si oju emi ati eti oye won ki won le mo O.

4. Gbogbo agbara ti o de won ni gbekun, e sofo danu pelu ina.

5. Emi Mimo, si ilekun igbala sile fun gbogbo awon alaigbagbo ni ayika mi.

6. Baba, fo gbogbo ipa ese lori aiye won ni oruko Jesu.

7. Jesu Oluwa, fun won ni okan titun ki O si tun okunrin emi won se ni oruko Jesu.

8. Nipa aanu Re Baba, to won lo si Kalfari fun igbala okan won ni oruko Jesu.

9. Baba mi, Baba mi, si oju emi awon elese ki won le ri oun tie mi.

10. Emi Mimo, gbe gbogbo awon ti won b wa si odo Re fun igbala wo.

7
ADURA LODI SI ALATAKO ALABASEPO – (O.D.12)
IJEWO

- Owo okowo mi oni doju bole. A danu o ni gbe owo mi mi. Panpe alatako o ni pa owo mi.

- Emi o ni gbe igbese ope ninu owo mi. Emi oni fi owo ara mi doju owo mi bole. Emi oni ko igba wole.

- A o ni di owo mi ku. Owo okowo mi, mi o ni padanu re. Emi oni padanu idoko mi, emi oni padanu ere mi.

- Okowo mi yi o lo si ipele ti o kan. Alabasowopo mi oni ba owo mi je.

- Okowo mi yi o maa lo layi ipa de ipa. Owo mi yi o ri atileyin lati oke gba. Gegebi Peteru, owo mi yi o ri opo, Oluwa yi o fun mi ni itoni lati oke.

KOKO ADURA

1. Oluwa be ipile ibi ti mo ti nsise wo, ki O si tu asiri alatako fun mi ni oruko Jesu.

2. Oluwa ma se gba alatako laaye lati dojo owo mi bole ni ibi ise mi ni oruko Jesu.

3. Oluwa gba awon osise mi ati alabasisepo kuro lowo ofa gbese ati iji gbese ni oruko Jesu.

4. Oluwa, pale ise mi mo kuro ni agbegbe ti ko faye gba itesiwaju ninu ikowo mi.

5. Oluuwa fo ajaga ati igbekun l'ori owo ibi ise mi ni oruko Jesu.
6. Oluwa fun mi ni isegun lori awon ti o fe run ti o si fe gbe owo mi ni oruko Jesu.
7. Jeki gbogbo agbara ti o fe gba isakoso okowo mi ya aro lesekese ni oruko Jesu.
8. Oluwa, oro Re so wipe iwo yi o ba awon ti o nba mi ja ja, gbe ija mi ja lori akowo mi ni oruko Jesu.
9. Oluwa fun mi ni ogbon ti o ga julo lori awon alatako lori owo mi ni oruko Jesu.
10. Oluwa fa igi le asotele ti o lodi si okowo mi lesekese ni oruko Jesu.

8

ADURA FUN AWON AKEEKO GBOYE TI NWASE (AISAIYA 14)
IJEWO

- Aiye mi o le wa ni ojukan. Emi yi o gba iranlowo ti o yato ni oruko Jesu.
- Aanu Olorun yio shawari aiye mi. Ilekun anfaani yi o si fun aiye mi. Oluwa yi o ma to isise me fun ise to lere nla ni oruko Jesu.
- Olorun mi yi o ranti mi fun rere. `Ilekun lati oke wa yi o si fun mi. Emi yi o ri ojurere nla gba ni oruko Jesu.
- Ise rere yio sawari mi; emi yi o sawari ise rere. Aanu Olorun, oju-rere ati ore-ofe yi o f'oun fun mi.

478

- Gbogbo iwe eri mi ati gbogbo iwe miran yi o ri onte ati ojurere nla gba ni oruko Jesu. Gbogbo ami ikosile ni ati mu kuro lori awon iwe mi ni oruko Jesu.

KOKO ADURA
O.D.1; DEUT.8:1-13

1. Baba, modupe lowo Re fun ipese ojojumo fun aiye mi.
2. Olorun aanu, jeki ilekun anfaani si sile fun mi ni oruko Jesu.
3. Oluwa o, jeki awon iwe eri mi ri oju-rere gba ni gbogbo ibi ti mo ba ko won lo.
4. Baba mi, Baba mi, pese ise rere ati ise ti o dara fun mi. Eyi ti yio fun mi ni aye lati sin o.
5. Gobgbo agbra ikosile lori aiye mi ati lori iwe eri mi, e so agbara yin nu ni oruko Jesu.
6. Gbogbo amin okunkun niwaju ori mi, a pa yin re pelu agbara to wa ninu Eje Jesu.
7. Baba, jeki gbogbo ikosile mi yipada si itewogba nipa aanu ni oruko Jesu.
8. Oluwa o, fun mi ni awon oun ti aiye mi fe nipa ise ti mo fe ni oruko Jesu.
9. Ni gbogbo ibi ti awon kan ti nba ijakule pade, emi yio ma ri ojurere gba ni oruko Jesu.
10. Pese mi sile Oluwa o, fun ise ti o wa ni iwaju mi ni ile ise titun ti mon lo ni oruko Jesu.

ADURA FUN AWON TI WON TI TO SE IGBEYAWO (AISAIYA 56)

IJEWO

- Emi ma se igbeyawo. Emi ki yio da wa lai nidi. Eni ti o da won, tako tabo lo da won. Emi yio sawari ololufe mi ni oruko Jesu.

- Gbogbo amin odi, tin se atako asopo emi ati eni ti Olorun ti ko mo mi, Eje Jesu we o danu.

- Eni ti o ba ri aya fe, ori ojurere gba lodo Oluwa. Oko mi yio ri mi. emi ki yio wa ni ipamo si oko mi.

- Amin itewogba, gbe mi wo. Mo ko ikosile. Mo so mo itewogba igbeyawo.

- Oko/aya odi, kuro ni odo mi. Oko/aya buburu, kuro lodo mi. ibasepo odi, kuro ni odo mi ni oruko Jesu.

KOKO ADURA

GEN.:18-24; O.D.19

1. Oluwa o, modupe lowo Re nitori O o ni je ki nsi oko/aya fe.

2. Emi Mimo, to mi lati yan oko/aya rere fun aiye mi.

3. Baba mi ni orun, fun mi ni eegun iha mi.

4. Olorun aanu, ma je ki nsileya nigba ti nba fey an ni oruko Jesu.

5. Gbogbo agbara idaduro ninu igbeyawo mi fo lori mi ni oruko Jesu pelu ina.

6. Olorun mi, fun mi ni ojo ayo ki awon eniyan ba mi yo.

7. Gbogbo amin okunkun ti ndi igbeyawo mi lowo, Eje Jesu fo danu.

8. Agbara ipile ati egun ti ki fi aye gba igbeyawo ninu iran mi, fo nisinsinyi ni oruko Jesu.

9. Ipa tin fi ilakaka igbeyawo sofo ninu iran mi, e sofo danu nipa Eje Jesu.

10. Ounkohun ti won ti se lodi ninu emi nipa igbeyawo mi, pare pelu Eje Jesu.

10
ADURA LODI SI IKU AITOJO (O.D.91)
IJEWO

- Aiye mi, ko iku ojiji. Ebi mi, ko iku ojiji. Ile mi, ko iku ojiji.

- Emi iku ojiji, awa ki se ti re, poora nipa ina Olorun.

- Owo Olorun, saabo lori emi ati awon oun to je temi ki o si pawamo kuro ninu agbara okunkun to nlepa lati pawa.

- Emi ati ebi mi yio wa labe aabo Eledumre. A yan iye. A ko iku ojiji. Awa fun ise ami asi wa fun ise iyanu.

- Ipa ti nberi awon eniyan layika mi, emi ki se eni to nwa, gbina be. Emi yio ye lati ma fi ogo Olorun han ni oruko Jesu.

KOKO ADURA

O.D.123

1. Oseun Oluwa fun gbese mi ti Osan lori igi Kalfari.
2. Gbogbo agbara iku ti njegaba lori aiye mi, so agbara re nu nisinsinyi.
3. Gbogbo okun ide ati agadagodo iku ni aiye mi, fo pelu ina ni oruko Jesu.
4. Olorun aanu, gba mi kuro lowo gbogbo iru iku ojiji ni oruko Jesu.
5. Gbogbo ofa iku aitojo iran, fi aiye mi sile pelu ina.
6. Emi iku, fi ise iranse mi sile ni oruko Jesu.
7. Gbogbo emi mujemuje, ti won ran lati mu eje wa nigba ti asun, gbina sonu!
8. Ore-ofe lati lo aiye mi de kikun ninu ife Olorun, gbe mi wo pelu aanu.
9. Emi Mimo, bo emi ati oun tin se temi pelu Eje Jesu.
10. Jehofa Nisi, je ki asa aabo re bow a mole ni oruko Jesu.

11

13. ADURA LODI SI OUNJE JIJE NI OJU ORUN –
(O.D.17)

IJEWO

- A o ni se oyun ayanmo mi. A o ni se pasiparo ogo mi. Alase oru lo ki o lo sonu.

- Ara mi je tempili Olorun alagbara. Ounje okunkun oni ba aiye mi je.
- Aya mi si mimo. Aya ile mi si mimo. Aya ibusun mi si mimo. Tabili ounje mi a yaa si mimo. Mo ko ounje okunkun.
- Emi o di pupo. Emi o di pupo si. Emi yi o dagba soke. Emi o dide. A o ni din mi ku. A o ni fi mi si ahamo. A o ni so mi mole.
- Emi o ni ku iku aitojo. Emi o ni je eniyan laasan. A o ni fi mi sofo. Amin

KOKO ADURA

1. Oluwa ya gbogbo alase oru ti o nse ounje fun mi ni oju ala l'aro ni oruko Jesu.
2. Oluwa ki ina bo gbogbo ile idana ati ile ita ounje okunkun ti ati n fun mi ni ounje ni oju ala mi ni oruko Jesu.
3. Oluwa da abo bo iyara ibusun mi lodi si gbogbo igbogun ti awon alase oru ni oruko Jesu.
4. Oluwa bu ifoju lu gbogbo agbodegba ti a ran lati bo mi ni oju orun ni oruko Jesu.
5. Oluwa ya ile mi si mimo, ki o si pa mimo kuro lowo gbogbo asoju alase oru.
6. Oluwa fo aiye mi mo kuro ni gbogbo idoti ati abawon nipase ounje ti mo ti je ni oju ala mi ni oruko Jesu.
7. Oluwa da gbogbo olumoni ati ogo mi ti ati se pasiparo eleyi ti o sele nipase ounje oju ala ni oruko Jesu.
8. Oluwa da awon ebun emi mi ati eso emi eleyi ti osonu nipase ounje oju ala ni oruko Jesu.

9. Oluwa fun mi ni ajesara lodi si gbogbo oro ato idibaje ni oju ala mi ni oruko Jesu.

10. Gbogbo majele ounje ti mo ti gbemi ninu ara ati ninu emi, Eje Jesu, fo danu kuro l'ara mi ni oruko Jesu.

12

1. ADURA FUN IDAGBASOKE ISE IRANSE ATI INA TUNTUN – (O.D. 27)

IJEWO

- Olorun wa ni iha wa. Enu ona orun apadi ko le boriwa. ijo ntesiwaju nipase Olorun wa. Awa yi o bori awon ota wa. A o ni teriba fun ihale okunkun.

- Ise iranse wa yio gbadun ise ami ati iyanu ti ko wo po. Olorun yio so agbegbe wa din la. Ofin okunkun ko le dawa duro.

- Idagbasoke je ami wi wa laiye. Idagba tumo si didagbasoke. Idagba tumo si isodi pupo. Oluwa yi o so wa di pupo ni gbogbo ona. Ise iranse wa ko ni duro si oju kan.

- Sioni je ibi ifokan bale. Oje ibi imupada bo sipo. Oje ori oke itusile. Itusile nla yi o sele larin wa. A o da ayanmo mi pada bo sipo. Ise amin ati iyanu ko ni di awaitl ni arin wa.

- Ina je iwenumo. Ina je irinse isodotun. Olorun yi o se iribomi ina tuntun. A o fi ina da ise iranse wa mo. Ina je irinse ti a fi nfo gbendeke. A o ni da wa duro.

KOKO ADURA

1. Oluwa modupe fun awon amin ati iyanu ti a ri gba ni inu ise iranse wa.
2. Ina tuntun Olorun eleyi ti yio gbe ise iranse yi ro ati gbogbo awon omo ijo, ba le ori aiye wa ni oruko Jesu.
3. Gbogbo gbara agbegbe eleyi ti o nsise lodi si ise iranse ati awon omo ijo, gba itiju nipase Eje Jesu.
4. Gbogbo agbo fin ro okunkun ninu ati nita ise iranse wa gba idajo Olorun ni oruko Jesu.
5. Orun awon ise iranse ti ko wopo eleyi ti o maa so ise iranse mi di nla ti o si maa so agbegbe mi din la si ni oruko Jesu.
6. Mo ko lati padanu gbogbo ohun alumoni ti e ti fun wa ninu ise iranse yala niti ara tabi niti emi l'oruko Jesu.
7. Gbogbo enu ona apaadi ti a ti gbega lori ise iranse mi o ni se rere l'oruko Jesu.
8. Gbogbo ami okunkun ti o n se ise fun awon ota ise iranse wa, e lo si se l'oruko Jesu.
9. Ore-ofe Olorun lati dagba soke niti ara ati niti emi bale ise iranse mi l'oruko Jesu.
10. Iwo ohun satani ti o n soro eke lori ise iranse mi ko ni se rere l'oruko Jesu.

13

ADURA FUN AWON OUN ELO OLORUN (O.D.23)
IJEWO

- Olorun lo yan mi; ore-ofe Re to fun mi. Emi wa lara awon iran tin sin Olorun. Emi ki yio rin lo.

- Amokoko yio mo mi. Emi aimo ni a o mu kuro. Lowo amokoko, emi yio jade dardara. Emi yio sin iran mi daradara.
- Emi yio je oun elo si ola nigbagbogbo. Emi ki yio je oun elo si ailola. Aiye mi yio wa si iyato si Oluwa titi lailai.
- Esu, oole ri aye ninu aiye mi. Gbogbo aye ninu aiye mi ni Emi Mimo ti di pa.
- Emi wulo. A fe mi. Aki yio ta mi danu. Aki yio so mi nu. Ni oruko Jesu.

KOKO ADURA
ISAI.61

1. Oluwa mi, modupe tori O yan mi lati je oun elo si ola lowo Re.
2. Baba, ya mi soto ki O si so mi ti eni mimo fun ogo Re.
3. Baba mi, je ki ore-ofe Re to fun aiye mi.
4. Jesu Oluwa, ranmi lowo lati mu ise iranse ti ogbe le mi lowo se.
5. Oluwa o, ro mi ni agbara fun akoni ise ninu ise iranse.
6. Gbogbo atako ota lori ise iranse mi, Baba, fun mi ni isegun lori won.
7. Gbogbo agbara to duro ti ise iranse mi, je ki won sofo danu nipa ina.
8. Baba, mo gbadura, ma je ki gbogbo laalaa mi ja si asan , ki emi ma ba di eni alupati.

9. Emi Mimo, ma se atoni mi ni gbogbo ona ti mob a gba.
10. Oluwa o, ke ji ife Re se ninu aiye mi.

14
ADURA LODI SI EMI GBESE (O.D.2)
IJEWO

- Ileri Olorun fun mi n iwi pee mi yio ma win orile-ede pee mi ki yio toro. Mo gba ileri yi ni oruko Jesu.
- Mo ko emi gbese. Mo ko emi yiya. Mo ko emi aini.
- Mo so pelu emi ani kun rere. Mo so mo emi imubopadasipo. Mo so mo emi akun won sile.
- Agbara ti ma fi ipa mu awon eniyan wo inu igbekun, so agbara re lori aiye mi nu. Eto isuna aiye mi, gba ina.
- Lati isinsinyi lo, eto isuna aiye mi, yipa da sir ere. Ni oruko Jesu.

KOKO ADURA
O.D.21

1. Oluwa o, modupe lowo Re pe O fa mi jade lati inu ikekun gbese.
2. Baba, jowo darijimi fun mi momo wo inu ikekun gbese.
3. Oluwa o, ro okoowo mi lagbara lati gboro.

4. Baba mi, Baba mi, di koto gbese ti ota wa si le fun mi.

5. Owo Olorun, fa mi jade lati inu koto gbese.

6. Baba mi, bukun ise owo mi kin le san gbogbo gbese ti mo je.

7. Mo gba ore-ofe lati je ibukun fun awon eniyan.

8. Mo gba ore-ofe lati je a funni lai se eni ti nya.

9. Mo gba ore-ofe lati ni ni anikun ati ani seku.

10. Baba, gba mi lowo emi eti.

15

ADURA LODI SI EMI IPEHINDA (O.D.51)
IJEWO

- Mo ko lati pehinda. Mo ko lati lo woro. Mo ko lati tutu. Emi yio gbona ma si ma yoruku fun Olorun.

- Mo ko lati je Dema. Mo ko lati je Judasi. Mo ko lati je Soolu.

- Emi Olorun, gbe mi wo fun ise to wa niwaju mi. Owo Olorun, to mi ni ona irin ajo tin je aiye.

- Abanirin oniwa bi Olorun, yi mi ka. Emi Mimo, yi mi ka pelu awon abanirin to ni wa bi Olorun.

- Ilakoja mi ki yio bori mi. Emi yio bori gbogbo ilakoja mi ni oruko Jesu.

KOKO ADURA
O.D.51

1. Oluwa o, modupe lowo Re fun sisi oju mi si awon oun ijakule tie mi ati ifasehin.
2. Nipa aanu Re Oluwa o, da ayo igbala re pada fun mi.
3. Tun okan titun se ninu mi ni oruko Jesu.
4. Tun igbe aiye emi mi se ninu adura, Oro ati igbe aiye iwa mimo.
5. Fun mi ni emi ti ma ke lodi si oun ese.
6. Gbogbo agbegbe aiye emi mi tin jo danu, Eje Jesu, di won fun mi.
7. Baba mi, Baba mi, ya mi ya awon ore tin fa mi sehin ninu emi pelu ina.
8. Jeki gbogbo awon okuta idigbolu kuro ni ona mi ni oruko Jesu.
9. Emi Mimo, gbe aiye mi wo ni oruko Jesu.
10. Emi Mimo, gbe mi wo pelu ore-ofe lati te siwaju ninu idanwo.

16

ADURA FUN AWON OMO WA (O.D.127)
IJEWO

- Awon omo mi wa fun ise amin. Awon omo mi wa fun ise iyanu. Awon omo mi je iyanu. Awon omo mi pe lola.
- Awon omo mi kin se omo beliali. Awon omo mi o ni emi esu. awon omo mi oni ku iku ojiji. Won ma ye fun ogo Olorun.
- Awon omo mi ma sin Olorun alaaye. Awon omo mi ki yio sin esu. Ni gbogbo ojo aiye awon omo mi, won yio ma ko orin iyin si Olorun.
- Awon omo mi gbon. Awon omo mi ni oye. Awon omo mi ni opolo. Awon omo mi ki se opoonu.
- Oju Olorun ni itoni awon omo mi. awon omo mi ki yio si ese gbe.
- O ti dara fun awon omo ni oruko Jesu.

KOKO ADURA
O.D.127

1. Baba, modupe lowo Re fun awon ebun rere (ini Olorun) ti O fun mi.
2. Eje Jesu, fo ohun rere si ara awon omo mi ni oruko Jesu.
3. Baba, ko awon omo mi.

4. Baba, je ki a fi idi awon omo mi mule ninu ododo. Je ki iponju jina rere si won ni oruko Jesu.
5. Baba, je ki awon omo mi mu ayanmo se ni orile alaaye ni oruko Jesu.
6. Baba mi tin be ni orun, ma je kin mo iboji awon omo mi ni oruko Jesu.
7. Oluwa o, je ki aseyori awon omo mi ya, ma je ki won radanu sinu ogo won ni oruko Jesu.
8. Emi Mimo, je ki emi ati awon omo ti Oluwa fun mi wa fun ise amin ant ise iyanu lori ile alaaye ni oruko Jesu.
9. Bi Oluwa tin be, gbogbo omo ti o ti ar mi jade yio je imole ati iyo ninu iran won.
10. Emi Olorun ati iberu Olorun, gbe gbogbo awon omo mi won ni oruko Jesu.
11. Ofa ki ofa ti a ta lu awon omo mi, pada si odo eni ta o ni oruko Jesu.

17

2. ADURA FUN IFINISIPO (O.D.90)
IJEWO

- Gegebi a ti soro Dafidi si ipo oba, Namani na si gba iyanu re ati iwosan lo si odo woli, emi na ma ri ifowo si awon orun.
- Emi yio de afin mi, ago ijoba mi ibi ti mo n lo ko si agbara na ti o le di mi lowo.
- A o gbe mi lo si ibi giga loruko Jesu, a o yi ipo mi pada, awon eyan nla yi o wa mi ri.

- Oluwa yio gbe agbenuso dide fun mi ni ibi giga, awon eniyan yio dide fun igbedide mi.
- Agbara okunkun ti satani lo lati di mi lowo ti dopin, ofin okunkun ko ni sise tako mi loruko Jesu, anfani ti Olorun sile fun mi ko ni ni atako, gbogbo atako ko ni sise lori mi ati lori okowo mi.

KOKO ADURA

1 Oluwa sanu funmi. So mipo mo eni ti yio ba mi ri ise ti okan mi n fe.

2 Gbogbo agbara airi ti o n sise tako gbogbo anfani ti mo ni lati sise, e gbina s'onu l'oruko Jesu.

3 Ororo lati ri oju rere fun ise ki ipade yi to pari, bale mi l'oruko Jesu.

4 Agbenuso ti e ti fi sipo lati soro mi ni ibi ti mo ma ti ri ise ni ibi giga. Oluwa ru soke lati ran mi l'owo l'oruko Jesu.

~~1~~5 Agbara ipile to ntopinpin awon anfani ti Olorun fun mi, eya afoju l'oruko Jesu.

~~2~~6 Gbogbo agbara airi ti o nyi okan awon eniyan pada simi l'ori aiye mi ati ise okowo mi, ma yaro l'oruko Jesu.

~~3~~7 Gbogbo awon ti Oluwa ti fi si ipo lati soro fun idagba soke ise iranse mi ko ni soro tako ise iranse mi l'oruko Jesu.

48 Gbogbo agbekale okunkun lati fa mi wale, Oluwa nipa aanu re, fi gbemi soke l'oruko Jesu.

~~5~~9 Mo gba ore-ofe lati ni imolara si eto ati ipinu Olorun fun aiye mi l'oruko Jesu.

~~6~~10 Gbogbo awon ti o nilo oun ti mo n se ati awon ti o nse oun ti mo nilo, e ma bo lodo mi ki a si sopo l'oruko Jesu.

18

ADURA FUN IJO OLORUN (O.D.133)
IJEWO

- Kristi ni Olori Ijo. Esu ki yio je olori re lailai. Ijo Olorun je ipe si igba ikehin yi. Ise re ni ki o yan, ki o ko, ki o sir o awon enia mimo ti nlo si orun.
- Ijo Olorun yio ma ti ipa de ipa nigbati agbara ibode orun apaadi yio ma re le.
- Ijo Olorun yio ma tesiwaju ninu iwa mimo. Gbogbo aimo ati aisododo ni a o o jade kuro ni oruko Jesu.
- A ki yio ti ijo Olorun. Yio wa ni sisi ti yio si ma ki awon eniyan kaabo ti yio si ma yi awon elese pada ni oruko Jesu.
- Ijo Olorun yio je ibi isadi. Ibi isinmi fun awon ti ore ati ibi ayo fun awon olokan wuwo.

KOKO ADURA
O.D.83

1. Baba mimo, a dupe lowo Re nitori Iwo ni Olori Ijo ti ibode okunkun ko le bori re.
2. Oluwa o, ma se je ki ibode apadi bori Ijo Olorun ni oruko Jesu.
3. Oluwa dide o, je ki gbogbo awon ota Ijo Olorun tuka ni oruko Jesu.
4. Gbogbo ikora jopo tabi ipade tabi ipanpa okunkun lori Ijo Olorun, e tuka ni oruko Jesu.

5. Gbogbo oun ija ti a se lodi si Ijo Olorun yio yaro ni oruko Jesu.

6. Oluwa, tu gbogbo asiri okunkun lori Ijo Olorun ki O si yida ni oruko Jesu.

7. Baba wa ti nbe ni orun, fun Ijo Olorun ni agbara lti ko Oro Re nigba gbogbo.

8. Emi Mimo, ro gbogbo awon adari Ijo ni agbara lati se aseyori lori ise won.

9. Gbogbo idojuko lodi si Ijo Olorun ki yio duro ni oruko Jesu.

10. Jeki gbogbo ise okunkun lori Ijo Olorun sofo danu nipa agbara inu Eje Jesu.

19

3. ADURA NIGBA TI AWA NI ILE AJEJI (AISAYA 54)
IJEWO

- Josefu kuro ni eniyan laasan o di eniyan Pataki ni ile ajeji. Danieli di ohun ni ile ajeji. Esteri de ipo ola ni ile ajeji. Ni ile yi ti mo wa, emi yi o di ohun.

- Ajeji yi o ko odi mi. Awon ti nko mo yi o sin mi. Olorun yi fi opin si ipongbe mi ni ile ajeji. Emi oni je ounje iponju.

- Ti Oluwa ni ile ati ekun re. Emi yi o mu oyan awon oba. Emi yi o mu wara awon olola.

- Nigba ti mo ba farahan, iberu yi o di await. Nigba ti mo ba nsoro, oju rere yi o dahun. Nigba ti mo ba joko, elegan yi o teriba.

- Rikisi okunkun ko le da Danieli duro. Potiferi ko le se aseyori lori Josefu. Olorun yi o so mi po mo Gosemu. Emi yi oje, emi yio si yo ni ile ajoji.

KOKO ADURA

1. Oluwa nipase aanu Re, so mi po mo ora ile ti ileyi afi ri orun lori re.
2. Oluwa mo dupe fun ipese re fun ipese aini mi l'ori ileyi.
3. Gbogbo agbara lati ipile mi eleyi ti o nduro de itiju mi ni ile, ina Emi Mimo sun ni oruko Jesu.
4. Oluwa mo sotele wipe mi o ni pada l'owo ofo ni oruko Jesu.
5. Ore ofe ti ko wope fun aseyori nla wa, si ori aye mi ni oruko Jesu.
6. Oluwa jeki ere ileyi bere si ni san wa si odo mi ni oruko Jesu.
7. Aanu Olorun ti odaju fun abo, wa si ori aiye mi ni oruko Jesu.
8. Gbogbo ibi ti on sise lori ile yi ko ni gbe emi ati ebi mi mi ni oruko Jesu.
9. Danieli se aseyori ni ile ajeji, Josefu la aluyo nipase ore ofe Olorun, mo gbodo lu aluyo ni oruko Jesu.
10. Ore-ofe ise-rere ni ile ajeji ni ilana ti Isaaki, ba le mi nisinsinyi ni oruko Jesu.

20

4. ADURA NI IGBA TI A BA FE GBA IWE IRIN AJO – (AISAYA 54)

IJEWO

- Ipinu Olorun fun aiye mi ni koni di asan ni oruko Jesu. Asobode okunkun ko ni se aseyori l'ori aiye mi. Ipa ti o da awon kan duro, ko ni dami duro. Nibi ti awon kan hasi, emi yi o tesiwaju.

- Josefu fi oju rere gba ni ile ajeji. Daniel ati awon ore re ri oju rere gba bakan na. A o ni ko mi sile. Oju rere yi o f'oun funmi. Mi o se daduro.

- A o yan mi fe. Nigbakugba ti mo ba farahan, won o ri Olorun ninu aye mi. Iwe irin ajo mi yi o ri ibowolu ati orun wa. Ko si agbara ti yi o le duro ni iwaju mi.

- Ileri Olorun fun aiye mi ko ni dawo duro. Ala ibi ko ni farahan. Gbogbo aseyori mi ti oju ala yi o wa si imuse.

- Awon iran ati ileri ojo pipe mi, yi o wa si imuse. Gbogbo ibere to ni se pelu aiye mi ni Olorun yi o dahun. Owo ko ni jami kule. Ore-ofe ni yi o je owo mi.

KOKO ADURA

1. Oluwa mo gba ore-ofe ti ko wopo lati rin ni ibamu pelu ipinnu Re fun aiye mi ni oruko Jesu.

2. Ilekun nla fun oju rere ti ko wopo si sile fun mi ni pase aanu ni oruko Jesu.

3. Gbogbo irinse alatako ni ona mi si itesiwaju, ya aro ni oruko Jesu.

4. Oluwa nipase aanu, mo gba enu ati ogbon eleyi ti a ko le tako ni oruko Jesu.

5. Gbogbo atopinpin okunkun ti a gbekale lati ya mi laro ati gbogbo ami anfani mi, eja kule nipase Eje Jesu.

6. Oluwa, jeki oun gbogbo sise ni rere fun mi niwaju awon ti o fe fi oro wa mi l'enu wo.

7. Gbogbo ami okunkun l'ori iwe irin ajo mi eleyi ti o nfa ikosile, Eje Jesu paa re ni Oruko Jesu.

8. Owo rere Olorun fun ojurere ti ko wopo bale ori iwe irin ajo mi ni oruko Jesu.

9. Gbogbo igba ti mo ba fi ara han ni iwaju awon ti o fe fi ijomitoro oro wadi oro lenu mi, oju rere f'ohun fun mi.

10. Gbogbo ami ikosile lori iwe iri ajo mi, Eje Jesu pare ni oruko Jesu.

21

ADURA FUN ITUSILE TI EMI (O.D.86)
IJEWO

- Eni ti Omo ba tu sile yio ni itusile ni toto. Jesu tit u mi si le. A tu mi sile nitoto.

- Okunrin emi mi gba itusile. Emi o si ninu iho ota mo. Awon onde tooto yio gba itusile ni Oluwa wi; emi yio gba itusile.

- Okan mi gba itusile. Emi ni okan to ye koro. Okan mi yio bori awon ero to lodi.

- Ara mi gba itusile. Okan mi gba itusile. Okunrin emi mi gba itusile. Emi papa ni ojulo itusile.

- Iho okunkun, po mi jade. Emi ki se ti e. Mo bo; lati se ife Baba mi ti nbe ni orun.

KOKO ADURA
AISAYA 41:10-20; JOB 11:13-20

1. Oluwa o, mom o riri Re fun itusile ti emi to pe to fun mi ni ori-oke Kalfari.

2. Ti Omo ba so e di ominira, iwo yio gba ominira ni toto! Jesu Oluwa, tu mi sile kuro lowo igbekun ti emi.

3. Ina Emi Mimo, tu aiye mi sile kuro ninu gbogbo ewon okunkun ti mow a ni oruko Jesu.

4. Gbogbo agbara ti ndi mi ni igbekun emi, e so agbara yin nu lori mi ni oruko Jesu.

5. Eni ti ngbe nu mi je eni ti ngbe inu aiye lo. Agbara isegun lati bori gobgbo igbekun emi, gbe mi wo nisinsinyi.

6. Eje Jesu (21x), tu mi sile kuro ninu gbogbo ikekun okunkun tin di aiye mi ni igbekun.

7. A da mi lati ma je gaba, lati oni lo mo gba ifami ororo yan ijegaba ni oruko Jesu.

8. Gbogbo agbara ipile ti ndari aiye mi, e sofo danu nipa agbara to wa ninu oruko Jesu.

9. Mo gba agbara lati ma gbe igbe aiye isegun lori igbe aiye ese lati oni ni oruko Jesu.

10. Gbogbo agbara ti a ti yan lati fi aiye emi mi sofo, e sofo nipa ina ni oruko Jesu.

PRAISE REPORTS

TESTIMONY is the Spirit of Jesus. When we encourage people to testify, we are not only appreciating the faithfulness of God over answered prayers but we are also using it to encourage others.

When you share your testimonies, someone somewhere will have hope that if God can settle your case, He will settle theirs too. This is why we encourage brethren whom the Lord has touched not to be silent but open up on God's faithfulness so others too can be blessed.

God is no respecter of persons, what He has done for one, He can do for others. We don't hide testimonies here. We beseech brethren to come forward, to appreciate God for honouring prayers and to give someone hope.

These testimonies are compilations of testimonies sent from people all over the world (especially our online partners) whom the Lord has remembered. My prayer for you is that the Lord will remember you for good in the name of Jesus. When this Prayer Manual comes out next year, your testimonies will be part of it in the name of Jesus. God bless you.

SALVATION OF OUR SOULS

I was a Muslim even an Alhaja but now, I am a born-again Christian. Last year I would perform Salat but now since January have become a Christian through Papa's morning prayers on Radio Lagos.

My children gave their lives to Christ before me; my first born in London, the other in USA. Now I am a Christian too.
Hallelujah!

TAX WOES RETRACTED

I want to share my testimony.

I have been listening to the services since the 26th day. In some cases where I didn't listen to the live services, I watch the reruns on YouTube.

Due to a mistake by my accountant (late submission of 2018 taxes) I got a very large tax bill and fine from the Swiss Tax authorities. I appealed against the odds but it took so long for them to confirm what the outcome would be. I was worried I would lose my home and although I had been praying I was very stressed.

Recently at the end of one of the services the Prophet asked us to ask God for just one thing which we needed. I was tempted to ask for all the other things I wanted from God, but this tax bill is what came to my heart. I prayed for favour from the authorities.

The very next day my accountant called me to say they had a final decision. They reduced the fine by roughly 90% so I only had to pay a very small amount. He said they would send official letter of confirmation. The letter came the next day.

This has taken almost a year and I thought I might lose everything including my home. Praise God for his goodness and for answered prayers and for your Ministry.

J. Adeyemi,
Switzerland.

MANTLE CANCELLED DEMONIC ATTACKS

I want to testify to the name of the Lord.

I used to have strange and demonic dreams. I bought 12 handkerchiefs for the mantle night, so that I can share with family and close friends. After the mantle night, God definitely turned my handkerchief to mantle. I slept with one mantle under my pillow and put another mantle on my face and went to sleep. Then, I dreamt that I was being attacked by a demonic entity, and I was being chased by it, but I stood, spoke in tongues and began to call the name of Jesus. This entity fell to the ground and was defeated. The God of angel armies, the God of Mercy Rain has delivered me. My deliverance will be permanent in Jesus' name.

Praise the lord. Amen

RESIDENCE PERMIT RELEASED

I have been praying for a response to my husband's British resident permit and I prayed specifically for it during the last 40 days retreat. And we received a post from the home office! They have granted it to him!!!!!! The letter was dated 7th October just 3 days after I said the prayer!!!!! This is just the beginning of my series of victorious testimonies please stay tuned!!!

May God indeed bless Papa and all LOCCIM

DIVINE HEALING THROUGH MANTLE

I want to thank God for His massive work in my husband's life, I was in the room yesterday night when I heard my husband screaming from the sitting room. So, I ran there and saw him rolling on the floor holding his stomach and crying, I was so scared, I ran to take my mantle and put it on his stomach. I didn't even pray. I was too shaken up to pray and immediately he was relieved. He started getting better immediately.

Secondly, this morning, I got a call from my aunt in London asking me to start preparing to come to London. I thought she has forgotten me, God is wonderful sir.
I give Him all the glory!

MANTLE NIGHT DELIVERANCE FROM BREAST CYSTS

Praise the Lord with me. I bless the name of the Lord for visiting me on the Mantle night. I was diagnosed of cysts in the breast and was told that I will need to do surgery to remove the cysts.

But to the glory of God, on the Mantle night I placed the Mantle on my breast as soon as we finish praying and immediately the lumps disappeared. This is what I call instantaneous healing.

I woke up one morning during this 40 Days Apostolic Prayer retreat with a very sharp pain on the right side of my ribs. The pain was so severe to the extent that I did not know what to do. I prayed on it and then read

those Confession on our prayer booklet, and immediately the pain is gone.
Praise the living Jesus!
Erhire,
 Lagos.

DIVINE RESTORATION FOR MY BUSINESS

I am a tailor. For a while now, my business hasn't been running smoothly. Things have not been going well in my shop as all my customers don't come to sew clothes from me anymore. In the 40 days program, I had a dream that a girl in my shop is using my charger to charge her phone. To God be the glory, I collected the charger from her and plugged my phone with it. And since then, my business has been booming. Things has changed for good.
Praise God!!!

GOD HEALED ME WITH THE MANTLE

I have been experiencing severe pains all over my body for long. I have used different medication but got no relieve. During the Mercy Rain Prayer, I believe the Lord has something for me. When it was time to get mantle, I prayed and got one. I then used it to rub my body. For the first time in a long time, I slept very well and all pains in my body disappeared. Thanks to the God of Mercy Rain 2020. I am grateful.
To God be the Glory!

BLESSED WITH GREAT JOB

- Good morning sir. God has been great in my life. He gave me a miracle job. I am here to appreciate God for another testimony. I wrote an international exam during the conference and I trusted God for assistance because the exam was hard. God surprised me miraculously and gave me my desired score.

- God really surprised me and gave me a good government job. I bless God for this because He promised to change my financial status and He did it in a miraculous way. I got this job without seeking for anybody's help, I could see the favour of God speaking for me.

- I thank the Almighty God for answering my prayer. During the 40 days prayer, one of my prayer requests was for God to grant my daughter a job, she has been looking for a job for some years. Two days after the program the Almighty did it. I give God all the glory. More anointing on your life sir.
- Esther Fatuyi.

- Thank the Almighty God for answering my prayers. During the 40 days prayer, one of my prayer requests was for God to grant my daughter a job, because she has been looking for a job for some years. Two days after the program the Almighty did it. I give God all the glory. More anointing on your life sir!
- Mrs A,
- United Kingdom.
-

FAITH SEED

Praise the Lord, I'm grateful to the Covenant Keeping God for He has given me my own testimony. I tied my 21-day seed to divine health for me and my children, and for a breakthrough in the life of my daughter. After the initial fasting and the anointing night, I started praying and confessing that I want to give my own testimony. I started applying the anointing oil on my leg and on my daughter's hand. I receive healing on my leg that was aching me with something that was crawling on the leg that was preventing me from movement. Now I can climb the stairs with ease. My daughter also got healing on her hand that was being scheduled for surgery. Also, this morning, people who have been owing my daughter started paying up. I give all glory to God Almighty, this is just the Lord's doing and it is marvellous in my eyes.

I'm Dorcas, Abba's beloved.

GOD OF MERCY CANCELLED IVF AND BLESSED ME WITH PREGNANCY

My husband and I have been trusting God for the fruit of the womb for years now. I have had miscarriages in the past and we had given up all hope. We decided and we were ready to go for IVF and all necessary medications obtained. So, I was just waiting for my period so I could begin the therapy.
Lo and behold, my period didn't come and just like that, our God of last minute showed up, I am

pregnant! I am a living proof that God is indeed a God of ELEVENTH HOUR Miracle, who would never share His glory with any man.

Glory to our God of MERCY!!!

Please join your faith with ours, daddy, that we will carry this baby (INIOLUWA) to term and deliver safely to the glory of God in Jesus mighty name. Amen!

ANOINTING FOR DELIVERANCE

I want to thank God for His healing and deliverance. About 4 months ago I had a dream in which I was in a struggle with some forces. On waking up, I found out that I had some scratches on my left palm and it felt like a spike and it was painful. Fast forward to last week, during one of the vigils which I joined for the first time. After the prayers on the anointing oil, I anointed my palm and the next morning, the spike feeling and pain is gone and the scratches began to heal. I Just want to thank God because evil deposits in my body is gone.

May the Almighty God continue to strengthen you sir.

Olayemi Festus

MERCY RAIN 2020 IS FOR ME

Several testimonies.

It's because of me that God allowed this 40 days happen in September because I only got to know about your ministry in July and since then I've been hooked and even sharing all the daily messages to everyone on my contact list.

My testimonies are;
I suffer from sickle cell and diabetes both with no cure. Every month I'm in hospital, since I had my child in 2018 I have not spent 2 months straight with her, I'm always in hospital, every month I have an exchange blood transfusion. Since I started this prophetic 40 days program, I have not had one single pain not talk of going to hospital even I didn't go for the blood transfusion in September and I'm still fine. I know God will perfect my healing.

Just within the first week of the 40 days Mercy Rain, all the benefit I was deprived of since February were given to me.

So many things have happened that I know this is God through this 40 days. I can't begin to list as it is endless. Because Satan couldn't get to me again, it started to attack my 1st born putting negative thoughts in her head and her thinking of committing suicide.
Please pray for my family as I am a single parent with 3 children here in the UK.

After Baba White came, I keyed into all the prayer points all the money owed to me got paid and I made sure I paid my tithe and offering to your church. Even though I don't work I still paid my tithe.

In this same September, I was called to come and do my biometrics after waiting since January and I have been granted my permit in the UK.

Praise be to God in Yeshua's name I pray. Amen.
Mr. Odusanmi
U K.

BLESSED WITH GOOD RESULT

Pls help me to thank God, for my son. He passed all his subjects in WASC, not just passing all but God answered my prayers, because he made his English Language with a B, which has been my prayer point. He does exceedingly well in all other subjects except English, this drop his marks in jamb. We have been telling God that if he does not pass the English language exam, he would not be granted admission into the university.
His examination result has been a prayer for me since the beginning of the forty days prayer retreat. And God is awesome and faithful to those who have total trust in Him. Thanks to Almighty God, to Jesus Christ, and the Holy Spirit. Amen!
Pst. Paul
Nigeria.

GOD MADE IT POSSIBLE

During the 40 nights vigils, I fasted for the 40 days. One of my major concerns then was the success of a conference I organized. People that ought to lend a hand of support refused because they didn't believe it would be possible.
As I have nowhere else to go, I turned to God in this Mercy Rain. I made it my prayer point. God has done it. The conference which lasted for 3 days has just

completed and we had 80.9% presentations. It was a huge success. I return all the glory to God.

THYROID DISEASE DISAPPEARED

I thank God Almighty that is directing our Father in the Lord to put 40days night vigil that that past down for us to know God more, glory be to His holy name (Amen).

My last born that has thyroid on his neck, the thyroid is gone by putting the mantle you prayed on it for us on line. Thanks Daddy more anointing sir, and more grease to your elbows in Jesus' name. Amen.

FIBROIDS CANCELLED

I want to thank God for His Mercy over my life and situations. I had serious fibroids surgery last year during the Lockdown (glory to God for its success) but the doctors were skeptical about its return in a year. During the 40 Days, I presented my case before God. I said God, please do not let this thing come back. Make it go away finally Father.
God heard me sir. It is past one year now and there is no trace of the tiniest fibroids in my system. Only God can do these things. I return all glory to Him.
Our daddy in the Lord (Prophet Olowoporoku), I thank you for all your prayers over us. They are really working. Thank you sir.

Divine Healing from Endometriosis

God is indeed faithful. I want to thank God for healing me of endometriosis. This condition gives me excruciatingly painful menstrual periods so much so, that I have to use usually large amount of pain killers from the first day of my period to the last day. I would also stool and vomit the entire time and find it hard to go to work. When I now go to work, I cannot concentrate because of the pain and will have to go home so I can roll on the floor in excruciating pain. I've had this condition for more than 20 years and the Lord has healed me through the 40 Days Mercy Rain.

Made in the USA
Monee, IL
29 June 2021